Tails of the Prairie

2007

To Sue + Betty,
Surprize, surprize!
Finally got the stories
printed in book form.
Thanks to newer
Technology than we
first put them together.
Hope you enjoy &
merry Christmas
Love - Bob

Tails of the Prairie

✦

My Life as a Small-Town Veterinarian in Wyoming

R. A. Baldwin, DVM

iUniverse, Inc.
New York Lincoln Shanghai

Tails of the Prairie
My Life as a Small-Town Veterinarian in Wyoming

iUniverse books may be ordered through booksellers or by contacting:

iUniverse
2021 Pine Lake Road, Suite 100
Lincoln, NE 68512
www.iuniverse.com
1-800-Authors (1-800-288-4677)

Because of the dynamic nature of the Internet, any Web addresses
or links contained in this book may have changed
since publication and may no longer be valid.

The views expressed in this work are solely those of the author and do not necessarily
reflect the views of the publisher, and the publisher hereby disclaims any responsibility
for them.

ISBN: 978-0-595-47637-4 (pbk)

ISBN: 978-0-595-91901-7 (ebk)

Printed in the United States of America

I dedicate this book to my wife, Harriet,
who was there in the writing of these stories in many, many ways.

Contents

Part II   THE GILLETTE YEARS

AUTHOR'S NOTE

All of the stories in this book are based on my actual experiences, as best as I can recollect them. However, many of the names have been changed because I thought that might be the neighborly thing to do.

ACKNOWLEDGEMENT

Many thanks to Kevin Quirk, who has guided me through the throes of "birthing" *Tails of the Prairie*. It had been in "rough draft" for several years, but a fortuitous event led me to his website, memoirsforlife.com. Without his suggestions, encouragement, and expertise it would still be as he found it.

INTRODUCTION

This book is an account of my experiences as a veterinary practitioner in Crook, Weston, and Campbell counties Wyoming, between the years 1951 and 1964.

Crook County, roughly fifty by fifty-six square miles, is the most northeasterly county in Wyoming, and borders both Montana and South Dakota. Sundance, the largest town and county seat, had a population of approximately 800 when my wife Harriet and I lived there from 1951 to 1955. That town sits underneath majestic Sundance Mountain, known as the Temple of the Sioux. The name, Sundance, relates to the history of the mountain, for there the Sioux held their councils and performed religious ceremonies. The nation's first national monument, Devils Tower, is located in Crook County. This monument, so designated by President Theodore Roosevelt in 1906, is a cluster of rock columns approximately 1,000 feet across the bottom and 275 feet across at the top. Rising some 1,280 feet above the valley floor it is more than 5,000 feet above sea level. Close to it are the three Missouri Buttes, and the headwaters of the Missouri River.

Crook County has hosted many famous personages in its time. General George C. Custer passed through on his way to the Little Big Horn in 1874. The Sundance Kid (Harry Lonabaugh), a member of Butch Cassidy's outlaw gang, earned his name in Sundance.

My wife Harriet was born twelve miles west of Sundance, on Houston Creek. Thus, when we decided to purchase one of the two drugstores in town and enter veterinary practice with her brother and sister-in-law, Dr. and Mrs. Rodney Port, her homecoming was like "The Return of the Native."

The first story, "Sundance," describes in some detail our living conditions during those four and a half years. As you read the various stories, we hope you also keep in mind the primitive nature of the roads and services at that time. Private telephone lines, kept up by ranchers and ranch hands, terminated at a central manually operated switchboard, owned and operated by a private individual. Connections to Mountain Bell, some thirty miles away, was also through the operator. Two-way radios or radio telephones were just being tried out in 1951. The only people who could afford them had sources of high, steady income.

REA, or rural electrification, was just coming into the area. Before it was completed, most ranch homes used a variety of mechanisms to generate electric power, ranging from diesel and gasoline powered generators to the lowly wind charger, which stored in batteries the electricity they produced. Those who were unable to afford these luxuries went to bed early, or used lamps, lanterns or flashlights. I did more than a few cesareans on heifers under the glare of my pickup's headlights or while someone held a lantern over the animal's back.

Most of the roads I had to travel were dirt roads. In the summer and fall you could judge your distances from another vehicle by the dust it raised. In the winter and spring, I spent a good deal of time under the truck … putting on chains or taking them off!

Before the town put in a sewage system, each business had its own method for handling wastes. We had a cesspool behind our place, and it never gave us any trouble. The restaurant a short distance down the street got along very well with its cesspool during winter and spring, but along with the coming of warm weather and the influx of tourists, the owners resorted to pumping the cesspool daily—I mean nightly around 11 p.m., after things had quieted down for the night. The owner would mount a huge empty tank on his old once-and-a-half-ton Ford flatbed truck into which he pumped the cesspool wastes. This might have worked just fine if the tank hadn't hung so far over the rear axle. From time to time, however, he pumped so much "waste" into the tank that the front of the truck raised into the air and the only way to lower it was to let some of the "waste" loose in the street. Well! As you might guess, Harriet and I, the closest recipients of this "fallout," were glad to vote for a referendum favoring a sewage system when the town council finally submitted the question for a vote.

Dr. J. F. Clarenbach was the one medical doctor in town, holding licenses to practice medicine, dentistry, and pharmacy.

The hospital consisted of a couple of rooms in a private home run by a practicing nurse. Sundance had a town council of which I was a member for a short time before we moved to Gillette.

We never lived in Weston County, but at one time had a "satellite clinic" there. The land area of Weston is a little smaller than Crook County, and it experienced a large run on oil drilling when we were there. It also supported several large bentonite mills. Bentonite, known in medicine as Fuller's Earth, is used for many things, including poultices. It is also used in lining reservoirs to make the earth impermeable to water, and in the manufacturing of Baby Ruth candy bars. This bentonite soil, indigenous to northeastern Wyoming and Montana, is processed by local mills and shipped by railroad to various parts of the country.

Weston County's two main towns—Newcastle, the county seat, and Upton—were both on the Chicago, Burlington, and Quincy Railroad line (now called the Burlington Northern).

For the most part, the "lay of the land" in Weston County is very different from Crook County. Weston County has gently rolling hills covered with short grass and sagebrush.

The livestock diseases I encountered there differed too. For example, "water-belly" (urinary calculi or stones) in steers was quite prevalent in Weston County, but seldom seen in steers in Crook County.

A fairly large population of Italian and Polish people lived in Weston County. Brought in to work the now defunct Cambria coal mine, they homesteaded the area around what is known as Fourcorners. They farmed as opposed to ranching, the occupation of almost everyone else in the county.

Weston County had a modern, up-to-date hospital and three or four MDs. Our son, Harry, was born there in 1953. The hospital bill amounted to about sixty dollars, but the doctor didn't want to accept payment for his services inasmuch as I had not charged him for taking care of his dog. Finally we prevailed on him, though, to accept at least the insurance allowance. We would still hear from him and his wife at Christmas for several years after we left.

Campbell County, directly to the west of both Crook and Weston, measures one hundred and twenty miles north to south, and sixty miles, east to west. Like Crook County, it borders Montana on the north. Like Weston County, it has lots of prairie and sagebrush. In addition, the wind blows almost 360 days of the year ... varying only in how hard! The other five days are taken over by tornadoes!!

When we were in Gillette, the county seat and main "trading post," it was the one major town in the county. It was named after the chief surveyor for the Chicago, Burlington, and Quincy Railroad and was platted in 1891.

Uranium and oil were discovered in Campbell County during our tenure there. Coal, however, was then and still is being mined in large quantities. The coal has low sulfur content and is mined from open pits. It is estimated there is enough coal in that area to supply our nation for the next 200 years!

Medical personnel and hospital facilities in town were adequate when we arrived. There were two physicians who owned hospitals located in houses. Shortly afterward, however, the county built a hospital and the private hospitals were closed. One dentist was already there, but later a young native, Dr. Jim Swenson, returned and established his practice. The county's only optometrist, Dr. Frank Hadley, was our closest neighbor.

At one time, I served as a member of the Campbell County High School Board, as well as the Campbell County Hospital Board.

We purchased a house with ten acres of land on the outskirts of the city of Gillette. There we built a veterinary hospital, then one of the few in the entire state. I was the first graduate veterinarian to establish a permanent practice in Gillette and Campbell County. Veterinarians employed by the federal government had, from time to time, been stationed there, and a couple of non-graduates were around the area when we first arrived. Soon, however, they stopped practicing. Times and knowledge were changing in veterinary medicine along with the other medical disciplines.

Our daughter Jen was born in Campbell County in 1956. The event took place after a night at the drive-in movie.

Following her delivery, Dr. Baughman, our MD, took me to the local truck stop restaurant for breakfast and to "chew the fat" (literally and figuratively). During our conversation I asked him if more babies were born at any one time than another, like lambs and calves. He sort of chuckled and replied, "Not necessarily, but I sometime think people have been at the same party nine months previously!"

Our practice would not afford the luxury of an X-ray machine because the times I needed one were few and far between. When I did need one, Dr. Baughman happily loaned his for use on small animals and the county hospital had a large portable X-ray, which I used on horses at the delivery platform at the hospital. Medically, we were one big happy family. Once, one of the MDs sent a patient of his to have me look at a lesion on her hand. He wanted to confirm what he suspected, and I did. It was cowpox. In fact, she caught the condition from her cow for which I had dispensed medication.

We lived in Gillette for nine and a half years. In 1966 we moved to Fort Collins, Colorado, where I attended Colorado State University as a graduate student. That ended the private practice years of my career and the many experiences that I much enjoyed. I share some of them here now.

PART I

THE SUNDANCE YEARS

SUNDANCE

Sundance, Wyoming, far in the northeastern corner of the state, was home base in the beginning years of my veterinary practice. For four and one-half years Harriet and I lived among 800 hearty souls in that sleepy little town, the county seat of Crook County, located at the edge of the beautiful Black Hills and nestled at the foot of the Sundance Mountain.

In 1950, just before my senior year in veterinary school, my brother-in-law, Dr. Rodney Port, asked us to join him in his veterinary practice, giving him more freedom to pursue ranching some twelve miles west of Sundance on Houston Creek. He honestly admitted that he had neglected the practice and suggested we would need to supplement the veterinary income with an additional business.

It so happened that one of the little town's two drugstores—the most profitable one, we were told—was for sale.

We agreed to its purchase in partnership with the in-laws, but not without fear and trepidation, for we had to use our entire savings and borrow a goodly sum in order to consummate the deal. I was committed to the work, however, and after I graduated in 1951 we moved from Michigan to Wyoming to take up residence over the newly acquired drugstore.

Home, a four-room apartment appended to the roof of the drugstore's (nobody called them pharmacies then) rear storage rooms, could be reached by a set of steep stairs leading abruptly up from the store. These stairs, with risers higher than usual and treads narrower, also made a sharp right angle turn at the last three steps, tending to throw the climber directly on his face into the tiny living room.

Fully furnished, the living room held only an easy chair and a sofa situated on opposite walls. When people were seated, they could easily play footsie. A heating vent, located next to the easy chair, provided a convenient space through which to observe activities in the store on those rare occasions when we were able to sit for a few minutes. Not adequate for heating or cooling our tiny rooms, the vent proved most adequate for allowing obnoxious medicinal odors from the drugstore and fetid odors from the surgery to waft their way through all the rooms, permeating our bedding, clothing and furniture.

An additional entrance to the apartment was provided by creaky, well-worn outside stairs at the rear of the building. A railing attached to the open side of the steps swayed with any strong wind and was of no help to anyone really needing assistance. Part of the year, when covered with ice or snow, they were, to say the least, a hazard. These steps led from the backyard, a grassless, deeply rutted patch of ground containing our dog runs, to a rickety porch. From this attachment to the building, which hardly deserves to be called a porch, a door led directly into our bedroom.

The bedroom consisted of a bed and a space heater. A tiny closet and bathroom were situated at one end of the room, and a door between the two led into our dining and kitchen areas. The space heater burned fuel stored in a Butane tank buried in the backyard. A barrel-like chamber housed the controls, regulating the flow of gas, and was buried in front of the fuel tank. Often in the spring, water from melting snow and ice filled the chamber and altered the flow of gas through the regulator to the space heaters. Incomplete combustion resulted, causing potentially deadly fumes to escape into the bedroom and to spread throughout the building.

This situation could be relieved only by removing water from around the controls. To remove the water, Harriet or I would grab the stomach pump I used to medicate horses or cattle, run to the backyard, ram the instrument deep into the control chamber, and frantically pump out the water. This routine, usually followed several times a day or night, became a part of life in our drugstore years.

Before taking possession of the store, we had increased its size by razing a wall between the drugstore proper and an attached empty building. This enabled us to merchandise and sell more veterinary drugs and equipment.

During this remodeling, we installed a rather large horseshoe-shaped ice cream bar and soda fountain. Located in the center of the two buildings, the "toe" of the fountain faced the front entrance of the store. The "heel" opened toward the rear, allowing entrance to the interior of the fountain from either of the two buildings.

Small-animal examinations and surgery were performed in a small room located at the back of the bigger building that also housed the veterinary merchandise.

Early on, we learned that only those hours before opening or after closing the drugstore were suitable to perform any kind of examination or surgery. Fumes from ether anesthesia somehow didn't "turn on" those having an ice cream soda at the fountain. Most customers also were not enthusiastic about dogs growling, wailing, or yelping, and cats shrieking and hissing. Large dogs coming into the store, even on a leash held by the owner, sent a wave of apprehension through the drugstore population.

The old crank telephone, located on the wall of the stairwell leading down from the apartment, was like a large rectangular box with a mouthpiece in the center front. The receiver was attached by a long cord through the box bottom, and the crank was situated on the right side of the box, approximately in the center. You see these phones now in antique stores selling for a large sum!

Placing calls was a trial. First you got the operator's attention by removing the receiver and turning the crank. The operator would come on the line and ask for the number, but then you waited. If the line was not busy, eventually you would hear the bells inside the box jingle as the operator rang the required number of short or long rings. When the call was completed, you hung up the receiver and "rang off" by cranking the phone. This signaled the operator and those along the party line that you were finished (as if they didn't already know!). All calls went through an operator who was always, somehow, fully apprised of your business.

The telephone system, including the transmission lines, in approximately a fifty-mile radius were privately owned. That is, they weren't owned by Mountain States T&T or any other big utility. The entire system was a good ten to fifteen years out of date, and many lines had deteriorated, but the owner allowed these conditions to exist because it was too costly to have it otherwise. Usually people listened in on their neighbors' conversations, and transmission along the lines was so poor, with two or three receivers off the hook, that it was virtually impossible to hear who was calling or what they were calling about. To obtain any kind of voice transmission over the rural lines, one was obliged to scream loudly. Often I thought I might just as well be on top of the building with a bull horn.

Many of the ranchers had no electricity to power water pumps or light their homes. Rural electrification was still a dream in many of those remote areas. Great distances made the cost of modernization beyond the reach of ranchers owning only a section or two of land.

It was to this rather primitive land of huge spaces, sagebrush, jack pine and scrub oak that circumstances and profession called us. While Harriet ran the drugstore, I plied my veterinary skills. The hard times, the fun times, and the sad times provided some of our most memorable experiences.

BEWARE THE MIGHTY HUNTER

The heat of the dog days and early September ended abruptly with the season's first heavy frost. The colorful leaves of the scrub oak and aspen had dropped with crisp breezes, and the air was filled with the smell of wood smoke from burning home fires. Harbingers, all, of the hunting season, that season I so dreaded, and the ranchers so dreaded for the safety of their livestock. Though the influx of eastern hunters brought needed dollars to our beautiful Black Hills community, it also brought danger to the livestock population.

"Bob, telephone. It's Clark Carroll. Someone shot his milk cow!" Harriet hollered out the back door of the drugstore where I enjoyed musing as I kept busy stocking medicines and cleaning equipment in my ambulatory truck on that day.

"Holy s—!" I said to myself. Leaving my task, I went inside to answer the telephone. "It's that time of year again when we are invaded by those gun-totin', fun-loving, whiskey-drinking, mighty hunters," I said to Harriet.

Harriet had just opened the front door for business about eight o'clock in the morning when the old crank telephone rang and Clark had shouted out his tale of woe.

When I picked up the receiver, dangling at the end of its cord, I heard youngsters crying and a woman shouting.

"What's going on out there, Clark?" I shouted into the mouthpiece.

"By God, Doc, you won't believe it. Someone shot our milk cow right in the guts!" As he responded to my question, he shouted at his wife and kids to shut up their hollering and crying so he could hear. "I milked her about six this morning, and turned her out in the pasture. About fifteen minutes ago, I was working on some machinery and I heard shots. I went around the corner of the barn to see who was shootin' so close to the buildings. That's when I saw a car on the highway start up and speed out of sight. The little cow was down on her side."

"Where was she hit?" I asked.

"On her left side, about a foot behind the ribs."

6

In the area of the rumen, I visualized. The first of the four compartments of a ruminant's stomach.

"She got up when I went over to her, but she acted a little dazed," Clark went on.

"Did you look at her right side to see if a bullet might have come out?"

"I looked, but there weren't no sign of blood on the right side."

That would mean the bullet had spent itself inside. Lord knows where it might be now or how much damage it had caused in the peritoneal or abdominal area.

"Think you can save her, Doc? I don't want to spend a lot of money on her if she's going to die anyway. May as well put her out of her misery now as to go to a lot of expense and have her suffer an' all."

His remarks caused wailing and hollering to begin again in the background. "Shut up, I can't hear what Doc is saying," Clark admonished his family.

"I really can't tell how bad it is or how much it will cost until I look," I answered. "I'll probably have to go inside her to see. That will cost at least twenty-five dollars. Then there are the drugs and the call out there. Likely be another twenty-five."

I heard him talking to his wife about the cost, and soon he said, "Okay, Doc, come on out. I'll try to get her to the shed."

"I'll need a couple of buckets of hot water," I said, knowing that one of the family would have to tote it from the house to the shed where I would work.

"They'll be ready as soon as you get here," came the reply.

By the time I hung up the receiver, several customers had come into the store and the pharmacist had arrived. Harriet was checking supplies at the fountain. I asked her to telephone Ruby Ferran that it would be early afternoon before I could make it out to her place to castrate her horse. If that didn't suit, she should set another time.

With a word of farewell, I returned to the truck and went through the Pandora bag to make sure I had all the instruments and drugs necessary to do abdominal surgery—a laparotomy in medical terminology.

Clark's ranch was about ten to twelve miles from town, and I arrived there just as he was urging the little Jersey cow through the shed door. His hands were covered with grease, as were his bib overalls, shirt, and lace-up boots.

"How unusual bib overalls are for this country," I said to myself, wondering why he was dressed in this manner. Glancing over the barnyard, I saw a combine near the shed consisting mainly of an array of disconnected parts. Obviously, Clark had been repairing the machine, and suddenly bib overalls seemed more appropriate to that task than the usual western tight-fitting shirt, slim-leg Levis, and high-heeled cowboy boots. Clark, who looked like a dwarf among the taller western men, sported a full-faced beard and was muscular through the chest and arms. His brown hair, usually contained under a cowboy hat, was tousled, and patches of grease here and there had cemented some of the hair strands together. Beads of perspiration stood on his forehead and his brown eyes snapped with anger as he greeted my by saying, "Sure is a hellava thing when they issue a hunting license to people that don't know the difference between a deer and a cow."

We entered the shed, followed by two or three children and a Collie dog. The children and dog spread themselves along the wall to watch. Clark's wife followed shortly with the two pails of water I had requested.

The little cow turned her head toward the dog and the kids. I could see she had a dull look to her eye. More ominous, she gave off a low grunt at the end of each exhale.

I took the stethoscope out of my hip pocket and started the physical exam. The heart was beating a little fast, but that would be normal in this situation. Lung sounds were normal, except for that expiratory grunt. Moving back along the left side, I found that the bullet hole was right where Clark had described it, about a foot behind the last rib and midway between the backbone and the lower-most point of her abdomen. He said she was "gut shot." I would say, more precisely, she was shot in the area of the rumen.

I continued the examination. No rumenal sounds. Normally there should be, but there were none. Nothing.

A little blood appeared around the wound. But then, I wouldn't have expected much because there are no major blood vessels in that area. More disturbing, but again, not unexpected, was a little greenish fluid coming from the wound. That meant rumen fluid had escaped or was escaping from the rumen.

The rumen, basically a fermentation vat, holds fifty or more gallons of material in big cows. Included are all sorts of bacteria and protozoa, along with water, grass, hay and grain, depending on what the animal has eaten. Escape of the fluid into the abdominal cavity would mean contamination of an otherwise sterile area. Its seriousness is great—something like a ruptured appendix in a human. To put it another way, the cow was in a life-threatening situation unless I could intervene successfully.

Examining the right side, I found again that heart and lung sounds were normal except for the expiratory grunts. There was no evidence of a hole where a missile could have exited.

"Well, the only way I can tell how bad it is, is to open her up," I said to Clark as I removed the stethoscope from my ears and shoved it into the hip pocket of my Levis. "If the bullet was stopped by all that hay and grass in the paunch, then I can sew up the hole, clean out the cavity, give her some drugs, and she should make it," I went on. "Anything else wrong in there will be bad news."

"Okay Doc, do the best you can," Clark said as he stared at his wife and kids standing nearby, no doubt silently saying to them, "We're trying."

"You put the halter on her and tie her as close to the wall as you can. Leave her left side exposed," I directed, thanking my good fortune that it was daylight. The daylight in the shed was difficult enough, let alone having to use light from a lantern in the dark. "I'll get my gear and be right back."

The cow was really gentle, so she tried to kick me only twice when I placed the three-inch needle along her spine, and between the side processes of the vertebrae, in order to inject the anesthetic drug next to the nerves running into the area where the incision would be made. While waiting for the anesthetic to take effect, I laid out the instruments in a white enamel tray, which contained a disinfectant solution.

That done, I tested the depth of anesthesia by pricking her side with a needle. She did not flinch or try to kick, so I proceeded to make a twelve-inch incision in her side with my sharp scalpel. The kids, who had watched in complete silence up to now, started to whimper and jabber. Clark promptly told them to be quiet or go outside. They obeyed at once, and the shed became completely quiet once more.

I had made my way through the skin and muscle, and when I entered the abdominal cavity I smelled, at once, the distinctive odor of escaping rumen gas. Placing my left hand into the dark cavity, I grasped the rumen wall and lifted it up into the incision. The rent made by the bullet wasn't very large and could be closed with a mere two stitches. Still inside, returning the organ to its correct position, I reached through to the right side. My worst fear was realized. Fluid was running into the abdominal cavity from a large four-inch tear in the lower portion of the rumen.

"Hell's fire!" I exclaimed, withdrawing my arm from inside the cow.

Up to that point, Clark had been telling me a story about a couple of hunters over in the Big Horn area who had killed a mule thinking it to be an elk. They had tied it on the roof of their car and proceeded happily on their way, unaware of any mistake until reaching a game checkpoint.

"It beats the hell out of me what people like that are doing hunting," he said, finishing the story.

Turning around, I held up my hand and lower arm for Clark to see. They were completely covered with a greenish brown ingesta.

"She's got a big hole on the other side of her paunch, Clark, and the juices are running through it into her belly," I said. "Now that we know about this, I don't figure there's much of a chance of saving her, but I'll sew up the hole and clean her out the best I can. Then, we'll have to hope for the best."

"Those sons-a-bitches! If I could catch them, I'd punch them right in the nose," he burst out, half sobbing and clinching his fists.

A week later, Clark called to tell me he had given the little cow all the medicine I had left, but that she was down and wouldn't get up. He wanted to know if there was anything else to do. If not, he would put her out of her misery.

"Nothing more that would help," I responded sadly. I thought of how much pain and suffering the little cow had already gone through and how much effort the Clarks had spent in nursing care. Slowly I added, "Best you take care of her as you suggest." Dejectedly, I hung up the phone, turned to Harriet and related the news.

"I know you care so much," she said, comfortingly. "But remember, Dear, you can't save them all."

GROWN MEN CAN CRY

During the years I spent in private veterinary practice, there were a few times when I saw grown men cry. Two such times resulted from bloat, once in a flock of sheep and once in a herd of cattle.

Bloat is an excessive accumulation of gas in the first compartment of a ruminant's stomach. Unlike humans and most other animals, which have simple or one-compartment stomachs, ruminants, such as sheep and cattle, have stomachs with four compartments. They are called the rumen, reticulum, omasum, and abomasum.

In its most devastating form, bloat can occur as a result of sheep or cattle grazing on legumes, such as clover or alfalfa. If these forages are eaten when wet, the incidence of bloat is higher than if they are eaten dry. Among other changes, gas accumulates until there is enough pressure on the lungs to suffocate an animal. Bloat, therefore, is always an emergency.

The first time I was faced with an entire flock suffering from bloat took place while in practice at Sundance. Early one fall morning, I had decided to finish the last of the painting on the first home Harriet and I would own. That house, originally located at the Keyhole Dam, some forty miles west of Sundance, had been used as housing for personnel overseeing the building of the dam. We had bought the house on a bid from the government, however, and had moved it over back roads and sagebrush flats and placed it on a cement block foundation early in the summer. We continued living in the apartment over our drugstore while completing repairs on the house. Naturally we were excited as this was our first home in the eight years of our married life. On the day of this incident, I had gone over early to work on it before calls came in and before the sun got too hot. Before long my plans were dashed!

Not half the bucket of white paint was used when I heard the roar of an engine and the honking of the horn in our old Jeep station wagon. Turning to look, I saw Harriet frantically waving her hand. Paintbrush in hand, I walked to the edge of the road in front of the house where she had stopped. Sticking her head out of the window, she half-shouted, "Johnny Cale's got a bunch of sheep sick. Vera just called. They both sounded out of their minds!"

"Did she say what was the matter?" I asked, hoping to get some clue as to what I might need in the way of drugs or equipment not ordinarily carried in my pickup.

"They said some were dead, some down, and others bloated. Johnny put them on the alfalfa hayfield last night in order that they might get some bloom on them. They were to go to market today!" she responded. While we were talking, I noticed Harry, our year-old son, still in his night clothes on the front seat beside his mother.

"It's only a couple of miles up to Johnny's. You follow me. If I need any more supplies, you can run back to get them," I instructed. With that, I threw the paintbrush toward the house and ran to my pickup.

The Cale ranch was located in a canyon just north of town, in a range of mountains known as the Bear Lodge. In five minutes we were there. Johnny jumped out of the corral when I drove in. He looked like a wild man: Levis covered with manure, his shirt soaking wet, the sweat running off his face, his lips and mouth covered with foamy, dry saliva.

"Christ, Doc, I've got into a real mess," he greeted me as I rolled out the pickup seat and ran around the back to get the equipment I knew would be needed. He followed me and repeated the story Harriet had related. Then he began to cry.

"How many lambs do you have?" I queried as I reached into the Pandora bag for the instrument kit containing a curved sharp pointed knife called a bistoury, and a trocar. A trocar is a tube-like instrument, similar in shape to an injection needle, but measuring about six inches long and half an inch in diameter.

Finally, I grabbed a stomach tube and mouth speculum. A stomach tube is a black plastic hose, approximately eight feet long. The speculum is a stainless steel pipe about eighteen inches long to place in the animal's mouth, through which to pass the stomach tube into the esophagus. Its purpose is to protect the tube from the teeth and chewing movements of the animal.

Bloat comes in at least two forms, and because I didn't know which kind these lambs were suffering, I took all those instruments to treat either kind. With regular bloat, the gas would be all in one pocket, like air in a balloon. The stomach tube or the trocar would work in that case. However, with frothy or foamy bloat, the air would be trapped as little bubbles, similar to soap bubbles, throughout the ingesta or food contents of the stomach compartment. The bistoury would be needed in that event, because I would have to slash open the animal's rumen to let the foamy ingesta out. Otherwise, the beast could quite possibly die of asphyxiation.

"We had ninety head of lambs last night," Johnny explained, once he got hold of himself. "Must be at least ten dead ones now." By that time, we were climbing into the corral.

"Let's get that one," I said, pointing to a lamb with its tongue out, gasping for breath, and whose left side, just ahead of the hips, extended over its backbone. When Johnny grabbed the animal, I quickly inserted the speculum and tube into its mouth and began to push the tube down the esophagus. When I felt that one end was in the rumen, I held the other end to my right ear and listened. Only a little air came out. Pushing the tube in and then out a little, I listened again. Still no great expulsion of air. I knew then that we were fighting frothy bloat and that this would be one tough day!

"It's foamy bloat, Johnny," I said. "That means we will have to open up the side of every lamb that looks like it is ready to go down and die. Have you a sharp pocket knife? If you don't, better get something sharp enough to open the side in a hurry. Here, I'll show you what I mean." With that, I pulled the bistoury out of my shirt pocket and made a six-inch gash in the left side of the lamb he was holding. Immediately, green frothy rumen contents shot out of the opening with explosive force. The lamb just stood there, but began to breathe easier.

I turned to Johnny. "I'll need to sew them up quickly, so it'll be up to you to open up those you think will need it. Don't be afraid to make a big enough hole to let the stuff out. You'll lose them if you don't," I told him. "I'll get my instruments and set up over in the shed. You bring them over to me the minute you can." There was no crying after that, just heat, dust, and hard work.

Ben Root, the trucker who had been called to transport the lambs to market, drove in during our conversation. He had a good sharp knife, so, with no fanfare, he too was pressed into service.

An incision into the rumen needs to be closed soon because of the certainty of peritonitis developing when ingesta spills into the abdominal cavity between the rumen and wall of the abdomen, contaminating an otherwise sterile area. I knew there would be some contamination, but if it wasn't too bad, I felt that any infection resulting from it could be controlled with penicillin.

It was now about six-thirty. Harriet, with Harry in her arms, and Vera had been watching us and talking quietly. I turned to Harriet and asked, "Do you suppose you can help me until it's time to open the store at eight? I need someone to hold those lambs while I sew."

"I'll take care of the baby," Vera volunteered, reaching for the now wide-awake thumbsucker.

Having had a father, a brother, and an uncle who practiced veterinary medicine, and having been brought up in a ranching environment, Harriet readily responded by handing the baby to Vera and heading toward the pickup to get two stainless steel water buckets. A veterinarian always needs water!

It didn't take long to set up and start to suture the wound I had made in the first lamb. First, I sewed the rent in the rumen, then cut away the contaminated tissue of the muscle and skin before finally closing the opening. Both Harriet and I were on our knees, she holding the animal around the neck with her left arm, in a hugging posture, leaving her right hand free to pass me the instruments I needed. The position for a real contortionist, and no place for an arthritic!

Three lambs had been surgically treated and repaired by seven-thirty when Harriet had to leave to open the store and get the baby bathed and fed. By that time, the crisis was abating and Johnny took over Harriet's job. Johnny and Ben had gotten all the live lambs into the corral, and had opened only nine more after the first one I had opened. Although many were still bloated, they were not bad enough to puncture.

By eleven o'clock we completed suturing and cleaned up. Earlier in the morning Vera had brought us coffee and rolls, which we devoured hungrily between patients.

Taking one last walk among the lambs made us all feel much better. In fact, Johnny was even able to add a little levity to the tragic situation. As we stepped over the boards of the corral, heading for the pickup, he laughed and said, "By God, Doc, I thought at one time I'd have to get my shotgun and shoot some of those lambs out of the sky. They had so much air in them, they looked like they would float away."

I smiled and handed Johnny a bottle of penicillin to use in the treatment of the ten surgically repaired lambs. Ben had left the Cales' about nine o'clock, and when I arrived back at the store, it was obvious by the crowd gathered inside that word of the tragedy had spread all over town.

The real tragedy of the situation was that the loss of those lambs took all of one year's profit from Johnny's ranching operation.

A near tragedy involving bloat occurred some eight years later in a herd of cows on the Jim Peters' place on the Powder River, north of Gillette.

One Friday afternoon, I attended the Gillette Livestock Auction in the capacity of a state official, inspecting the livestock being sold for health. When animals were sold, it was my duty to issue a health certificate attesting that the animals had been checked and were free of any infectious disease. I had just gone in to my saleyard office from the yard when Harriet called from our large animal clinic.

"Bob, you've got to go right out to Jim Peters.' His wife just called to say they have about twenty-five bloated cows. They broke into the alfalfa field sometime this morning after Jim had seen them. He's out now trying to get them into the corral."

Suddenly, my private practitioner hat was back on.

"I'll be up in a few minutes to get some drugs. You call Betty and tell her I'm on my way. If Jim is able to put any cows in the chute, have him tie a stick in their mouth, like a bit. It should be the diameter of a broom handle and about a foot long. They will chew on it, and the movements could help them relieve the bloat until I can get there."

I slammed the receiver back in its cradle, jumped up from the desk and said to Budge While, the brand inspector seated at another small desk in the office, "I've got to go out to Jim Peters' place to treat some bloated cattle. I've inspected the stock here, and everything is okay, except for those in the quarantine pen. Will you go ahead and fill out the blanks on the health certificates so folks can get the ones they bought out of the yard before I get back? I've signed about twenty certificates. That should be enough. Any animals going out of state will have to wait until I return and check the book of regulations."

He grunted agreement without removing the well-chewed cigar from his mouth. I slapped on my Stetson and left in a rush.

Only in emergencies such as this did I break the rules and let someone else fill out the health papers. It was then, and still is, acceptable only for the inspector to complete the paper work. Nevertheless, I rationalized, I had indeed looked at all the animals in the yard and filling out the document was just a formality. The next closest veterinarian to the Peters' was seventy-five miles on west! I really had to tend to Jim's cattle.

It was twenty-five miles up the Powder River road to the Rockypoint turnoff, and I was there in twenty minutes. Record time. The Peters' place was another ten miles over dirt road.

Dust rolled as I passed a half dozen pickups and Jeeps parked along Jim's drive. Pulling to a stop, I jumped out of my truck, ran over to the corral and climbed up to get a look at what was going on. Two or three neighbors were at the chute placing a stick in a cow's mouth and securing it with baler twine behind her ears. The cow chewed on it furiously.

Jim and two other men were trying to separate those cows with huge swollen abdomens from those who seemed less distended. Most staggered, and their tongues dangled. They grunted and gasped for breath as they were pushed forward toward the chute. Two dead cows lay in one corner.

Jim hollered, "We're trying to get those sticks in their mouths like you told Betty, Doc! Havin' a hellava time gettin' them in the chute, though." His face was red and sweaty, and he was half crying.

Running back to the truck, I got the stomach tube, pump and speculum, as well as a gallon of mineral oil and some anti-foaming agent. I knew what kind of bloat I was dealing with without a preliminary test with the tube.

When I reached the front of the chute, the men had another cow caught in its head-catch. She was really slobbering and grunting as she gasped for breath. Her left side in front of the hips was extended higher than her backbone. Quickly, I rammed the speculum into her mouth and threaded the tube through it into the rumen. Only a little air came out of the tube, but she was chewing frantically on the speculum and air came out around it when she eructated or belched. Wanting to hasten the process, I had one of the men pour some of the anti-foaming agent and a half gallon of mineral oil into a nearby bucket. I rammed the tube into my pump and hurriedly began to pump the liquid from the bucket, pumping it dry in only a few minutes. I continuously worked the tube in her mouth—out a foot, in a foot—attempting to "mix" the medicine with the ingesta in hopes of speeding up the palliative remedy. This procedure worked well on a single case of bloat, but was taking far too long in this situation. Six more highly bloated cattle waited to be treated! With no further delay, I pulled out the tube and speculum, reached for a stick and jammed it into the cow's mouth, securing it there with baler twine.

When we had finished the sixth, the crisis was pretty much over. Often in cases of frothy bloat, moving the animals about does much to relieve the distress.

The sticks were removed from the cows' mouths when their sides returned to normal, but it was necessary to run all of them back through the chute in order to accomplish this.

As I was leaving the corral, Jim, who was standing by one of the dead cows shouted, "Hey, Doc, will you come over and show me where you're supposed to stick a critter that's bloated? I was afraid to do it to these two, or I might have saved them."

I put my equipment down and walked over to where he was standing next to the cow with the greatest amount of bloat. "Loan me your jackknife and I'll show you," I said. Others were gathering around to watch the demonstration.

I opened the knife to the sharpest, most pointed blade, and gripping it in my right hand, I said, "Now what you do is find the highest point here on the left side, right between the front of the hip and the last rib." I outlined the area with my left hand. "Then just plunge the knife into the hilt and rip a four- to six-inch gash in her side. Like this." I drove the knife into the dead animal's side and opened up a six-inch hole. Jim and one of the neighbors were so intent on seeing the exact location of the incision that they were bent over the cow, peering down at almost the precise point of the knife's impact. Green foamy, putrid-smelling ingesta exploded through the hole, and their peering faces caught the full force of the flying material. Their hats, faces, and shirt fronts were a sight to behold!

Other men who were watching fell back convulsed with laughter. All tears had vanished and the sadness of the situation was momentarily forgotten.

"Don't be afraid to open them up good," I chuckled. "They're going to die if you don't. They can always be sewed up, and most will live."

GUMBO: EPISODE 1

Gumbo, by dictionary definition, is a fine, silty soil of the Western prairies, which becomes sticky and nonporous when wet. A polite way of saying gumbo is that substance of onerous properties, the likes of which this Easterner had never encountered. It took one car engine and one four-wheel-drive Jeep clutch assembly to give me a real understanding of gumbo's power and might.

I'd been in the Bayhorse, Montana, region about five days testing cattle and vaccinating for brucellosis, a disease that causes abortion in cattle. The same organism that is responsible for the disease in cattle causes undulant fever in humans exposed to the milk and excrement of infected animals. This poses not only a public health and animal health problem but also creates an economic disaster for ranchers who depend upon getting one live calf from each cow every year.

Controlling the disease, at that time, consisted of blood testing the cows and bulls to determine those infected, removing those showing a positive test, and vaccinating the ones that tested negative. Today, vaccinating adult cattle against the disease would result in severe reprimand, if not revocation of one's license.

It had been a long and tiring week for a greenhorn right out of school. Each day I'd stood in front of a cattle chute taking blood from the jugular vein of each animal and every evening titrating the blood samples drawn. The serological test performed required lots of pipetting, and I hadn't been to bed before midnight for four consecutive nights. We rolled out of bed at four-thirty every morning to start the momentous routine all over again.

Friday, the day to go home, finally arrived. One to two inches of rain had fallen in the night and it was still drizzling in the morning when we started to wind up our work. Around ten o'clock the sun came out. Work had been organized so I could leave for home directly after lunch.

At the dinner table, one of the ranchers looked up at me. "Doc," he said, "you'd better wait an hour or two before you leave. Don't think that little car of yours will make it to the blacktop unless you do."

I looked at him quizzically. It hadn't rained that much and the ground was drying out rapidly. I did notice with some wonder, however, a couple of other heads nodding agreement to the rancher's statement. In spite of my wonder, I responded, "I've been in wetter places before with that little car, shouldn't have any trouble now. Besides, if I don't leave shortly, it will be late afternoon when I get home." I thought to myself: thirty miles to the blacktop, fifteen miles to Gillette, and seventy-five more miles to Sundance. Three hours with any luck at all. Only later would I reflect on that obtuse warning, offered me so warmly. Only later would I know what it truly meant.

The little car was a 1950, six-cylinder, two-door, bullet-nosed Studebaker. Harriet and I bought it the fall before graduation with no thought of where I would practice. We purchased it through a classmate's father who had a car agency. It paid to have contacts in those days because cars were a scarce commodity. We figured we had better avail ourselves of the opportunity while we could afford it; the first few years in practice could be financially unpredictable.

Folks in the Bayhorse area had different kinds of vehicles for their transportation. Most had powerful four-wheel-drive Jeeps, similar to those the Army used during the second world war. Some had regular rear-wheel-rive pickups, and some had cars. Four-wheel-drive pickups were rarely used in those days, but the fact that some of the more well-to-do ranchers possessed them gave me food for thought a little later on. Ranchers, of course, had quarter horses to ride when working livestock, and teams to drive when feeding cattle. All, however, were experienced enough to stay home, or stay right where they were, when the "gumbo was rolling."

Dinner over, I said my good-byes and headed down the road toward home. The road was kind of greasy or slippery in places for the first ten miles or so, but otherwise it seemed okay. "Drying out real good," I said to myself. "Wonder what those folks at the dinner table were worried about?" No sooner thought than, suddenly, I realized the little car's engine was laboring more than it should.

Heading down a slight incline, I heard mud hitting the fenders and was aware of a slurpy sound coming from the floorboard under my feet. Soon the little car slowed perceptibly, even though I was pressing more and more on the accelerator.

Finally, I decided to see if something was wrong. I stopped, got out of the car, and started to walk. Halfway around the car I cleaned the mud off my boots, commandeering a nearby stick for the job. Continuing back toward the open door, I found that in a few steps it was necessary to clean the mud off my boots again. To my amazement, what was worse, I found the underside of all the fenders filled almost completely with a gray, clay-like mud. Only about two inches of space remained between the mud-packed fenders and the tire tops. The same material was sticking out, perpendicularly, a good eight inches from each tire. I couldn't believe it!

"Some way, I have to get that stuff out from under the fenders," I reasoned. Dragging my muddy boots, I proceeded to the car's trunk, opened the lid, reached into the tool kit and pulled out a long screwdriver.

Scraping the tires wasn't too bad, though I needed two hands to push the screwdriver through the mass, and the force of my whole body to pull it free. By the time I finished, my screwdriver looked something less than straight.

"Now for the fenders," I said to myself. Kneeling down I jabbed the screwdriver upward into the drying mass and tried to pry it loose. It wouldn't budge. With all the force I could muster, I pushed and pushed. Suddenly the screwdriver bent into a neat right angle and freed itself from the handle with a loud crack.

What a bitch this is, I thought. Guess I'll have to use my hands.

The mud felt slick, like it wouldn't stay in your hand if you didn't hang on with a firm grip. I managed to grab a fairly large chunk of the goo, pulled it out and away from the fender and opened my hand, sure the mass would slip quickly away. But there it stayed.

Shake it off, I thought. When I shook my hand a little, the gumbo budged only a little. It just sort of rolled over on itself and stayed right there, as if loath to leave. A mighty shake helped more, the other hand helped even more, and the stick I'd used to clean off my boots finished the job, such as it was. By the time I'd finished cleaning the fenders out, I had journeyed often to the edge of the road to rid my hands, arms, and boots of the clinging stuff. I used the sagebrush and grass nearby and even the fence posts to wipe free of the metallic looking adhering mire. Each time I'd return to the car, even though it was a mere twenty-five feet away from the grass, my boots were again laden and needed scraping.

Fenders fairly free, I decided to move on. I started the engine, threw the shifting gear into reverse, thinking: maybe if I can back up the hill, and then get a running start, I'll be able to keep going. To make a long story short, I moved about a mile, then had to repeat the cleaning procedure all over again.

At one point I had the car in low gear going down a very steep incline. The engine overheated, and smoke poured out around the clutch. Finally, we moved no more.

Stopped and stuck, I hoped someone would come along. A vain hope, I knew, as I said to myself, "Ranchers are too smart to venture out when gumbo rolls!"

It was late in the day by now, and I knew Harriet would start to worry when darkness came. I sat in my mud-caked clothes and wondered: what next? For half an hour I rested, then I became restless and decided to try moving out once more.

I walked around the car to assess the situation and noticed the gumbo was not sticking to my boots as it had earlier. "Maybe the same thing will happen to the tires and fenders," I hoped. Again, I cleaned tires and fenders as best I could. Incredibly weary from the chore, I climbed into the car once more, cranked the engine and stepped on the accelerator. We moved! The little car moved and kept moving! In half an hour we reached blacktop, and I heaved a sigh.

Two hours later, out of pitch blackness I walked into the office at the drugstore. Harriet looked up from posting the day's receipts and said, "Where have you been? I've been worried silly!" Then her eyes fell on my hands and clothing. Her face took on an understanding look as she said, "Oh, I know. You've been in the gumbo. You poor dear."

The next morning I tried in vain to remove the mud from under the car's fenders and off the floor boards. Mostly, it remained there, and only time and travel removed it. When we traded for a pickup truck six months later, some still remained.

GUMBO: EPISODE 2

Two years after Episode 1, I knew that two-wheel-drive pickups and little cars, though economical to operate, were not the answer to prairie practice.

Always at the mercy of rapid and unexpected weather changes, four-wheel drive vehicles were better suited for some road conditions. For this reason we had purchased a second-hand, four-wheel-drive station wagon Jeep.

One rainy spring day, a rancher called saying he had a good registered cow in trouble. "Doc, I gotta cow who's cast her withers!" he yelled into the phone. "Can you come right out?"

"Casting her withers" meant that a cow had calved and, during the process, had strained and continued to strain until she had pushed not only the calf out of her body, but also her uterus. A cow's life, under these circumstances, is in grave danger. Exposing a large internal organ, roughly the size of a washtub, to cold exterior air often produces shock, which must be treated rapidly before the condition becomes irreversible.

Cows with such a condition can become frantic and start to run, or move restlessly about, shaking the bleeding calf bed in such a manner that interior major blood vessels may burst, causing the animal to bleed to death.

My client's ranch was twenty miles from the blacktop. When I went in around eleven in the morning, the road was slippery (greasy, the natives would say), and deep ruts all along the road kept me from slipping sideways off the route. In fact, it would have been impossible to leave the deep ruts even if one made an extreme effort to do so.

Once at the ranch, I completed my task in less than an hour. It took only a short while to replace the uterus, and because the cow was gentle, the organ had not been traumatized.

Finished, I stored my equipment in the Jeep, walked over to speak to my client, and suddenly I knew the gumbo was rolling!

Now I remembered from my first episode with gumbo that when it rolls, you better stay where you are. Don't move—stay put. In a couple of hours the earth would dry enough to allow travel over it; before that time, doom was inevitable.

But this was spring—calving time in the West, a busy, stressful time for ranchers. The time a veterinarian is greatly needed and much in demand. Not a time to sit around and wait for the caprice of gumbo!

"Guess I better put chains on. Just in case," I said to my client.

"Best if you wait an hour or two, Doc," he replied. "Should be okay by then."

"I really need to give it a try," I answered, knowing full well he was probably right. "I have so many calls waiting, it will take me, with luck, until midnight to finish."

"Better stay for a bite of dinner, anyway. You gotta eat somewhere," he offered good-naturedly, while helping me chain up the Jeep.

"Sure would like to," I said, "but I better keep going." A feeling of gloom settled over me as I slid behind the steering wheel and started the engine.

Waving my hand, I accelerated a bit, swung left off the drive and onto the rutted road. Oh, the gumbo was rolling!

With the front wheels already in a drive mode, all I had to do was change the gear ratio with the shift stick located on the floorboard next to my right leg. Simple: increase or decrease the gear ratio with a stroke.

Even with a fast start down the road, the engine began to labor in just a few minutes. I reached down and slammed the shift stick into a lower gear.

The wagon ground slowly and laboriously down the road. Only when water stood in the ruts could any acceleration be noticed. I thought: if only the ruts were filled with water, we'd make some time!

Grinding along mile after mile, I at last reached the steep incline leading to the blacktop. A few short yards up the hill the Jeep stopped. I shifted the gears to several different positions but to no avail.

Turning off the engine, I climbed out of the machine onto the monstrous mud. The sun was beating down now, and it was extremely warm. All the fenders were caked with mud and a good four inches of the stuff was sticking all around the tires.

"The chains are holding it," I reasoned. "I'll remove them, and that will give the clearance needed to make it to the blacktop."

An hour later I had the chains removed and the fenders cleared. I felt as though the mud removed from the Jeep had become an integral part of my hands, face, arms, hair, coveralls, and whatever.

I shucked my coveralls and shirt, threw the heavy mud-laden chains in the back end of the wagon, got behind the wheel, started the engine, shifted down to low gear and moved ahead maybe a hundred yards. Dead stop.

"Back up," I said to myself. "Then give it a run!" That I did. Back, and then forward until stopped. Back, and then forward until stopped.

Smoke began to rise around the clutch assembly and come through the floorboard. The engine roared, and the wagon moved no more. The clutch was gone—burned up! Fortunately, a friendly ranchhand soon came driving up the same road I had just traveled.

"How come you are able to go in your truck when I got stuck in my Jeep?" I asked incredulously.

"Well," he said, "for one thing, the treads are pretty well gone on my tires, and for another, the gumbo stopped rolling about half an hour ago!"

"Maybe someday I will learn," I mumbled.

"By gollies, Doc," my friend said, "I seen a lot of crazy things happen when gumbo is rollin'. Remember one time we were loggin' up on the ridge. We had two big teams of horses hooked to an empty loggin' wagon on the level ground. The gumbo was rollin'. Now, you can believe it or not, but the gumbo piled up on those wheels so bad, they began to turn backward! Made the thing worse than pullin' a sled on dry ground. The gumbo stuck to the horses' feet, too. They finally got so tuckered, they just couldn't go no more. We unhooked the big fellas and called it a day!"

By the time he finished his story, we were entering the small nearby town of Upton.

"Just let me off at the garage," I said. "I'm sure glad you came along, otherwise I'd still be walking. Many thanks."

The Jeep was towed to the garage, where several days and many dollars later, a new clutch assembly was installed, and it once again became a serviceable vehicle.

Prairie practice to me is synonymous with gumbo. The saga of these two episodes is only a sample of many such experiences.

I was always dumbfounded to realize that gumbo, that soil which grew the best natural pasture and hay anywhere in the country, which grew the finest hard wheat and kept ranchers in business through long periods of drought, could be so fickle. One minute it was benevolent and benign, but another minute, when given a little water, it turned into a gluey, gummy, cohesive substance, monstrous in character. A veritable Jekyll and Hyde! The sticky characteristic of silly putty, cotton candy, or flypaper is pale compared to gumbo.

Old-timers and homesteaders in the West have a saying about gumbo: "If you will stick to the gumbo when it's dry, it will stick to you when it's wet."

THE WRECK

Sometimes people would ask and pay for advice they wouldn't take. Not often, mind you, but when they did, once in awhile it ended up in a wreck!

The event I remember most vividly involved a shipment of "drouthy" cattle from Texas. These cattle had been under severe drouth conditions for over a year. Finally, they were sent to market before they died on the range. One of our local ranchers, Matt Wenger, went to Texas, bought them at an auction, and had them shipped by rail to Upton, a good forty-five miles from his ranch. He planned to trail, rather than truck the animals home. I didn't see the cattle until they had been on the trail four or five days. I wouldn't have seen them then except that Matt sensed some trouble and dropped in at the drugstore to talk to me about it. It was about eight in the morning, I remember, because Matt was the first one in the store after Harriet unlocked the front door. I had just come down the stairs to go to the office when I heard him greet Harriet and say, "Is Doc around? I need to talk to him."

"He just went into the office. He's on his way to a call," she responded. "Bob, Matt Wenger is here to see you. Can you wait a minute before you leave?"

I turned and went back into the drugstore. "Morning, Matt. What can I do for you?"

"Got some cattle out on the trail that are acting funny," Matt replied as he hoisted himself onto one of the bar stools at the soda fountain. "Do you suppose you can do any good if you come out and look at them?"

This was a different way to start a conversation to be sure, but then, Matt was different, too. "How are they acting?" I asked.

"Well, most of them are doing all right, but some are just standing around grunting, like they are over-full, but they're not. There's a couple of dead ones, too," he answered. Harriet had poured us each a cup of coffee and set it before us while we were talking.

Early in the fall of the year, it was not uncommon to have outbreaks of Pulmonary Emphysema. In fact, the call I was headed to sounded like it. This atypical pneumonia is associated with a change of forage, such as when cattle are brought from their summer range and turned onto a field or meadow that had

25

been cut over for hay. It hits them hardest if they are hungry and gorge them-selves on the new pasture.

The thought crossed my mind that Matt didn't do much haying, so I won-dered where he could have cattle that might have the disease, if that is what it turned out to be. "Where have you got your cattle?" I asked.

"They're in a field out on the Upton road. I got it leased from Jim McGov-ern," Matt replied. Then he told me about his trip to Texas, about buying ninety head of cattle and having them shipped to Upton. He rented the field that had been cut over for hay and was letting them rest and fill up before going on to his ranch.

"Well, it sounds like Pulmonary Emphysema to me," I offered. Then I told him what it was and that I could get out to look at them as soon as I got back from the other call, likely first thing in the afternoon. In the meantime he should try to move them real easily to the nearest corral.

"There's no corral; it's a hayfield," Matt explained.

"Better get some snow fence or something to make an enclosure," I suggested. "We'll need to have some way to examine and treat those that are sick."

"How much is it going to cost?"

"Well, fifteen dollars for the call and whatever drugs it takes." I got off the stool, anxious to be gone since I was already late getting started. "The drugs are pretty expensive. Probably run about ten to fifteen dollars a head," I added, just to make sure Matt would have a chance to mull it all over before I started any therapy. He could be one to let nature take its course, with a little assistance from a rifle, if something was going to cost too much.

"Well, okay. You come out and have a look when you get back. I'll try to get something rigged up to catch those that are the sickest, then we'll decide what to do after you figure out what they got," he replied, finishing off his coffee and ambling toward the door.

It was close to two o'clock before I made it to the snow fence corral in the middle of the hay meadow. Matt was sitting in his pickup, chewing on the stub of a cigar, along with his hired hand, a stranger whom he never introduced. I counted twelve head of the thinnest cows I had ever seen in my life just standing with their tongues hanging out, gasping for every breath of air. At the end of each expiration, I heard the characteristic grunt that went with Pulmonary Emphy-sema. I studied them for a minute, then turned to Matt and said, "They have what I told you about this morning, but gosh, they are awfully thin."

"If you think they're thin, you should have seen the ones I didn't dare buy for fear they wouldn't make the trip. Hell, these are in good shape!" came his retort. "You say it's going to cost ten to fifteen dollars a head to treat them?" he went on.

"Yep," I answered. "The drugs are antihistamines and corticosteroids, some of the most expensive we have now. They are the only thing that seems to work. There have not been any controlled studies to support the use, but they seem to do better than doing nothing. Unless we have to run them around to give them the drugs, then it's probably better to do nothing. They seem to drown in their own lung fluids when this happens."

"Well, let's try it on them," Matt allowed. "If it doesn't work too well, we won't treat anymore if they get sick."

With that, I got the drugs and syringes together to give them the shots. The two men crowded each animal against the snow fence with their bodies and held them there until I'd given the medicine. The cattle were too sick to fight, except for an occasional kick when I stuck in the needle. When we got through, I turned to Matt. "We better go look at the rest. Could be more by now."

"Well, if there are, we're just going to let them go. I'm going to start trailing them out of here toward home tomorrow," he responded.

I was a little taken aback. "That's the worst thing you could do, to move them when there's likely another twenty-five or thirty in the early stages of the disease. The best thing for you to do is to bring some good hay into this pasture and give them some "cake"—anything to dilute that meadow grass in their stomachs. Otherwise, I'm afraid if you force them onto the trail when they still have the toxin that causes this, plus the dust and heat, you'll really have trouble."

"Well, I'm going to see how they are, come morning. I'll make up my mind then," he stated.

"I'll come out about seven in the morning to look at these we just treated, and to see if there are any more."

"Suit yourself. We'll be on the road by then, if I decide to move them."

Driving among the cattle in the meadow, I saw about five more with signs of the condition that should have been treated. Matt said he would leave them until morning and see how they looked. Obviously he was all through with treating anymore.

The next morning at six-thirty I was on the road to the hayfield, which was only ten minutes out of town. As I breasted the hill before the meadow, I saw the first of the cattle trailing along in the "bar pit," or ditch, alongside the highway. When I got to the top of the hill, I could see them strung out for a half mile. Those on the "drag," or end, moved very slowly. Matt on horseback was driving them. Another rider, in the meadow, looked as if he was trying to move several more toward the gate leading into the bar pit. When I got to Matt, I pulled over to the side of the highway. I could see that a half dozen of the cattle directly in front of him were breathing pretty hard even though it was still cool. I got out and went over to him. "I see you decided to move them," I spoke first.

"Yep, couldn't just let them stay in there and die. Had to do something," came his reply. "Lost two of those you treated yesterday. More are sick this morning. Figured it couldn't be much worse!"

Matt didn't figure it could get worse, or maybe he just hoped it wouldn't, but he soon found out it could! He hadn't gotten the drag a mile up the road until five had gone down and wouldn't get up. That was on top of the two he lost in the night, the ten others still alive in the makeshift corral, and those the hired man was trying to bring out of the meadow. I stopped where he was after checking on those in the corral. He was off his horse looking at one of the "downers," adjacent to a set of wooden corrals owned by rancher Sid Cooley. Without looking up he said, "Well, I guess I better get them into Sid's corrals. He's got some water in there, and I can bring them some hay. I'm sure he won't mind as long as they haven't got anything that's catchin'."

"I'm sure he won't," I responded. "Have him talk to me if there's any question. What are you going to do with those cattle that have gone on ahead? The lead ones must be a mile and a half down the road by this time."

"I'm going to let them go on toward home and catch up with them later. If they feel that good, they must not have gotten too much of that toxin, or whatever is causing this," he retorted. "You go and treat those that are down, and I'll go on ahead and bring those back to the corral that are not looking too good. It sure is a mess. Maybe these cattle won't be all that cheap by the time I get them home." With that, he chomped down on his cigar stub, swung into the saddle and rode up the bar pit to open the gate into the corral so he could run in the ones he wanted.

When I finished my treatments, I drove slowly toward town, looking over the cattle still headed that way. I hollered to Matt that I would be back in the morning if he wanted.

"Okay, Doc, check on us in the morning!" he shouted back, reluctantly.

By the next morning, two more were dead—two of the five I'd treated. When I opened them up, the alveoli or little air pockets in the lungs were full of blood and other fluid. All of the passageways for air to travel from outside the body to the lungs were also filled with the material. They had suffocated in their own fluids!

Before he got through, Matt lost ten or twelve head out of the ninety he started with. I never did get the final count. He just stopped having me out and kept pushing a few more toward home each day. He wasn't the kind of person who would volunteer information, especially when it must have hurt so badly. I always felt he could have had half the loss and grief if he had heeded the advice he paid me for. I doubt that he even learned from the wreck. But that, too, is part of practice.

SAM

Sam was a Boxer—fawn-colored-black-faced-white-chested, with four white feet. He had a big tongue, too. He was the first of several dogs Harriet and I would own and he came to us through a client after Harriet had lost her first child. He was very special to us because of that, and really, also because he was such a character.

I had just brought Harriet home from the hospital after her miscarriage, and she was pretty blue. Maybe Mary sensed it, or maybe it was coincidental, but the day after Harriet got home I received this telephone call.

"Doctor, this is Mary Early. I have one pup left from Sally's last litter that I'd like you and Harriet to have. Do you think you would like it?"

Now Mary Early lived over in Newcastle, and she had a Boxer male and bitch from which she produced a litter of pups once a year. Nearly every Boxer in Newcastle came from this pair. They were fine specimens of the breed.

One problem she had in selling the pups or giving them away was the amount of cosmetic surgery they required (tail-docking and ear-trimming) in the absence of a veterinarian close by. Further, in those days, not many veterinarians in that part of the country were trained to do ear trims. The closest were either in Rapid City, South Dakota (90 miles), or Casper, Wyoming (100-plus miles).

Soon after Harriet and I had moved to Sundance, Mary brought over a litter of six puppies for me to give their shots and dock their tails. At that time, she approached me about doing the ear trims, too, when it was time.

"I don't plan to do ear trims," I told Mary. "I don't like to do that kind of surgery."

She was somewhat taken aback, but responded at once by asking if there was someone I would recommend.

"I'll call a colleague in Casper for you and see if he can do it," I offered. "I'll let you know in a couple of days."

Well, I made arrangements for the surgery and didn't hear anything more from Mary for about six weeks.

"Doctor, this is Mary Early," a faintly exasperated voice came through the telephone. "I have some sick puppies I want you to see. When can I bring them over?"

It was my turn to be taken aback. "You can bring them over this afternoon," I responded. "What seems to be the trouble with them?"

"You'll see when we get there. It's pretty sad."

Well, it was pretty sad, indeed. All the pups had runny noses and diarrhea. Their eyes were glazed over with purulent material—pus, laymen call it. These were signs of canine distemper, which is fatal ninety percent of the time. Another five percent get neurological after-effects, and, more often than not, have to be put to sleep or suffer a painful death. The sight was really pathetic, especially since they had just had their ears trimmed and still had the stitches in them.

I took one look and said to Mary, "What happened? I gave these pups their first distemper shots. That should have held them until they had their ears trimmed. The vet in Casper was to give them their second shots!"

"Well, I don't know what happened, but two or three days after we got them home, they started sneezing. They've gotten progressively worse," came her answer. "Is there anything you can do for them?"

That's when I told her about the poor prognosis, even with the best and most expensive treatment. "Do what you can," she said in resignation.

One pup out of the six lived. I decided right then that even though I didn't like cosmetic surgery (and still don't), I owed my clients the best service I could give. Particularly when, as in this instance, breed standards required such surgery, and also because I had the latest training in the technique. Thus, by the time the next litter came along, including Sam, I had the equipment on hand and was ready to do ear trims.

When Mary offered Sam to Harriet and me, we talked over the pros and cons of having a puppy under less than perfect circumstances: we lived in an apartment over a drugstore; having him included the task of housebreaking; and even worse, when he got older, having him included the possibility that he would scare clients' dogs and cats. Even with these considerations and other minor ones, we decided to take him; as often happens, the decision to own a pet turned out to be a mixed blessing!

First of all, housebreaking wasn't too bad—at least I didn't think so. But of course, I wasn't home all the time, either. Harriet might have something else to say on that score! Next, however, came time for the ear trim. By then, I too, had become attached to him, so it wasn't easy to put him under anesthesia and do the surgery. I still remember Harriet holding him in her lap as he was coming out of the anesthesia, obviously feeling much pain. Anyway, we passed that crisis, and he began to grow out in good shape—habit and character wise, as well as physically.

He grew very fond of chocolate cake with chocolate frosting, which was pretty much a staple in our house during those early years. One night at dinner when Harriet and I had just finished the main course and were preparing to have our cake, we both were called downstairs to the drugstore, which was not uncommon. We went down leaving the dishes on the table, as well as a newly baked cake, and Sam who had been waiting patiently beside the table. If Sam had been hoping for a sliver of cake, he must have decided the opportunity had come. In any event, when we returned a half-hour later, the dishes and tablecloth had all been rearranged and our nice, well-frosted chocolate cake was half gone! I quickly looked under the table. No Sam, just crumbs. I roared "SAM!" That was the wrong thing to do for when I finally caught up with him in the bedroom, he was so scared, he made the normal puppy evacuations all over the rug! The mess diminished our desire for chocolate cake that night, and Sam's desire forever, unless it was given to him properly.

When Sam got old enough to ride without getting car sick, I took him on calls with me. He seemed to enjoy sitting up to look out at the passing scenery, and he liked it, too, when I would let him out to run. He wasn't much for running livestock, but rather just taking in all the wonderful odors that go with a ranch. So I let him out quite often. One of those times was at a perfect place for a good run—at a set of corrals away from the main ranch, with no cattle around. I had been called to the place to conduct a post-mortem examination on an insured bull that had died suddenly, so the insurance company could get a report. Unknown to me, of course, the rancher had butchered a beef at the corral some two weeks earlier and had thrown the offal (stomach and intestines) behind the windbreak at the back of the corral. Naturally, Sam found it! When I was ready to go and called him, he bounded over to the pickup, with what looked like a big smile on his face. Further, his haircoat was matted with what I knew to be contents of one portion of a ruminant's stomach. As he bounced up to me, I knew from his odor that those ten miles would be a long ride home. The rancher went into a fit of laughter. Well, it was a long and odious ride home. Although the weather was cold enough that I needed the heater to keep the pickup reasonably warm on the way to the ranch, I had to drive home with the window open on my side, while Sam sat on his side, looking around and taking in the sights, as if nothing had happened. What a trip!

Most of the time, Sam didn't have a very expressive face. He would just sit with his black face hanging out, absorbed with any activity that happened to be going on. At least, that is the way it appeared to me. Once in awhile, however, I thought I could detect a little slyness to that apparent lack of expression. For instance, after we had a clinic in Gillette, Sam turned into an official greeter of clients, sort of the PR or "front" man. Not too far from the front door of the clinic, a set of stairs led up to the dog runs at the back of the clinic. Sitting on the top step, Sam could survey the comings and goings of clients and their animals. He sat there often, I suppose, because it was always warm there and out of the wind. At times, he became interested in a particular client or happening at the entrance, and would saunter down to be petted or have a sniff or two. Sometimes, I swear, he got off his haunches and came down to the front door, just for devilment, just to molest folks.

One such time I attribute this mood to him was a quiet Saturday morning in the summer. A client had called from Moorcroft, thirty miles away, and wanted to know if I'd be there to vaccinate her cat if she brought it. As usual, Sam was sitting on the top step studying the car as it drove in. He didn't show much interest, however, until the lady got out of the car with the cat in her arms. At the time her husband got out, too, and started up the walk beside her. Sam raised up off his backsides and ambled down the stairs. He met the folks about halfway up the walk between their car and the front door to the clinic. Instead of holding his head out and sniffing, he raised up on his hind legs and began to smell the cat. Well, you can just imagine what happened next! The normally tame and quiet domestic shorthair turned into a wild cat with all claws bared! In trying to get away from Sam's advances, the cat climbed onto the now distressed lady's shoulders, using its front claws for leverage.

As a further result of the long ride and its fright, the cat began to urinate down the front of the woman's dress. The husband, seeing this, tried to wipe the cascade of urine off her dress with his hand, all the time trying to make Sam stay away, and calling out for someone to help. That's when I arrived on the scene to call Sam off and give him a scolding. Although he acted rebuked at the moment, I knew when I saw him sitting on that top step after the clients were gone that he felt okay about himself.

Sam loved to play. Most of the time playing meant he would be on his hind legs trying to get a stick or a pair of gloves away from me, or from anyone who wanted to play, or from anyone who Sam thought wanted to play! He developed the habit early in his life when he and I would get into a tug-of-war with an old rag or piece of rope. This led to gloves, however, because after a few rope burns to the hands (and because of the cold weather), I almost always wore leather gloves. Thus, they were a handy plaything for a rambunctious puppy as well as a mature dog, and our neighbor who ran the Ford garage next door also played with him the same way. So whenever Sam saw anyone remove a glove from his hand, it was his signal to play, whether that person wanted to or not!

The older Sam got, the more aggressive he became in his play habits. All of this led to some funny incidents. Like the time we were preparing to build our clinic in Gillette. The man who was to dig the foundations arrived early one morning with his backhoe mounted on the back of an old truck. Looking out the kitchen window at the time, Harriet got a good look at what happened next. The man climbed out of his truck and walked toward the contractor; Sam, as usual, was watching all of this activity. Suddenly, the backhoe operator took off one glove and waved it in the direction where he would park his truck to start the digging, evidently wanting the contractor to guide him into position. The next thing Harriet saw was Sam charging toward the operator, and the operator making a lunge for the cab of the backhoe, reaching it just as Sam made a flying leap past him. Harriet called Sam back, at the same time telling the distraught operator that Sam just wanted to play. The man wouldn't believe it at first, but after a few days on the job, they became fast friends; that is, after the operator loosened up a little and relinquished an old glove in the bargain!

Boxers are short-haired dogs, of course, and not well adapted to the bitter cold we often had in Wyoming. So, when the temperature fell to ten to thirty degrees below zero, I didn't take Sam with me unless I knew I would not be away from the truck very long. Even with the heater going full blast, in that kind if weather he shivered and shook and I would throw an old lined jacket around him to keep him warm. He liked that, I can tell you!

When we got our clinic in Gillette, we decided that it was warm enough for him to stay there rather than at the house. He had a good place there next to the coal furnace and he didn't mind until it got really cold—like thirty-five degrees below, with the wind blowing forty miles an hour, when pipes froze and snow on the ground was real scrunchy underfoot. That's when Sam and two of the barn cats took up a symbiotic relationship—a relationship that took place only during such times. While Sam lay on his mat beside the furnace, two of the three barn cats would get on top of him, kneading him real easy-like with their claws. The third cat was not allowed in the pact, just the favorite two. When it was not cold weather, Sam would sometimes chase those two also. He was real people-like now and then!

Sam wasn't much help as a working stock dog. If anything, in such situations, he normally made matters worse. Like the time I was working on some calves in the basement of an old barn at a ranch west of town. I had taken Sam with me but left him in the truck, with the window open, as I had done many times before. He was about a year old and until then had been well-behaved. On this ranch, owned by an old maid former schoolteacher, every animal was a pet, including a shaggy old ewe that must have gotten too close to the pickup. As a neighbor and I worked with the calves, and the woman looked on, we suddenly heard a commotion together with a lot of bleating, coming from the yard where the pickup was parked. The old woman stuck her head out the door and let out a blood-curdling scream like you hear sometimes in a horror movie. The neighbor and I couldn't imagine what was happening, but dropped what we were doing and followed her out the door. There I saw Sam with a mouthful of wool, almost on top of the old ewe he was chasing. The other sheep, probably a couple of dozen, bleated in fright. Some were facing Sam and stamping with their front feet, while others ran around in panic. All the time, the old maid was screaming at the top of her voice, "Get that dog! Get that dog!"

Well, except for the hollering and a few thatches of wool pulled out of the old ewe, there wasn't really any harm done. More harm was done to my composure and Sam's backside (when I caught up with him). The old ewe had so much wool, Sam's teeth couldn't get through to the skin so she didn't suffer much. You can guess, however, that I was told Sam was not welcome back there again! I guess you would suspect, too, that much to my chagrin, the story was repeated with great mirth the countryside over.

Sometimes, though, Sam came in handy. If Sam was with me when I picked up hitch-hikers, which I usually did, he had a tendency to keep everything honest in the event the passenger had any random thoughts of taking over me and the pickup. From the time the stranger reached for the door handle to get in, until the time he got out, unscathed by a sixty-five-pound, black-muzzled pooch, sniffing and pushing him as far as he could move against the door, there was only polite talk. No hint of a takeover!

Well, like anyone who has owned a real good dog, a trusted friend and playmate, albeit, not human, there is no end to the tales I could tell. Suffice it to say, Sam was our first dog, and I still have many pleasant memories of him.

THE HORSEBACK RIDE

It was my second spring in practice. After the first spring, I figured there wasn't anything more I could experience. I was wrong. Spring is the time of year when most of the cows, ewes, mares, bitches, queens, and various other pregnant females have their young, and although most of this occurs without the help of man, thank goodness, there is always the odd event that calls for the help of a veterinarian.

Spring was the time of year, too, when the weather in Wyoming was the most unpredictable. It could snow eighteen to twenty inches or rain three to five inches in one week. You could always count on bad roads. If it wasn't deep snow, it was deep mud. I learned real early that when it was necessary to get off the hardtop (which was most of the time), it was best to stop and put on the chains. Otherwise, I'd still end up putting them on, but in very unfavorable circumstances, perhaps in a snowdrift or in mud up to the axle. How I'd talk to myself and the Almighty when that happened!

Something else would happen to the roads in spring. From time to time, parts of them would just disappear. The water would take them out, or worse yet, would cover them just deep enough so you couldn't get a vehicle through for a few days. When that happened and you still had to travel, it was necessary to go by horseback. Folks who lived out on the ranches were used to such happenings, and I finally got used to it too. But it wasn't all that much fun because saddles weren't designed for Pandora bags, calf-pullers, a gallon jug of mineral oil, and such other paraphernalia as I felt might be needed to aid in the delivery of a fetus.

Close to ten o'clock one spring night, just after Harriet and I had gotten into bed, the telephone rang. I got up to answer it, as Harriet said, "Oh, no!"

"Doc, this is Buster Bancroft. You know, out west of Oshoto." The voice was barely audible, yet I knew he was shouting into the mouthpiece. "Got a heifer out here that needs attention. Got a calf stuck in her. We've been working on her since six o'clock, but haven't been able to get it. Can you come out?"

I'd been to the ranch a number of times in my two years of practice. It was a good twenty-five miles from a hardtop road, and five or eight miles from a good graveled road. Just before you got to the house, which sat on a little knoll, the road passed through a meadow for about 100 yards. Sometimes after a heavy rain like we'd had during the week, and were still having at that minute, the meadow would be flooded. I was visualizing all of this while Buster was talking.

"How's the road?" I shouted back.

"Real bad. I'll have to meet you with a horse if you can come. I'll be watching for lights up on the ridge above the meadow. You just wait there, and I'll be right along. I'll have the horse all saddled and ready. Better wear some warm clothes. The wind is up and can chill you pretty fast."

"Okay, I'll leave in a few minutes!" I hollered. "Should be there in a hour if all goes well."

"Do you really have to go tonight?" Harriet agonized. "You know if they've been working on that heifer since six o'clock, the calf will be dead. Another few hours won't make that much difference. It'll be daylight then, and you won't be so apt to get stuck or slide off the road or something."

"I'd best go. By morning there will likely be more calls. That will put me just that much further behind," I responded. "I should be back by two or three in the morning, if all goes well."

By that time I was about dressed and ready to leave.

"Better have a piece of that chocolate cake we had for supper," Harriet sighed. "It will tide you over till you get back if they don't offer you anything. But knowing them, they'll feed you when you get done."

As I went by the kitchen, I grabbed a slice of cake and ate it on my way down the stairs and out the back door to the pickup in the garage. The rain didn't let up all the way to the ranch. The bottom had dropped out of the gravel roads as well as the mainly dirt road that let to the ridge. I had but one deep rut to follow for the thirty miles or more, and it was midnight before I got to the ridge overlooking the meadow. I blinked my lights a number of times after wiping the mud off the lenses. The rain was letting up a bit and the wind had become a Chinook, but it still had a chill to it. The meadow had become a riverbed, and I could hear the roar of the water running through it. In about fifteen minutes, I could make out a horse and rider splashing though the water, close to midstream. Another horse was being led by a halter rope. Pretty soon, they were at the side of the pickup.

"By golly, Doc, it's a hellava night!" Buster shouted out from the turned up collar of his slicker. "Thought maybe you'd got stuck."

"The roads are worse than I thought they'd be!" I shouted back. "How deep is the water down there?" I started to get the equipment out of the box on the back of the pickup.

"Belly deep!" he yelled back.

Because I didn't want to carry more than necessary I asked, "Do you have a calf-puller?" I hoped I would not have to take mine.

"We got one, but we broke it trying to get the calf. Bent the rod in a U-shape," came his reply. "Then we hooked a set of wire-stretchers on it and still couldn't get it out. The heifer's down and can't get up. That's why we called you."

"Boy," I muttered to myself. "This is really going to be a pistol." It would mean lying on my belly and cutting the calf out one piece at a time. The procedure is called an embryotomy. In those days, I didn't often do a Cesarean because it was a relatively new surgical procedure to perform under field conditions. Furthermore, it is best not to use it when an animal is in a weakened condition.

We finally got underway after Buster handed up the Pandora bag, which I tied to the horn in front of me, and he swung into his saddle with the calf-puller and gallon of mineral oil. The horses didn't like entering the cold water, and it took some urging to get them through. We arrived at the shed where the heifer was, in about twenty minutes. I was half numb with cold and glad for protection from the wind, especially since I had to strip down and work in bare arms. The heifer was down, all right—she wouldn't even lie up on her brisket!

It was a tough job and nearly three in the morning before I finally finished and washed up in now ice cold water. All the time I was working, Buster was telling me about the old days, before they had a licensed vet in the country. First they'd use the fence-stretchers. If they broke, then they'd use a horse or tractor and try to pull out the calf. If all that failed, they'd have to shoot the cow. "It wasn't pleasant, but it had to be done," he stated matter-of-factly.

We tried to get the heifer on her feet, but to no avail. She was just too worn out. She did, however, lie up on her brisket, and we propped her there with a bale of straw. She drank a little water from a bucket and ate some range cake we offered her. Good signs, both.

"Well, Doc, suppose she'll make it?" Buster queried.

"You'll have to keep turning her from side to side so she won't get paralyzed. In a day or two we should know," I answered. "Keep giving her some penicillin so infection doesn't set in."

"Well, let's go over to the house and have a bite to eat before you leave. It's been a long night. Mother will have something ready, I know."

I knew, too. Mrs. Bancroft always had something good to eat. Though she was in her seventies, she had waited up most of the night to fix us bacon, eggs, fried potatoes, and hot biscuits. She was born and raised in the South and had all the charm of a southern lady. She had experienced hardship and sorrow out here in the west. After losing her husband some years ago, she stayed and ran the ranch until her children were old enough to take over the responsibility.

That wonderful breakfast gave me a new lease on life, and before long we were once again on horseback, heading toward the truck. It still wasn't daylight, so going was treacherous. Again, the horses didn't want to enter the water. Mine was particularly stubborn, and I wasn't in a good position to urge him on since I had to balance the Pandora bag on the horn of the saddle with one hand and hold the reins in the other. I kicked him in the ribs, but he would turn one way and then the other, not quite getting into the water. Buster had gone ahead, but turned his horse and came back. He got behind my horse and, with a holler, he struck him on the rump with his reins.

What really happened is hard to recapture now, but for sure it was a wild ride the next few minutes. All I remember is that the pony stuck his head between his front legs and began to buck. On the first jump, the bottles and equipment in the Pandora bag began to rattle. On each succeeding jump they rattled louder. If the horse wasn't scared when we started, he was before long. Although I tried desperately to stay in the saddle and keep hold of the bag, I soon decided it was either me or the bag. I managed somehow to throw the bag clear of the water, and it landed in the mud while I was "pulling leather," as they say in rodeo circles, trying to stay astride my horse. After what seemed forever, but was actually only a few seconds, the horse stopped bucking and settled down after a few snorts.

Buster rode over to see if I was all right. "He'll be okay from now on," he laughed. "He's got sort of a cold back, but as soon as he warms up, he's a good horse. You just wait here and I'll get your bag. I'll carry it on my horse and you take the calf-puller."

As I really hadn't gotten over the shock of the experience, I was glad just to sit there on the horse while Buster put things back together.

When he had retrieved the bag and was ready for the second assault on the water, we returned to the edge of the torrent. This time Buster stayed behind me and the horse walked in without hesitation. The perverseness of animal behavior never ceased to amaze me.

"See, Doc," Buster hollered, "he's a good horse once he gets going!" Although I could not hear him, I knew he was chuckling to himself. It would be a good story to tell the next time he was in the barroom!

It was at least four o'clock before I got the pickup loaded and turned toward home. Still dark, still raining some, but the wind was warmer. "Well, Doc," Buster said by way of parting, "thanks 'til you're better paid. Send us a bill."

"I'll do that, and you let me know if you think she might need some more help!" I shouted through the open window, and then revved up the engine to hit the ruts once more.

The morning was still pitch black when I ground past Oshoto, so I found it necessary to run in second and third gear most of the way. I had only about five miles more to the hardtop when my front wheels hit something in the ruts with such force that they jumped out of the rut. Before I knew what was happening the front end of the pickup landed in the ditch on the left side of the road. When I tried to back out, the rear end slid sideways into the ditch. The truck stopped at a forty-five-degree angle, lying against the ditch bank.

It didn't take me long to decide I had had enough. No use fighting this night anymore. It was warm enough that there was no danger of freezing, and since the nearest house was a good two miles away, I judged the best thing to do was get some sleep. A road crew or someone with a four-wheel drive would likely come along after daylight. That would be enough to get out of this pickle. Then, too, I knew Harriet would be worried by the time she got up and would put a tracer on me. I had never stayed out before without calling her. So, using an old jacket for a pillow, I flopped over on the seat and fell sound asleep.

A couple of hours later (though it seemed only a few minutes) I was awakened by someone hammering on the door next to the road. "Hello, in there," came a man's voice. "Do you want help to get out?" This fellow lived in a camp back up the road toward Oshoto. He worked on a seismograph crew doing oil exploration in the area and was on his way back to the campsite after a night on the town.

I raised up sleepily. "Ya, I sure could use a pull if you've got a big enough piece of equipment," I responded. That's when I noticed he had a four-wheel-drive Dodge Power Wagon pickup with a heavy duty winch mounted in front. Just what it would take, I thought to myself.

"Well, let's give it a try with this; if it doesn't work, we got some other equipment at the camp that will," he replied. "Out in this country, a man needs all the equipment he can get."

With that, we hooked a tow chain to the front axle of my pickup and to the winch. He backed his outfit down the road a piece, set the brakes, and started the winch. I got the pickup started, put it in low gear, and let out on the clutch. Slowly, we were extricated from the ditch. I made it to the hardtop about eight o'clock, and rolled into Sundance close to eight-thirty. Harriet was wild-eyed when she saw me.

"Where in the world have you been? I've been frantic since I woke up about six and you still weren't home! I called the Bancrofts' and they said you left close to four-fifteen. Then I called a couple of places along the Cabin Creek road where I thought they might have seen you go by. Nobody had seen the truck until eight-thirty when Mrs. Heizer called to say that Allie had just seen you go by when he was at the barn feeding. Look at that truck! It's mud all over. Were you stuck or something?"

I guess she finally ran out of wind, so she stopped talking long enough for me to recount the events of the night. In particular, she laughed when I told her the epic of the horseback ride.

"Well, you better get upstairs and wash up. I'll get you some breakfast. You have two calls waiting. Both are calving cases."

Just like that, one day ran into the next. It was the spring of the year. Everything wanted to get out and around, and I just had to help. Besides, it was fun!

CRUDE OIL AND CATTLE
DON'T MIX

If there's anything that puts a veterinarian "between a rock and a hard place," it's crude oil poisoning. The reason for this is that when ranchers lose a lot of cattle at once instead of an odd critter here and there, they are looking for something or someone to blame (you really can't blame them!). If there is an oil rig on their place or one they have leased, logic points to that as the culprit. Oil-drilling outfits know what it is to be blamed for everything from the milk cow drying up prematurely to a daughter getting pregnant. Thus, as we say in scientific circles, "there is a built-in bias" on both sides. Too, the vagaries of crude oil poisoning are such that it isn't easy sometimes to point to crude oil as the definitive cause of death when only one or two animals are involved. There are many causes for death of cattle on the range, where they are only seen every two or three weeks. If they have been dead for several days or weeks, the cause is next to impossible to determine with any certainty.

You would think that anything as black and tarry as crude oil would be easy to identify almost anytime a post-mortem examination is conducted, whether it be in an hour or in two weeks. But not so. An hour or even a day isn't too bad, but often it would be two weeks or even up to two months before the vet was called in. With time, post-mortem changes cause the stomach linings to disintegrate, giving them a black as well as a greasy look. Even the odor of crude oil was often difficult to discern after remaining in an animal's stomach over a week.

Another problem is the time of death in relation to the time of ingesting the oil. The crude from some wells gave the animals only a good case of diarrhea, while the oil from other wells resulted in the animals' prolonged and lingering death. Then there is the crude that kills cattle within a few hours after ingestion, and those cases were easy to solve. Massive evidence, like the "smoking gun," made for little or no argument. The company paid!

When the cause of death of a bunch of cattle is not obvious, and the oil company is not convinced they are at fault, then it's a setup for a lawsuit. And that's when the "heat" is on the veterinarian. If he has been called early in the case, he has a lot more factual information than if he was called only after the company and the rancher had been arguing for two or three weeks while the animals were decomposing. When I was called early, I never had an oil company challenge my findings. They would make some settlement with the rancher if I said I had the evidence. When animals had been left to decompose a long time before I was called, however, and I couldn't be sure of the cause of death, then it was likely to go to court if the number of animals represented a large money settlement.

Such was the situation one morning in the spring of the third year Harriet and I were in practice in Sundance. A rancher west of Newcastle, sixty miles away, called for me to do a post-mortem examination on some ten head of cattle that had died over a two-week period four weeks previously.

"Doc, this is Joe Altman," came a plaintive voice over the long-distance line. "Need to have you come over and check on some cows that have died. I'm sure it was drinking oil that killed them, but the oil company won't pay up. They said they had the rig fenced off and there was no way for cattle to get near it."

"How long have they been dead?" I asked, having had experience with this type of call before.

He answered with a description of the circumstances.

I thought about it a minute and said, "Well, I don't think I'll be able to tell much from any examination. The only thing I can do is open up their paunches and get a sample to send to the laboratory. If they can't find anything, you'll probably be out of luck."

"Well, come on over anyway. I've been fooling around with the company for over three weeks and they're not going to budge. I figure on suing them."

That put a bit of a different light on the subject. A lawsuit was time-consuming as well as grueling, especially when one isn't used to it. Being an expert witness was not taught in veterinary school. You learned by experience and this was the first of several such learning experiences for me.

"Okay, I'll be over this afternoon," I told Joe. "But I want to tell you right up front what I tell everyone else in this kind of fix, and that is that I'm going to call it like I see it. If I don't think they died from crude oil poisoning, I'm going to say so. And if I think they have, I'll say that too." The reason I made this known at the start was to ward off anyone's attempt to influence my decision. That, too, I learned from experience. When money is involved, people do strange things and think strange thoughts.

"Wouldn't have it any other way, Doc," came Joe's reply. "See you this afternoon then."

After I rang off I turned to Harriet and told her about the call.

"How are you going to see anything recognizable in animals that have been dead that long?" she asked incredulously.

"Well, it has been pretty cold these past weeks. Maybe there will be something that isn't completely decomposed," I responded.

"Make some good notes when you get through," Harriet advised. "If you're going to be involved in a lawsuit, you'll be glad you have them. I learned that much from my Dad when he was State Veterinarian."

I arrived at the ranch about two that afternoon. I had made a call to deliver a calf on the way over, and the delivery wasn't easy. The calf had to be taken out in pieces. I was tired.

"Where are the animals?" I asked Joe after the usual howdys.

"They're over that divide," he said, pointing west. "I had them rolled into a washout over there. Didn't want them lying all over the place."

We took off across the sagebrush flats and over the divide, he leading the way in an old beat-up World War II Jeep. Looking over the edge of the washout, which was more like a pit, I saw the animals all jumbled together. True to my expectations, they were obviously in various stages of decomposition.

"Well, there's no way I can do any kind of a decent post-mortem examination on those animals," I said as I turned to Joe. "Like I said on the phone, I will get some paunch samples to send to the lab, and I'll want to look about the oil rig, too, before I leave."

I put on my rubber boots, took the post-mortem knife and some plastic bags, and climbed down the wall of the washout among the carcasses. Because of their positions, I was able to get paunch samples from only seven of the ten animals. Needless to say, it was an odorous and onerous situation, sticking the knife into the animal's left side and reaching into the hole to extract the sample. Joe stood on the edge of the washout.

"God, Doc, how can you stand it?" he said half gagging.

"We get that in the last course we take in vet school," I replied, only half jokingly. One learned real early in practice that he has little control over the environment or conditions in which he has to work, unless, of course, he has a clinic.

After climbing out of the pit, storing the samples in the pickup, and washing, we headed back over the divide to the oil rig. Sure enough, the rig had a good barbed-wire fence around it, better than most I'd seen. It didn't look as though it had just been put up, either. A good metal gate leading into the rig was closed and locked. The rig was not running and there was no one about.

"Is there a way we can get into the enclosure to look around?" I asked, looking at Joe.

"We can climb through the fence, but they won't like it."

"Well, I can't help that. We need to see of there is any evidence that cattle have been around the rig and especially the sludge pit. If the cattle didn't get into oil, they might have got to the sludge. Sometimes it contains poisonous chemicals. I need to tell the lab what to check for."

With that, we climbed through the barbed-wire fence and had a good look. There were no signs that cattle had been in the enclosure. No droppings. No hoof prints. No evidence that the ground had been disturbed or cleaned up, either.

"I don't see anything out of the way," I said, turning to Joe.

"I don't either," he said half dejectedly. "I still think this rig has something to do with them dying, though."

"Is the rest of the herd still in this pasture? I'd like to see them."

"No, I moved them out after all this started. Haven't lost anymore, either. I'll take you to where they are. Just leave your pickup here and ride with me. It's pretty rough country."

Climbing into the Jeep, we headed south along an old trail. After about twenty minutes we came to a barbed-wire gate, which I got out and opened. It was stretched tight, so it took me a bit to open and close it. We drove over to a windmill, which was the power source to pump the only water in the pasture. Twenty-five or thirty head of cows and yearling cattle milled around it, either drinking from the tank or licking on the mineral blocks scattered about. The animals were thin, but otherwise had shiny hair coats and looked alert. The grass was practically non-existent. "How many cattle do you have altogether?" I asked Joe as I continued to look about.

"This is about it for this pasture. The bulls and steers are further on in another pasture."

"How much feed are you giving them?"

"They each get about a pound of forty percent cake and then I throw out to this bunch about ten bales of hay a day, too. I know that is little enough, but they also have some pickin' here and there. You know we've had a real tough winter out here. Never got above zero during the day for close to ninety days and when it was down to thirty below, the wind blew thirty to forty miles an hour. You know that takes a lot out of cattle. You could see them shrink every day when that was going on."

"Yes, I know it's been a tough winter, all right. I was out most every day vaccinating heifers. Sometimes the vaccine would freeze right in my pocket. Had to use handwarmers from time to time to keep it from freezing. Even then, it some-times froze in the needle before I could get it into the heifer.

"Do you have any old dumps in the pasture where those ten died?" I asked, changing the subject.

"Nope, the dump is over where the bulls and steers are. We haven't lost any of them, either. They are thinner than this bunch, but we haven't lost any."

"Well, let's get back to the pickup." Since the sun was already going down and it was beginning to snow, I wanted to get on the road home. "I will send these samples into the lab and hope they can find something. Like I said, though, those animals have been dead so long I have my doubts."

When I got back to Newcastle on the way to Sundance, I called Harriet, as usual, to see if there were any calls in the area or on the way back. Sure enough, I had to backtrack to Osage to deliver a calf from a heifer at a ranch near town. By the time I got home at nine that night, we had two feet of new snow on the ground. I was beat. Harriet had just closed the store and was becoming worried about me. The snow continued most of the might and the next day, making every back road in the county impassable. I slept until close to ten o'clock the next morning and was probably the only one in the county who was glad for that much snow with the reprieve from the calls that it gave.

Two weeks passed before I heard from the laboratory at Laramie that they had found nothing of significance. When I relayed this to Joe, he said he was going ahead with the lawsuit anyway. It just had to be something about that oil rig that killed the cows.

Not until early summer was I contacted by Joe's lawyer for a deposition. He wasn't too happy that there was no laboratory evidence to support Joe's case. Nor was he enthralled that I had nothing very definitive to say, either. In spite of this, I was called as an expert witness and had to take the stand. The oil company had hired another veterinarian from South Dakota to testify for them. When we go through, the only thing Joe had going for him was the local jury. Even then, he lost the case. He was hurt and angry, and never did pay me for the time I spent with the lawyer or at the trial. In fact, it was close to a year before I was at his place again, and that was just to vaccinate his heifer calves against brucellosis. He was pretty cool toward me, too.

Yep, nothing puts a veterinarian between a rock and a hard place more than a case of crude oil poisoning of livestock—especially when you can't find it!

FOLLOW THE RULES

One thing a practitioner learns, soon or later, is to follow the rules. Although the great emphasis in veterinary medical training is toward the diagnosis, treatment, and prevention of disease, as well as the public health implications of animal disease, when one begins to practice, he soon learns that regulatory veterinary medicine plays a large role in his clinical activities. If the work is not done correctly, and the forms are not filled out properly and not sent to the proper state or federal office, it might just as well not have been done at all! There was no forgiveness for failing to follow the rules. This was in contrast to a surgery, for example, where one could fail to follow the exact procedure outlined in the surgical text and sometimes still have healing take place.

Early in my practice, I allowed a shipment of cattle to go to Illinois before they had been tested properly for evidence of tuberculosis. I had filled in as saleyard veterinarian for my brother-in-law at a Friday sale in Gillette, some seventy-five miles from Sundance. A buyer who bought a railroad carload of breeding cows at the sale wanted them shipped out on the train the next day. Now a TB test takes seventy-two hours. First, one has to inject the antigen tuberculin into the skin at the base of a cow's tail. Then, in seventy-two hours, you must get the animals back in the chute and feel the injection site for evidence of swelling. If there is swelling, it means the animal has the disease, and a whole new set of procedures go into effect. If there is no swelling, the animal is negative and free to be moved across state lines.

Now, trying to be accommodating is were I "screwed up," to put it in the vernacular. I thought it perfectly reasonable to inject the cattle, allow them to be shipped, and have the buyer's veterinarian "read" or feel the injection site, since the animals would be at their destination in seventy-two hours. Since Wyoming was a Certified Tuberculosis Free state, which meant it had less than a one percent infection rate at that time, I thought it was highly unlikely that any of the cattle would test positive. If they were, however, it was closer to ship them to slaughter from their destination than from Wyoming. Furthermore, the buyer assured me his veterinarian was very helpful and would not mind the task. Accordingly, I injected the animals in the proper place, filled out the "health certificate" with all the required information, and wrote across the bottom that the TB test would be completed by the veterinarian at destination. The cattle were loaded on the noon train the next day, Saturday. The same day, I mailed the certificates, along with all the other paper work to the State Veterinarian's office in Cheyenne. I always forwarded paper work promptly because there's nothing that makes regulators angrier than getting reports late, unless they are sloppily prepared or illegible.

It took just about two weeks for "all hell to break loose." First, I received a long distance call from the State Veterinarian of Illinois, telling me that was the dumbest thing he had seen happen since he became chief, ten years previously. Also, he placed a quarantine on the cattle and was having one of his deputies retest them. To make matters worse, if any of the animals showed up with TB, he would recommend to his board that all the cattle be slaughtered, not just the one that had the disease! Finally, he was writing a letter to the State Veterinarian of Wyoming recommending that I be placed on probation as far as writing health certificates was concerned. Needless to say, it was not the best day in my short practice experience! I learned right quick there is no place in regulatory veterinary medicine for compromise or accommodation. You either live by the rules or you forget it; it's as simple as that.

Close to two years later I was called upon to test a shipment of cattle destined for Ecuador. By that time, I was getting to be an old hand at reading and interpreting the book of regulations issued by the state and federal government, which told us the health requirements for shipping any animal into the different states and into foreign countries. Since this was my first experience in qualifying animals for a foreign shipment, I read and reread the rules for sending cattle to Ecuador. Just to make sure, however, I called the federal veterinarian at Cheyenne to confirm his reading of "the book" also. Since the book was two years old, he decided to call the federal veterinarian in charge of foreign shipments at Hyattsville, Maryland. He wasn't certain, either, so he in turn called the embassy of Ecuador in Washington.

It's a good thing he did, too, for indeed there was an additional requirement not spelled out in "the book." All animals had to be checked out of the U.S. by a federal veterinarian at a port of debarkation. In this case, it meant that even after I had conducted all the required tests, filled out the proper papers in the appropriate manner, sent them to Cheyenne to be "certified" by the federal veterinarian, and had seen the animals loaded on a cargo plane at Newcastle, the flight still could not go directly to Quito, Ecuador. Instead, the plane was required to land at New Orleans, where a federal veterinarian would go aboard and check the number on the metal eartag I had placed in each animal's ear, verifying that these indeed were the animals identified on the papers.

Clearance to ship was finally given about two weeks after I had completed all the test and initial forms. It was then that I called the businessman/rancher who owned the cattle.

"Leroy, this is Doctor Baldwin. I finally got the okay to ship the cattle. When do you want to load them out?" I asked.

"By golly, Doc, I was just about ready to call you to find out what was going on. The cattle have broken out of the pasture two times since we tested them. I thought for sure you guys had forgotten all about me."

"Well, I'm sorry it took so long, but you know this doesn't happen every day. They tell me this is the first shipment of cattle to Ecuador in over four years, and the rules changed in the meantime. In fact, you won't be able to ship them direct. The pilot must put down at New Orleans to check them out of the U.S."

There was silence on the other end of the line. Finally Leroy said, "God, Doc, that's going to be an added expense I didn't count on when I sold them. I gave the man a price delivered at the Quito airport."

"Well, that's the word I got, and it's been my experience that you best follow the rules; otherwise, there's a heap of trouble."

"Okay, Doc. I'll get hold of the airline and arrange everything, then I'll get back to you with load out time. Probably be within a week."

Sure enough, Leroy called the next Sunday evening, just six days after the previous call. "Can you be at the Newcastle airport by ten o'clock tomorrow morning?" he asked me. "The plane is in now and the trucks are lined up for eight in the morning. We should have them all at the airport and ready to load by ten at the latest."

"Yes, I can be there. Be sure not to load any until I get there, though. I need to recheck those tags," I instructed.

"Gotcha, Doc."

Fortunately, I arrived at the airport at nine-thirty the next morning. Things had gone better than usual at the ranch, and all the cattle were at the airport. Leroy was "faunching at the bit" (as they say out there when someone is worked up), ready to get on with the task.

"By golly, Doc, I'm glad you got here early. Everything's ready soon as you give the okay."

I looked at the two semis, one backed up to an unloading chute that led to a small "catch pen," the other waiting close by. A ramp led from the catch pen up to the open cargo door at the side of the plane. The airliner crew, the captain, the copilot and the cargo chief stood at the catch pen talking with the truck drivers and Leroy's hired hands. The state brand inspector was there, also. They all looked my way when Leroy greeted me. I walked over to the pen, identified the captain, and pulled the papers out of the manila envelope I was carrying.

"Captain," I said, "these are the papers you'll need to get these cattle into Ecuador. You'll also have to put down at New Orleans and have the Feds check you out of the U. S. They have a copy of these papers there. You can radio the New Orleans airport when you get airborne and tell them when you expect to arrive. They said they'll be waiting, no matter what time it is. Shouldn't take them over thirty minutes from start to finish."

"Okay, Doctor. I got the message," the captain responded.

I turned to Leroy. "Let them come," I said, looking up the unloading chute.

"Let 'em out easy, boys!" Leroy hollered to the truckers and his own hired hands.

I stood outside the catch pen, making sure there were just thirty-five head, because that was the number on the health papers. I noted also that each had a new metal tag in the right ear, the tags I had inserted about three weeks ago. Each had a different number, although they were sequenced. The numbers corresponded to the numbers on the papers. They would be used by the federal inspector at New Orleans as well as the Ecuadorian authorities to identify the cattle.

About an hour later the last animal was pushed up the loading chute and the cargo door closed. I handed the manila envelope to the captain saying, "Don't forget to stop at New Orleans."

Again he said, "Okay, Doctor. I got the message."

I waited with Leroy and the rest of the crew as the airliner taxied to the head of the runway and took off. It seemed slow to get airborne, but finally, amidst all the dust and the roar, the big plane lifted—a sight to behold, especially when you knew what was in it!

It was close to lunch time and though I didn't always eat lunch, I accepted when Leroy offered to take us all into town for a bite to eat. I always enjoyed the camaraderie that occurred among a group of men in a relaxed mood after they had completed a task.

Two days later, I received a call from the federal veterinarian in Cheyenne. "Doc, where are those cattle you said would be going through the port at New Orleans? They called from down there and wanted to know what was going on."

"Gosh, we loaded them out two days ago. I told the pilot twice he had to stop and be checked out," I replied.

"Well, maybe you can call the rancher and find out what happened, then let us know," came his answer.

"Yes, I'll do that," I responded. "It's got me wondering, too. Surely there would have been something in the news if a plane-load of cattle went down somewhere between here and New Orleans."

Immediately after hanging up, I called Leroy long distance. When he came on the line he said, "Doc, is that you? I was just going to call you. I just got a call from Quito, Ecuador. From the buyer. He said the government there had slapped a quarantine on the cattle and was sending them all to slaughter. The pilot didn't stop at New Orleans to check them out of the country; therefore, the authorities in Ecuador said they had entered illegally. They want to kill them all! Is there anything you or the federal vets can do to clear this thing up? If you don't, I stand to lose my—on the whole deal."

I thought to myself: what a mess!

"The reason I called you was to find out what happened to the cattle," I answered. "The vets at New Orleans have been on the alert for the past two days waiting to check them out. When they didn't arrive, they started checking. I'll call Cheyenne and tell them what happened. If anything is going to get done, I'm sure it will have to be through the higher authorities in Washington. Chances are they'll have to contact the embassy officials. I suggest you do the same or get the Wyoming congressman to do the same. If the Ecuadorian authorities are so bent on slaughtering the animals, it's likely going to take some big pressure to make them back off."

"By golly, Doc, that's a good suggestion. I'll call Washington right now. I know the congressman personally. I'll let you know how I make out," he responded before hanging up.

I returned the call to the federal vet at Cheyenne. He was dumbfounded by what I was telling him. He said he would call Hyattsville to see if they could do anything. We agreed it was more than a mess, it was a disaster. When I hadn't heard from Leroy for over a week, I stopped at his business office one day in Newcastle. He wasn't very happy to see me either.

"Doc," he greeted me, "the deal's gone completely sour. They tell me the cattle will be sent for slaughter and they'll send me a check for what they bring. Isn't that a hellava note? I was to get $450 a head. That's $200 more than they would have brought here. For all I know, the buyer could have paid off the authorities down there, and he's laughing all the way to the bank." He was obviously despondent.

"Can't you sue the airlines or the pilot or something?" I offered, trying to provide some hope for recovery of the loss.

"Well, I'm thinking about that now," came his reply, "but that costs money, too."

Like so many other things that happened in practice, I never heard what finally happened in that case. I did work for Leroy from time to time over the years, too; I was even an expert witness in a case he brought against an oil company for the death of some cattle. But he didn't offer me information on what happened in the Ecuadorian venture, and I didn't ask. All I know is what I said in the beginning. When it comes to regulatory work, either live by the rules or don't take the job.

SAVING THE BULL

About ten o'clock one morning in mid-July, with the sun already pounding down, I was restocking the pickup in the driveway behind the store. Harriet, as usual, was doing the books in the little office at the back of the store when I heard the screen door open. "Bob, there's someone here to see you!" she called out.

Stepping out from behind the big red box mounted in the bed of the pickup, I saw an elderly man heading toward me—fiftyish, I judged. Instead of the normal blue jeans, cowboy boots, western shirt, and straw hat, he was wearing bib overalls, a blue work shirt, black high-top laced shoes and a bluish billed cap like the railroad men wore. As he got closer, I extended my hand, expecting him to do the same. Instead, he stopped, looked me up and down in a manner I used to call the Wyoming Stare and said, "Are you the vet?" Then after a second or two, still staring, "You don't look old enough to know anything."

This was my second year of practice, and by then I wasn't completely taken aback by such unabashed observations. After all, on more than one occasion I was mistaken for Harriet's son. When we first arrived in Sundance, old and grizzled ranchers were afraid I wouldn't be able to do them much good at calving time "because you have to have a long arm to reach inside an old cow and get the calf out." None of them minded saying so either. So I laughed a little and asked, "What seems to be the problem? If I don't think I can help, I'll tell you." I really thought that was fair enough, without directly responding to his observation.

Not to be distracted so easily he went on, "I came over here to see Dr. Port, but your wife tells me he'll be gone for another day. I know he'd know what to do."

My patience began to wear thin. We were standing there in the hot sun, and this guy was not backing off a bit. Besides, when we got close, I could see the front of his overall legs caked with dirt, as though he had rubbed his hands on them without washing. I looked at his hands and they were dirty, too—I mean, old dirty. The bill of his cap was the same. His shoes were only half laced. "If the problem won't wait until Dr. Port gets back, there is a veterinarian at Spearfish, 30 miles east of here, and several at Sheridan, 150 miles west," I offered, hoping he would either take his problem and leave or tell me about it so I could help him.

"Well, I guess you'll have to do. I live thirty miles south of Gillette. Any of those other fellows would charge too much to go that far." Gillette is seventy-five miles west of Sundance so that meant a hundred miles one way to his place. If I was to go there, I quickly figured out I'd have at least four hours in travel time. Lord knows how much longer if his place was far off the main road.

In a sort of a mumble he began to speak again. "I got this bull down there that's not doing good. Bought him last year. Paid twenty-five hundred dollars for him. He was doing fine until last week when I noticed he wasn't keeping up with the cows or the rest of the bulls. Just sort of lies around not eatin'. When he gets up to get to water, he sort of staggers along and breathes hard. Got any idea what it could be?"

Now, although I had not seen an animal with the disease during a year of practice in Sundance, I surmised it might be Anaplasmosis. This is a parasitic disease involving the red blood cells of cattle. It is something like malaria in humans. The parasite destroys enough red blood cells so the animal is deprived of oxygen, resulting in a severe anemia. The disease is endemic in certain areas, and Gillette was one of those areas although it was very rare in Sundance.

"Well, it sounds like Anaplasmosis to me, but I can't tell without having a look," I advised. "If it is, the only treatment that has been successful is blood transfusions. Have you got any cows handy in case that's what it is and we need blood?"

This was going to be one of those calls to make me regret I'd ever taken up being a "vetinary," I thought to myself.

"What about a horse and a hired hand? Do you have those?" I asked hopefully.

"Nope. I'm all alone. Got a tractor is all. Don't even have a pickup. Anyway, I don't know if I'll have you come over or not. How much are you going to charge?"

"We charge fifty cents a mile, one way, plus the drugs."

He shuffled his feet, jammed his hands into his pockets, looked down, and said, "That's a real steep price. Fifty dollars at least, the way I figure it. Are you sure you can cure him if that's what he has?"

"Can't be sure of any cures in this business," I replied. "With that disease, twenty-five percent are going to die no matter what, twenty-five percent will get better on their own. That leaves fifty percent where treatment might help. If we have to run him around to catch him, though, it lessens his chances."

Almost an hour had passed, and I was anxious to get on the road if he wanted me; therefore, I did not keep the conversation going.

"Well, I guess I'll take a chance," he said after a period of silence. "When can you leave?"

"I'll leave within a half hour. Just give me the directions so I won't get lost." I was glad he'd made up his mind at last.

After giving me the directions to his ranch, we went into the drugstore through the office. I told Harriet I was going on the call and it would likely be five o'clock before I got back. The old man shuffled through the store and out the front door. He got into a new Cadillac DeVille sedan. It was green, I thought, though it was hard to tell because it was so filthy.

This is going to be some call, I thought to myself. And from that standpoint, I was absolutely and totally correct.

When I went back to the office, Harriet said, "Who was that? I don't think I've seen a dirtier man in my life! And did you see the car he was driving? He doesn't come from around here, does he?"

I told her his name was John Lambeth, and he lived thirty-five miles south of Gillette.

"Well, I was born and raised in this country, and he beats anything I ever saw," came her reply. "Do you want me to pack you a lunch?"

I thought for a minute what I had to load into the pickup. "No, I'll just grab a couple of Milky Ways and a Coke. That should get me through," I answered.

In those days, there were no "ready-made" containers or anticoagulant solutions available for the collection of blood. All of this had to be put together "from scratch." Thus, I had the pharmacist prepare enough material for two gallons of blood. I then obtained two one-gallon bottles that had contained alcohol, rinsed them with sterile water, and packed them into a cardboard box. The needles were in the instrument case. I was on my way in about twenty minutes.

I seldom had trouble finding a ranch provided I was given proper directions. This was no exception, even though the place was a good seven miles off the main-traveled road. I looked for the green Cadillac and was beginning to think I had the wrong place when I saw it coming over the hill. John had gone into Gillette for a bite to eat, thinking I'd not get started when I said. It was now one-thirty.

"Where is the bull located?" I asked John as I looked around for signs of cattle.

"Oh, he's over that hill about a mile," came the response. "I'll just ride with you and open the gates. Anything you think you'll need before we leave?"

"I forgot to bring water. Is there a place to fill a cream can?" I asked.

"Right down at the stock tank," he answered, pointing to the corral. "There's also a reservoir over in the pasture."

I could just see trying to dip water out of the stock pond. "We'll stop by the corral. Hop in," I answered.

The road was rough, and we had two gates to go through. It took about fifteen minutes to get to the place where the bull was lying. When we drove up to him, he didn't let on he saw us. Unusual for any animal not accustomed to having people around, especially strangers. We walked over to him. The white part of his eyes had a yellow tinge. He was breathing heavily. I reached down, grabbed him by the muzzle, and opened his mouth. The inside of his lips and his tongue were sort of off-white instead of the usual pink color. A sure sign of anemia. I went back to the truck and got a hypodermic needle and a halter. Returning to the still reclining brute, I slipped the halter on him.

"Here, hold the end of this rope and don't let him swing his head toward me. I'm going to tap his jugular vein with this needle," I said to John, handing him the end of the halter rope. Reluctantly, the old man took the rope and pulled the animal's head around. I leaned over the bull's neck and shut off the flow of blood in the jugular with the fingers of my left hand. In my right I held the needle. As soon as I saw the blood rising in the jugular, I popped the needle in the vein. The blood that came out was watery and a dirty brown color, nothing like the appearance of normal blood.

"This guy is sure enough anemic," I said to John. "It's likely Anaplasmosis. At least that's what we are going to treat him for. I'll take a sample and send it to the lab, just to make sure. Is there a halfway gentle cow we can catch without too much trouble?"

"Well, they're not too wild, but they are range cattle, and you know how they are around strangers."

We drove close to where a cow and her calf were grazing. She looked at us briefly, looked around for her calf, called it and started to run off.

"Not much chance of catching her afoot," I said to John. "Let's try to find something gentler."

We drove around for about ten minutes and finally spotted a fat cow without a calf. She looked gentle enough in that she just stood and watched us drive up. I got out of the pickup, got the lasso out of the back and walked around to the side where she was. She continued to watch us curiously. I made a big loop, figuring I would have only one chance to catch her when I threw the rope.

Now I wasn't raised with a rope in my hand, like a lot of the folks out there. I had never done any competition roping; mostly I roped out of desperation and there seemed to be plenty of that! Also, there is a considerable difference in who has the advantage when you rope a cow from the back of a horse or when you are afoot. So when I threw the loop and caught her, a whole predictable and distressing set of events took place. Realizing she was caught, she took off running. Since I didn't have a post or tree to dally the end of the rope around to stop her, I had to hang on, hoping she would soon tire and slow down. Thus, I was dragged like an anchor thrown from a fast-moving boat. Old John jumped out to help me, but stumbled and fell in the sagebrush, so he didn't get to help much on the initial run. When the cow slowed down a little and I was able to get a little breath, I found a clump of sagebrush to try to dally around. It didn't work the first couple of times, but did slow her down considerably, especially since the noose tightened around her neck and shut off her air passage to some extent. Finally, she headed into a patch of greasewood, which are much taller and stouter bushes than sagebrush. At last I got a good dally around one of them and she stopped. John came grunting up about that time.

"Here," I said, handing him the end of the rope. "You hang onto this and I'll go get the pickup," which was a good 200 yards away. Walking back to it, I knew we still had plenty of work to do: throwing the cow down, drawing a gallon of blood, and then catching the bull. The hot sun was really coming down, and needless to say I was not the picture of the clean and well manicured veterinarian you see in advertisements. It was fun at the time, though. Real emergency veterinary medicine—saving an animal's life like I was trained to do, even though it was not in a nice clean clinic. Neat!

Two hours later I pulled onto the Douglas Highway heading toward home. I was a real dirt-ball by that time, having all that roping and wrestling of the animals to do in the dust. There was nothing sterile about the procedure and no blood typing either. We were taught that with animals you could most likely always have one blood transfusion without the trouble of anaphylactic shock and death from mismatched blood. However, you should never give the second transfusion without cross-matching. In this case, as in most cases involving large animals under range conditions, you didn't have to worry about the second transfusion since it was very unlikely you got to treat an animal the second time. One call and one treatment regime was the rule. At times, animals didn't even get that depending upon the cost of treatment.

I finally got back to Sundance after stopping at a gas station in Gillette to get another candy bar and Coke. It was 6 p.m. when I drove into the driveway behind the store. Harriet met me at the back door, and we walked up the back stairs to the apartment. I told her all about the afternoon as I got ready for a shower.

"Do you think the bull will live?' she asked.

"Sure hope so, especially after all that work." I went on to wonder out loud how it's possible to operate a ranch with 300 brood cows and not have a horse or a hired man. Not even a pickup but a new Cadillac!

"Did he pay you?" Harriet finally asked as I stepped into the shower.

"No, he said he'd send the money over as soon as he got a statement. I told him it would be fifty dollars. Better make out a ticket on it when you go downstairs. I forgot to."

At the first of August we sent John a statement. We hadn't heard from him by the first of September, so we sent him another one. One day in mid-September the old man showed up at the store. I was a little surprised he'd drive that far to pay a bill when it only took a three-cent stamp and an envelope. It didn't take long to find out why.

"Hello, Mr. Lambeth, how'd the bull get along?" I asked, hoping against hope that the animal lived.

With his hands deep in his dirty overall pockets, he looked down at his feet and mumbled, "The bull's all right, but the cow died. Don't know why I should pay you. I figured you killed that cow drawing all that blood out of her."

Naturally, I was glad the bull lived, but was sorry about the cow. I was dumbfounded by the reasoning not to pay the bill. "Well, I'm sorry about the cow," I said after I recovered from the onslaught. "When did she die?"

"Oh, about six weeks after you were there."

"Have you lost other cows this summer?"

"Yep, at least a dozen. They all acted like the bull, including the cow you bled out."

"Well, it's obvious you just went through an acute outbreak of Anaplasmosis. That's the way it acts. Hits a herd all of a sudden, and hard. You get these kind of death losses. Chances are that cow would have gotten the disease whether we took blood from her or not. The amount of blood taken from her was no more than if you'd given a pint of blood to someone that needed it." I felt much better now. If anything hit me in the pit of the stomach, it was hearing an animal died that I treated and expected to live. Never did get over that.

"Well, I still reckon that taking that blood and all that wrassling around had something to do with her dying, so I'm not going to pay you, and you can quit sending any more bills." He didn't pay either. We finally took the fifty dollars off our income tax. I believe we made all of $8,000 that year.

ALTERNATIVE MODES OF TRANSPORTION

Very early in my career in the hills and on the prairie I learned that I had to be flexible. Now that wasn't easy for me—still isn't. I soon discarded my wrist watch because I was "fighting time" too much. I would hire a pilot to fly me to a call every chance I got. I was trained to respond rapidly to calls and the car or truck seemed too slow sometimes. Before I got through the first winter and spring in that Sundance country, however, I was introduced to alternate modes of transport. In addition to horseback, airplane, and occasionally my own two feet, one of the most memorable was a trip on a hay sled behind a "green" team of matched Belgians.

It was the middle of February, 1952. We had had a lot of snow during the winter, and it was still pretty deep in some parts of the county. Deep enough that ranchers had to leave their wheeled vehicles near the hardtop and go the rest of the way to the ranch house and buildings by horseback, sleigh, sled or foot.

I was in the pharmacy of the drugstore talking to old Midge, our pharmacist at the time, when the telephone rang.

"That you, Doc?" came a distant voice through the receiver.

"Sure is!" I hollered into the mouthpiece.

"This is Ned Smiley," the voice went on. "We got a milk cow out here having trouble calving. Can you come right out?"

"Yes, I can come out. What seems to be the problem?"

"She's up and down, strains a little but nothing happens. We tried to get a hand into her, but there doesn't seem to be any opening. Can't figure it out."

I knew where the ranch was and doubted that I could drive in, so I asked, "What's the best way to get into the place?"

"We'll have to meet you at the road end with a team. You let me know when you are planning to leave, and we'll plan to be there."

"Let's see. It's about four-thirty now. How will it be if I meet you about five-thirty? That will give me a chance to get my gear together and get a bite to eat."

"That's fine. See you then."

The only work I had ever done on the Smiley ranch was to vaccinate heifer calves against brucellosis or contagious abortion. They did all of their own "vetinary work" as they called it. Some years earlier, Ned had had a real bad experience with another veterinarian, and he wasn't about to use one unless he had no choice. A registered Brown Swiss milk cow was something special, and this was to be only her second calf.

It was almost dark when I arrived at the road end and parked the pickup as far off the road as I dared. I could just make out a team and hay sled coming up the grade from the meadow below. Two people were standing on the rack with their backs to the team. That would be Ned and one of his boys, probably Paul.

By the time they got to the road, I had the gear I felt I would need. This included a cream can full of hot water, which wouldn't stay hot long because it was already close to zero with a little breeze blowing.

"Hi, Doc. Ready to go?" Paul hollered through the scarf around his face and neck.

"Just as soon as I throw this stuff on," I responded, while I placed everything I planned to take at the back of the rack.

When he saw I was all set, he spoke to the team. They turned and headed back toward the ranch. About that time, Ned began to talk about how he used to be able to do all this kind of "vetinary work," but since he got the "arthereetus" he couldn't work inside a cow like he used to. "Besides, when you got your hand and arm inside and they strain, the pain and numbness finally make it so you can't stand it anymore," he volunteered. "You fellows give them a shot in the tail so they can't strain. That's a big advantage."

I didn't say anything to his observations. I was getting cold. Sure wish I'd put on more clothes, I thought to myself. Suddenly one of the horses fell on its side in about four feet of snow, and floundered to get up. My stowed gear was thrown into the drift during the melee. When the snow is deep, horses' hooves and sled runners make a track that builds up as it snows, and the team and sled pack it down. As long as the horses follow the track precisely, everything goes fine, but if they step too far to one side or the other, they plunge into deep, soft snow. Then, it's a matter of getting their feet back up on the track. An old team seldom gets in this predicament unless the snow starts to melt and the track breaks down. But this was a young green team and they had to learn their lessons the hard way.

It took us a half hour to rescue my dumped gear and proceed to the barn where the cow was stanchioned. I had not seen a milk cow in a stanchion since I left school the previous June. In fact, it had been awhile since I saw a milk cow that looked like a milk cow. The ones I saw since arriving at Sundance mostly had white faces—Hereford crosses of some kind. As for a stanchion, there weren't many of those around, either. The normal method of restraint was a lasso or "throw rope."

"How long has she been trying to calve?" I asked as I took off my coat and shirt in preparation for donning my OB or obstetrical suit.

"I noticed her acting funny yesterday," Paul explained. "She held her tail out and strained a little, but she didn't really get down to it until this afternoon. That's when we went into her and couldn't find the opening to the calf."

The cow was on her feet and stepped around a little as I placed the one-and-a-half-inch needle into the epidural space, just in front of the tail head, and injected 10cc of procaine hydrochloride, an anesthetic agent.

As I waited for the anesthetic to take effect, I tied her tail along her side with a piece of baling twine around her neck. The examination revealed my worst fear. She had a torsion of the uterus. That is, the uterus was turned 180 degrees from normal, toward the left. This meant that whenever the cow strained to expel the calf, the cervix and vagina became smaller instead of enlarging. Something else was wrong, too. I felt what I thought was a tear in the uterine wall, and when I withdrew my hand, it was covered with blood. It had to be a tear.

"How long did you work on her?" I asked, turning to Paul.

"I'd say not over twenty minutes. I kept trying to get my hand and arm in, and she would strain pretty bad when I did. Why, is there something wrong?"

"I'll say there is. She has a twisted calfbed, and it's ruptured. The only way out of this is a Cesarean. Even then, I don't know if we can save her. Infection sets in pretty fast when something like this happens. She's in a little shock already."

"What will it cost?"

"Twenty-five dollars plus the drugs. Probably about forty dollars altogether."

He looked over at Paul and then turned to me. "Go ahead. Do the best you can. She's a good cow. I'd hate to lose her."

In those days, doing Cesareans on cattle under field conditions was a rare event. It was mostly a last-resort procedure when all else had failed. That meant, in many cases, a cow or heifer was down and couldn't get up due to excess manipulation, including use of wire stretchers or even a tractor in trying to pull the calf from the animal. In this case, the cow was not down and exhausted, but the rent in the uterine wall made it equally dangerous. One thing in our favor, however, was that the barn had electricity and was fairly warm and clean. I felt, too, that she would have the best of care following the operation.

I had a choice between two surgical approaches, mid-line or left flank. The mid-line approach involved throwing the animal so that its right side would be on the ground with its front and hind legs stretched out and tied in opposite directions. The line of incision would extend from in front of the udder to near the umbilical area. Since the uterus on a pregnant, near-term cow is normally the first organ encountered after incising through the skin and abdominal wall, it is easy to get directly to the calf and to sew the uterus and wall. The disadvantages, however, include working on your knees, or worse, in a bent-over position for forty-five minutes to an hour. There is also chance of wound contamination both during the operation and following it, and greater chance of the animal's struggling during the procedure, further complicating an already compromised aseptic operation.

The left flank approach takes a little longer, since there is muscle to incise and re-sew, but wound and abdominal contamination is not such a problem. You can stand up during the procedure, and, in this case, where there was a tear to repair in the uterine wall, it would be easier to reach it through the flank than the midline. Thus, I chose this approach.

Getting the clippers out of the bag, I handed them to Paul. "Here, will you clip the hair off her side while I get the instruments ready?" I showed him what area to clip and while he was doing that, I prepared the instruments and gave the animal a shot of penicillin. After he had finished, I washed the surgical site with disinfectant soap. Following that, I made a series of injections of procaine hydrochloride along the nerve pathways affecting the area of incision.

All during this time, Ned rattled on about how it was different now than in the old days. "Didn't have all this medicine then. We'd have just shot her in those days. Might still have to, but at least there's some chance," he mused. "Didn't have electricity or a warm barn then either. I remember this country before REA (Rural Electric Association) or telephone or anything like that. Didn't even have a decent road to town. When I was a boy, things were different."

Paul looked over at me and winked. "How about the girls, Dad? Were they different, too?"

The old man smiled, knowing Paul was kidding him. "Haven't been out with many lately, so I can't tell you."

Before the conversation ended, I informed them that there were still parts of the county as well as places in southeastern Montana that didn't have electricity. At least not REA, or telephones. I had already done one Cesarean by the light of a kerosene lantern and another by the lights of my pickup.

I picked up the scalpel and tested the depth of anesthesia by touching the skin with the sharp end of the blade. The animal didn't move. "We're ready to go.

When I get the hind legs out through the incision, each one of you get hold of a leg and lift upward. If it's alive, get a sack and rub it good and hard until it's breathing good." I cut through the skin, muscle and lining of the abdominal cavity, releasing a woosh of air when I entered the cavity. Because of the difference in temperature between the air inside the animal and the air in the barn, a goodly amount of steam came out through the incision. From then on, the operation proceeded mainly by feel.

As it turned out, the calf was alive and vigorous. Before I left, the cow was licking it and the calf was trying to get to its feet. I found the tear in the wall and closed it, despite not being able to see it. Ned and Paul were tickled with the outcome, so far.

"By golly, Doc. I believe she's going to be all right," Paul opined when he saw her mothering the calf. "She doesn't act as if anything happened to her."

"She hasn't any pain yet because of the anesthesia. She might show a little sign of pain later on, but it's amazing how few do," I stated. "You'd thing that with that big an incision and the lifting, pulling, and cutting on the uterus, they'd have some pain and show it, but they don't seem to. Doesn't appear to hurt them as much as dehorning does."

It was now eight-thirty. Paul had gone to hitch the team to the sled, while Ned and I cleaned my gear and placed it near the door, ready for the return trip to the road.

"If you like, Doc, we can go to the house for some coffee and something to eat. It's been a long evening," Ned offered.

"No thanks," I responded. "I'll get something when I get home. We still have a way to go and I don't know what will be waiting when I get back." About the only time I would stop to eat was either late at night after an exhausting ordeal or at noon when it was scheduled in the course of vaccinating or testing cattle. Most times it was real good eating, too: roast beef, or venison, or antelope steak, and plenty of vegetables with hot rolls and gravy. Once in awhile, however, I had to gag on every mouthful, especially when I had to sit beside the slop bucket in a dirty kitchen. On some occasions, too, there were only vegetables to eat since the folks didn't have money to buy meat or kill one of their own animals for food.

Soon we heard the tramping of the horses' hooves and the squeak of the sled runners on the snow. "It must have gotten colder," I said to Ned. "The squeaking of the runners sounds like it."

"The radio called for ten-below tonight. Probably getting down close to that by now," he responded. Then he went on to tell me how it was in the old days, before the automobile, when you were exposed to this kind of weather most winters, in open sleighs or on horseback to boot. I surely wasn't looking forward to that ride to the highway, nor did I take any solace in how it was in the old days.

The ride back to the truck didn't take as long as the coming in, thank goodness, but it was colder. None of us spoke; we just stood on the rack, swinging our arms from time to time to keep warm. Neither horse fell off the track on the return.

As I was loading the gear back in the pickup, I told them to let me know how the cow got along and if anything went wrong, to give me a ring.

"Okay, Doc, send us a bill, and thanks 'till you're better paid," Paul sang out as he turned the team and started down the slope.

A week later Paul called to make an appointment for me to vaccinate their heifers. After setting the date, I asked him how the cow and calf got along.

"Neither missed a meal," he laughed. "Dad's still talking about it. He keeps telling people he can't see how she lived, exposing her guts to the cold and all."

"Well, I am really glad it turned out. Certainly, nothing like that ever happened in the old days!"

For a moment the line was silent, then Paul let out a hoop. "I'll tell Dad. He'll get a kick out of that."

Before I left my prairie practice, I had many more rides behind a team of horses—most of them cold; some wet, others muddy; but all memorable. Memorable because it always meant an emergency—the "lifeblood" of the young practitioner.

PINE NEEDLE ABORTION

An acute power of observation is indispensable in the practice of medicine, be it animal or human. Next in importance is the meticulous recording of those observations. These two details are the essential ingredients for medical advancement. Thus, it was William Withering of Birmingham, England, who observed and recorded the beneficial effects of an old woman's potion that led to the widespread use of digitalis, both as a diuretic and later as a treatment for congestive heart failure, a condition for which it is still prescribed today.

One intriguing disease problem among cattle in the Sundance area was characterized by abortion. Keenly observing and recording events leading up to the abortions was the easy part; convincing learned colleagues was more difficult. That, too, has been the history of medicine. Every winter and early spring that we practiced in Sundance I'd get a call.

"Doc, I got a bunch of cows out here that don't seem to be doing right. Can you come out and look at them?"

"Sure, I can come out, but what seems to be the problem? How are they acting? It would help to know so I can bring the right medicine," I'd respond.

"Well, some of them have slunk their calves. Others go around with their tails in the air and straining. Those that lost their calves don't seem to be cleaning right either." The reply would always be the same.

I practiced a couple of years before I finally convinced myself and my brother-in-law that cattle would eat pine needles from boughs within their reach, and some toxic elements in the needles was causing abortions. I'd prepare for the call by making sure I had plenty of specimen containers and blood vials because the laboratory needed to help confirm or rule out certain known causes of abortion.

In later years, especially when I knew the owner, the herd, the vegetation on the ranch, and the management practices including the herd health status, I'd ask the caller when the cattle were turned into the pines or into a place where they could reach them. If they had been in the pines all winter, then I'd ask when the animals had been given "cake," a compressed form of grain. In either case, if it had occurred within the last two weeks, I'd have the diagnosis pretty much in mind.

I first encountered this about the last of February, the first year Harriet and I were in practice. Late March to the end of May was normally the time most ranchers in the area had their cows calving. Thus, when Rene Fromm stopped in at the office one snowy afternoon and told me some of her cows showed signs of having calved prematurely, I thought first of brucellosis, a common bacterial disease that results in abortion. Or possibly it could be one of several other bacterial or viral diseases. She said she could have all the cattle in by the next afternoon if it stopped snowing; otherwise, she would call to set up another appointment.

After she left, I got out my book on infectious diseases of livestock as well as the book dealing with nutritional ailments and made a list of all conditions that could cause abortion in cattle. Brucellosis, leptospirosis, aspergillosis, trichomoniasis, vibriosis, listeriosis, pasteurellosis, pseudomonas, corneybacterium, streptococcus and staphlacoccus were mentioned, plus the statement that there are many causes of abortion for which no diagnosis can be made. No mention was made of needles from the Ponderosa Pine. (Vitamin A deficiency/viral diseases were just being identified.) I could see immediately that getting to a definite diagnosis in this case would be quite a challenge.

The snow stopped during the night, and I didn't hear anything from Rene, so at noon the next day I headed for her ranch, about eight miles from town. The day was bright and sunny; however, the temperature was about freezing, and the wind was beginning to blow the eighteen inches of snow on the ground into banks of snow in the roadway. I was glad the corrals were located down in a swale from the highway, because I had to push snow all the way down the hill from the hardtop. I would have to chain up to get out, though.

Rene and her hired man were just working the last of the herd into the corral when I pulled up beside the chute. Both were so bundled up with scarves partially covering their faces, that I was a little uncertain who was who until they got off their horses and tied them to a corral post.

"Well, here they are Doc!" Rene shouted above the din of the bawling cattle.

I had gotten out of the pickup and was making my way through the snow to the corral. Climbing up the side, I perched myself on the top board and began the process of observing the cattle and getting the history of the herd. I judged there were about fifty cows in the bunch. They appeared to be in good shape, nutritionally. They were "in good flesh" and full. However, about a dozen or so had placenta hanging from the vagina.

"When did you first notice something wrong?" I asked Rene without looking at her, but still watching the animals as they moved about.

"About a week ago, when we were feeding, I noticed a dead calf on the bedgrounds. It looked like it came early. Didn't have much hair on it. The cow didn't claim it either. I didn't think anything about it because that happens once in awhile, but when I found a couple more the next day, it began to worry me. Now in just a week we've had twelve or fourteen. That's close to a twenty-five percent loss. That's more than the rest of them will make for us this year."

"Let's work those off with the retained placenta, and I'll examine them or treat them while we talk," I suggested, knowing it would be a long afternoon until we finished with the collection of samples as well as the treatment. Besides, by the time I finished, I just might have the answer. It's always gratifying to find the answer to a diagnostic problem right on the spot without having to send in specimens and wait several weeks for an answer.

As we worked the twelve cows with retained placentas through the chute, I removed as much of the material as I could, treated each one with penicillin and a sulfa drug, and then took a blood sample from the jugular vein. Nothing was particularly diagnostic. A couple of them still had dead fetuses inside them, which I removed and saved to be sent to the laboratory.

"Have you had these cattle in this pasture all winter?" I asked as we were letting one cow out of the chute and letting another in.

"No," came the hired man's reply. "We had them down in the meadow until about three weeks ago. There was quite a lot of pickin' down there, and we fed them all the hay they'd clean up too. Then we decided to move them here closer to the corrals and shed so if any of them got into trouble when they started calving, it would be handy to take care of them. Besides, there's more protection from the weather up here. They can get in among the pines. We started to 'cake' them too. Sort of build them up for calving."

"When we get through here, I want to ride around a little to see if there is something they can be getting into," I stated. "There doesn't happen to be a dump in this pasture, does there?"

"Yes, there is a dump but it hasn't been used in years and it's been covered with snow most of the winter," the hired man replied.

"What about an old homestead shack or something like that?" I went on.

"I'm living in what was the homestead shack," came Rene's lighthearted reply, "and if this keeps up, it'll be as vacant as some of those others around the county."

I smiled to myself and thought: these Western women can sure handle adversity.

The sun was going down and the wind coming up when I finished treating the last cow. As I washed my gear and my hands in the now ice-cold water, I asked, "Which of those two horses is the gentlest? I'm no bronc rider."

"Better get on mine," the hired man offered. "Rene's is a one-person horse. Besides, I doubt that you'd smell too good to him about now. He can be a little snakey from time to time."

With that, Rene and I swung atop the horses and started through the snow toward the herd, which was now in the field at the edge of a heavy grove of pines and scrub oak.

"Take me to the dump first!" I called out to Rene. She reined her horse around and started toward a wash-out not too far away. When we arrived, it was obvious the cattle had not been around it, at least not in the last twenty-four hours. Only rabbit tracks were evident in the snow. The area was very steep, too, making it unlikely that any but the occasional animal would get near it.

"Okay, let's go along the pines at the edge of the meadow," I said to Rene. With the sun going down rapidly and the wind coming up again, I was getting chilly. I was not dressed for riding in this kind of weather.

As we neared the pines, I noticed that most of the boughs were eaten off about as high as a cow could reach. In fact, one "old sister" was munching on one.

"Have you noticed the cattle eating the needles before?" I asked Rene.

"Oh, once in awhile I see one doing it. I figure there must be something lacking in their diet to make them do it, even though they get all the feed and minerals they want," she responded.

"Well, I don't see anything out of the way, except for those boughs being eaten off, so let's get back. I'll just have to send the specimens into Laramie and hope they can help us with the diagnosis."

When we got back to the pickup, the hired man and I began the process of putting on the chains, which wasn't an easy job. The chains were quite heavy because I had an extra link placed between the standard links to give me plenty of traction. To put them on we had to shovel out the snow from around the rear wheels and feed the chains over the tires so I could back onto them. Finally, we finished the job, and I started up the hill to the road. The tracks I'd made coming in were drifted full of snow and packed solid, so where possible I made new tracks because that is always easier than following old ones. I made it to the highway about dark and rolled into town a few minutes later.

The next day I sent the fetuses and other specimens to the lab, asking them to call me if they found anything significant. I went back to the books to see if I could find any reference to pine needles and abortion. Nothing. A week later I received a call from Laramie that they could find nothing to account for the abortions in this herd. I asked them if pine needles had ever been associated with abortion. They stated that from time to time, some of the veterinarians and ranchers had suggested them as a cause, but that no studies had been made on the subject.

The college people had the opinion we were probably dealing with a Vitamin A deficiency if the animals were eating needles which are supposed to contain goodly amounts of that vitamin. Otherwise, it was likely to be Bang's disease or some other infectious disease. Most experts didn't believe a cow would eat pine needles either, unless they were starving.

Well, I had three more such episodes that spring, and it was most frustrating. It didn't become any easier either when I brought it up at a veterinary meeting during the summer and had a college professor just about laugh my brother-in-law and me out of the room for suggesting that a cow brute would even eat pine needles, let alone that they could cause abortion. He contended it was probably Bang's or some other infectious disease, and we just didn't collect or handle the samples correctly.

Just before calving began the following year, an abstract of a paper on pine needles abortion appeared in one of the veterinary journals, reporting on a controlled experiment conducted in Oregon. Sure enough, the researchers found that cattle would indeed eat pine needles from the Ponderosa Pine, even though they were on a balanced ration, and abortion resulted in a high percentage of the cows.

Elated, I wrote for copies of the entire paper, one of which is still somewhere in my files. The rest I distributed to colleagues in academe. You can be sure that my list included the professor who took great glee in chiding us at the summer veterinary meeting!

CANINE ENCOUNTER—THE WORST KIND

One of the absolute nemeses of the canine world is the spine hog or porcupine. Usually, one encounter with this slow-moving, apparently coarse-haired creature is enough for most dogs. Once in awhile, however, you run across a mutt who will not give up—something, like an angry old man. This is the story of one such dog, a Boxer called Mike.

The first time I saw Mike, he was sitting in the front seat of a yellow Cadillac convertible, watching the chauffeur and me come out of the office and approach the car. He looked for all the world like a canine Prince Albert, the quills sticking out of his muzzle like a thick beard. As we got to the door on his side, I could see quills even up under his eyes.

"This guy really got into them. Wonder what the porcupine looks like?" I asked rhetorically.

The driver, opening the door and getting hold of the dog's chain collar, said, "If it's like most porcupines, he just lost a few quills."

Mike jumped out of the car and entered the surgery without hesitation. When we got him on the table and started to insert the needle into the vein of his right front leg in order to give him an anesthetic, he kind of looked down to see what I was doing; otherwise, his expression didn't change. Soon he collapsed and was snoring soundly. It was then I opened his mouth. Quills were embedded in nearly every square centimeter of his lips and tongue, as well as the roof of his mouth.

"Going to be at least an hour before I get through with this job," I told the chauffeur. "If you want to leave him and pick him up tomorrow, it might be best. Then I can see how he comes out of the anesthesia."

"Okay, Doc, but take good care of him. The boss thinks a lot of him. Wouldn't want to have anything bad happen to him."

It took more than an hour and a half to remove all the quills I could reach. Some had broken off and were so deeply embedded, surgery would have been necessary to remove them. Since the membranes were already badly damaged, I decided to leave them, knowing they would either stay where they were or "work out" in time. It was another two hours before Mike began to come around, but an hour later he was on his feet looking for a drink of water.

The owner called that evening to see how Mike was doing, and the chauffeur was at the door at eight o'clock the next morning to pick Mike up. The dog had eaten a good supper and had just finished his breakfast when the chauffeur arrived. Other than for some swelling of the lips, he seemed "little worse for the wear."

"Better tell the owner he had best keep the dog in during the evening. That's when the porcupines are most likely to be out. This fellow may want to finish the fight. Boxers have that way about them," I said to the driver as he got behind the wheel after seeing that Mike was comfortable on the other leather seat.

"I'll tell him, but it probably won't do much good. The boss thinks Mike can do no wrong and just about lets him do what he wants to do. If it happens again, we'll be back."

They left, Mike sitting there looking straight out the windshield and the chauffeur waving goodbye. With the top down on the convertible "it was a sight for sore eyes," as my mother used to say.

Two days later, when I returned from a calving call around two in the afternoon, the first thing I saw was that yellow Cadillac convertible. Must be something wrong with Mike, I thought. I looked over to the outside runs and there in all his glory sat Mike. He had on his Prince Albert beard and mustache! About that time the driver came out of the office where he had been talking to Harriet while waiting for me.

"Hi, Doc," he greeted me with a grin. "He's gone and done it again."

"When did it happen this time?" I asked, thinking perhaps I'd given him a "bum steer" about porcupines more likely to be out in the evening than another part of the day.

"The boss said he was gone all night. When he showed up this morning, this is the way he was. Can you believe it?"

"Yes, I can believe it. We own a Boxer, too, and he'd do the same thing if he had a chance."

"Do you want me to leave him?"

"Yes, I'll need to watch him closely for sure this time. The liver has to detoxify the anesthesia and because this is so soon since we put him under the last time, it might not have had time to recover fully from the process. He'll be ready to go home tomorrow morning. I'll call the owner if he's not."

After helping me get Mike onto the table and under anesthesia, the driver departed, and once again I went through the procedure. There were just as many quills as before but he bled more this time—the aftermath of the previous encounter. This time it took more anesthetic to get him to a surgical state, and it took an hour longer for him to recover to the point of drinking water. He didn't eat his supper, but did eat his breakfast, after a fashion. Instead of sitting up in the seat when he left, he lay curled up in it. Again, I admonished the driver about not allowing the dog to run around unchecked.

Less than a week later Mike's owner called—again!

"I'm sending Mike over again," his owner, Sam Huddleson, told me. "He's gotten another snootful of quills. The driver will leave this minute if you are going to be there."

"I'll be here," I answered. "You sure must have a time keeping that rascal in."

"We kept him in every night until last night. When he came in this morning, this is the way he was. Don't know what we are going to do with him."

"Well, send him over, I'll see what I can do."

An hour later, the yellow convertible drove in with Mike sitting in the passenger seat looking straight ahead, as usual. This time I had to give Mike about a half more drug than recommended to get him down and to a place where he did not feel the pain of extracting those barbed needles. Although his breathing was normal, it again took him a long time to recover and get to his feet. In fact, it was late afternoon; he should have been up early in the afternoon. I knew the liver was having a time getting rid of the drug. I called Sam and told him I wanted to keep Mike an extra day, just to make sure he was getting along. When he left, however, he was sitting up in the front seat like his old self.

Four days later, the Cadillac arrived in the driveway with Mike. Sam had not called, and I was to be gone all day testing bulls for fertility. After calling Sam, the driver decided to take Mike on to another veterinarian thirty miles away.

Perhaps a month later, I happened to see the chauffeur of the yellow Cadillac at a filling station. "How's Mike?" I asked jocularly, thinking he would come back with a retort about how stupid he thought the dog was. Instead, he looked away.

"Mike's dead. He never came out of the anesthesia the time you weren't there and we took him to the other vet. Sam's still sick that we didn't leave him for you."

I was sick, too. The Boxer courage had been Mike's undoing.

THE GENTLE COCKER

About a year after Harriet and I had been in practice, "Black Gold," better known as oil, in greater than expected quantities, was discovered in Weston County just south of us. Newcastle, about sixty miles from Sundance, and Upton, about thirty miles away, were the two main towns in that county. Most of the commercial activity accompanying the oil boom was centered in Newcastle, where the executives and "ramrods" located. They were the ones with a steady income, the ones with enough money to afford the amenities of life, like owning a dog or cat and sometimes both. Once in awhile a horse or pony was also part of the scene.

Soon after the strike, Harriet and I noticed the volume of services for small animals had picked up, and most, if not all the increase was coming from Newcastle. Although Newcastle was about sixty miles away, we had the closest available veterinary service. It was only a matter of time, therefore, until we considered establishing a satellite clinic at Newcastle. Eventually we did open it, but before doing so I stopped there to treat pets from time to time when I was going through to a large animal call south of there. I also held rabies vaccination clinics there.

Sometimes I even picked up a bitch someone wanted spayed and carried it back to Sundance for surgery. That way, the owner had to make only one trip. I did this a number of times with no untoward events. I'd just stop by the home, the owner would put the dog on the seat of the pickup beside me, say some sweet words to it, and off the two of us would go. Usually, for the first thirty miles or more the dog would be so mesmerized by all the new odors it was picking up, it didn't miss the owner. For the last thirty miles it would just look out the window at the passing scenery. Sometimes, however, it didn't quite work out that way. The animal would get overexcited, then carsick. At times like that I swore I would stop extending the courtesy, especially since winter was coming on and weather was getting too cold to leave a window open!

The worst time was with a nice, gentle cocker spaniel named Mitsie. The owner had made an appointment to have her spayed. I had previously given this blonde, long-eared, good-natured and imminently trusting little canine all of her

73

shots, and it never batted an eye. In fact, she was usually curious, watching intently, but without fear, as I prepared the lypholized vaccine for injection and then gave it to her under the loose skin at the side of her neck. She'd wag her stub of a tail afterward and liked to have me scratch her behind the ears. Thus, I was quite unprepared for the reception I received that Wednesday afternoon when I stopped to get her while on the way back to Sundance from a particularly taxing call I had made thirty miles south of Newcastle.

I had driven around to the back of the house and parked the truck, but I left it running since I expected to be there just a few minutes while the owner and I placed Mitsie on the front seat. What a laugh that turned out to be! When I arrived, I saw a note pinned to the door. It read: "Doctor, I had to leave and will be gone about two hours. Mitsie is inside, and the door is unlocked. Just gather her up and call me when you want me to come after her." The time on the note was one-thirty; it was now two. I could hear Mitsie barking excitedly just inside the door, so, as I opened the door, I spoke her name over and over in an attempt to allay her fears. The barking increased in frequency, and the tone became frenzied.

"Here, Mitsie, Nice Mitsie," I chanted over and over again as I walked through the door. She would have none of this "Buddy, Buddy" business, but stood her ground, and the sound of her barking became one of fury with a snarl thrown in from time to time when I attempted to reach out for her. She also began to urinate on the floor.

"Well," I said aloud. "I'll get the leash from the truck and try to 'rope' her with it. If that fails, the owner will just have to bring her over."

That didn't work either. Furthermore, before it was over we had been all over the kitchen, through the living room, and into the master bedroom, where Mitsie finally took refuge under the bed. There was no way I was going to reach under there to pull out that snarling, frenzied animal. Besides, it was now two-thirty, the truck was still running, and it was past time to be home.

I removed the note from the door and penciled another on the back. "Couldn't get hold of Mitsie. She is just too much watch-dog. Sorry about the mess. Call me when you wish to bring her over."

That evening the owner called to make an appointment, and I told her about the ordeal. She laughed hysterically. "I thought veterinarians had a way with animals so they could do just about anything with them," she explained.

It would not be the last time a "gentle" animal would face me down in its own way!

THE STATE POLICE VS. THE TRUCK DRIVER

Not everything one does as a veterinarian is necessarily to his liking. The lofty vision of spending my life helping animals (which kept me going back into the chemistry classroom to beat my brains out, term after term, when I was in veterinary college) was badly dashed one hot August day, the second year I was in practice.

Close to eleven o'clock in the morning, the store was full of tourists licking up sodas and malted milks and pawing over postcards and souvenirs. Already the thermometer outside the back door read ninety-eight degrees Fahrenheit. The wind was not blowing, either, which was unusual for that country. The telephone had been quiet all morning, and since I did not have a call, I had spent the time making out an order for drugs. Just after I finished that and sat down in the rocking chair in the office to read one of the monthly veterinary journals that had arrived two days earlier, the phone rang. Jake, the pharmacist, answered it.

"Doc, it's for you!" he hollered, not bothering to take the few steps to the door of the office where I was sitting. We'd been having a little trouble with him about his insolent conduct with customers and I had to have a "heart-to-heart" talk with him about it the night before.

I could tell the second I put the receiver to my ear that it was long distance.

"Doc, thank God I found you!" the voice blurted out. "You don't know me, but my name is Sid Spaulding. I'm calling from Sioux Center, Iowa. One of your classmates here gave me your name and location. You still there?" A little panic was coming through.

"Yes, I'm still here. What's the problem?"

"I've got a double-deck trailer full of butcher hogs held up by the police over in a town called Newcastle, Wyoming. They are on their way to Seattle to be slaughtered. The driver told me he got stopped for some minor infraction of the law, and when the police checked his papers, he found out the driver didn't have a health certificate to transport the hogs across the country so he's got him held up. Been tied up since nine o'clock this morning. The policeman said he didn't know where there was a vet, and I've been 'till now trying to find one out there. God, Doc, those hogs have been in that trailer since yesterday afternoon. It'll kill them and me both if we can't get them moving. Probably already lost more than they're going to make."

"Did the driver say where he had his rig parked?" I queried. "It's mighty hot out here, and there aren't many trees to park under for shade."

"Yes, he said he was parked close to the railroad station."

I knew just where it would be. In fact, it was the only shade in town large enough for a trailer full of hogs. About that time, it dawned on me that someone should have the fee handy for such a call. After all, it was unlikely I would ever see or hear of them again, once I had conducted the inspection and got the hogs on their way. Close to sixty miles one way, the trip would take a good two-and-a-half to three hours to make the round-trip.

"Has the driver got the money to pay for the call?" I asked, hoping I didn't sound too mercenary, considering the plight the fellow was in.

"No, he hasn't, but you tell me how much it is, and I'll wire it to you as soon as I hang up the phone. I just have to get those hogs moving or I'd tell you to wait 'till you received it. You can trust me, Doc. I won't cheat you out of it."

From the sound of his voice and my limited experience with livestock dealers, I believed him. "It'll be thirty dollars," I answered.

"Okay, Doc, I'll get it right off to you. Can you leave right now to check them out? Like I said, they've been on that truck since yesterday."

"Sure enough. I'll leave the minute we hang up. No use to wire me the money; the closest telegraph station where I can collect the money is thirty miles away. Better, you let me send you a statement and then you pay me. Let me have your full name and address."

"By God, Doc, if you will do that, I'd sure be much obliged. This is a hellava spot for both of us to be in." With that, I got the particulars. The easiest part of the ordeal was done.

After placing the receiver back on the cradle, I went to the front of the store where Harriet was working at the cash register, told her where I was going, about what time I expected to be back, and that I would call her before leaving Newcastle in case I had another call over that way. Before long I was headed toward Four Corners on the prairie and Newcastle. I didn't stop until I got to the railroad station. There, I saw a semi parked under the trees. "That has to be the outfit," I mumbled to myself. When I pulled up beside it, I knew it was! I could smell those hogs before I turned off the engine of the pickup.

All the way over to Newcastle, I kept trying to figure out where I could have the animals unloaded so I could inspect them, because a proper inspection called for observing them moving about on their feet in order to recognize any lameness or other evidence of infectious disease that would manifest itself. In this case, in particular, a contagious disease among pigs in Iowa was causing the animals to be lame as well as to have lesions or sores in the mouth. As a result, all livestock health authorities and state police across the country had been alerted. The trooper who stopped this trucker had evidently read his bulletins because he knew enough to ask for health clearance papers. After talking with the trucker, whom I found at the pool hall up the main street away from the railroad station, I had reason to believe the trooper wanted to enforce some law on him, too.

The only nearby place close where a double-deck semi could be unloaded was the pens in the railroad yard. Short of that, I would have to do the best I could, which meant observing them through the slat openings on the side of the trailer, or crawling in among them, or both. The driver and I talked it over and decided he would approach the station master. I should have known the answer before starting, considering this fellow's personality, the fact that the hogs were moving by truck instead of by rail, and that if indeed the animals had some sort of disease it would mean cleaning and disinfecting the railroad pens. As I might have suspected, he returned to tell me there was no way the agent was going to let his yards by used.

By that time, the temperature must have been ninety-five without a breeze. The hogs lay stretched out the best they could, as crowded as they were, and all of them were breathing with their mouths open. I told the driver to raise the end gate high enough for me to crawl in.

"Okay, Doc, but you won't like it," he said with a grin as he reached for the rope to pull up the door. He raised it about two feet. A couple of old sows got to their feet, stared me right in the face and began grunting loudly, almost like a bark. That raised an alarm amongst the rest. Soon all the hogs, some weighing as much as 300 pounds, were on their feet, panting, grunting wildly, and moving around enough to start the trailer rocking.

"Drop it down!" I hollered, at the same time motioning for the still grinning trucker to close the gate. "All we'd need now is to have some of these big things get loose!" I was yelling to be heard above the din of the aroused porkers. He seemed glad to comply. With that, we stepped off a little ways so we could talk without shouting.

"What are you going to do now, Doc? Looks like you're pretty much up against it." He went on like he thought this was all a bunch of nonsense, anyway.

"Only one thing left to do," I said, responding to his challenge. "I'll look at them the best I can through the cracks in the side of the trailer. If everything looks all right, I'll issue the certificate so you can get these poor things on the road. However, I'm going to call ahead to the veterinarian in charge of the slaughtering establishment to tell him what happened and how I had to inspect them. I'll ask him to look them over well after you unload. If anything is wrong, he'll probably quarantine your truck until it is disinfected." That wiped the grin off his face.

"God, Doc. I'll never get home if I keep getting run around like this."

To make a long story short, I completed the "inspection," issued the certificate, stayed until the patrolman was satisfied the papers were in order, and saw the trailer load of hogs heading west on Highway 14. All the way back to Sundance I could smell those hogs, even though when I stopped at a gas station to call Harriet, I had washed the best I could. The inspector at the packing plant was very appreciative of the call and thanked me for my concern. Two weeks after I sent the statement of fee to the livestock buyer, I got a check and a nice note, again thanking me.

There was no tip for compromising an inspection procedure, not to mention being barked at by a bunch of hot, smelly butcher hogs!

TEN EIGHTY

As I look back on it now, poisoning was a significant factor in the loss of livestock in those practice years at Sundance. By poisoning, I mean inadvertent as opposed to deliberate poisoning, which occurred, too, but was confined to dogs. In the spring, there always seemed to be some loss of sheep from a weed called death camas. Later on, Larkspur poisoning was a problem, especially in sheep, but it also occurred in cattle grazing in the Bearlodge, on government lands. Animals eating moldy, sweet clover hay could succumb by hemorrhaging to death. The toxic agent, dicumarol, is better known as the rat poison Warfarin. The same agent, in highly controlled and refined amounts, is used in human medicine as an anti-clotting drug in heart disease patients, for example.

Chemical poisoning usually occurred from carelessness or ignorance, as illustrated in the case I am about to relate. It was different, however, in that it happened in a group of about twenty hogs, a number of pigs I had not seen collectively in three years of practice, and the poison was one used to kill coyotes.

Late in the spring when calving and lambing were about over, I resumed the scheduling of spays and other elective surgery in dogs and cats, which I had mostly suspended during the busy time. My feeling, which often turned out to be a "snare and a delusion," was that once in awhile with careful planning and forethought I could conduct such surgery during the day, rather than after the store closed at 10 p.m.

This was about nine o'clock on one of those well-planned mornings. I had spayed two dogs and was in the middle of surgery on a third when I heard the telephone ring. This was about the third time it had rung since the store opened at eight, but evidently none of the calls were of such importance that they needed Harriet's or my attention because our help had not interrupted us. The two bitches I had completed were sleeping peacefully on a thick pad on the floor where I could glance at them from time to time. Everything was going well as far as this last surgery was concerned, too. I had located the ovaries with no problem and had the two horns of the uterus and the ovaries up through the incision about to clamp them off when someone knocked on the door. Mrs. Binney stuck her head in.

"I'm sorry to bother you, but one of the Stymus kids just called in from the Oshoto Store. They were out playing and found eight dead hogs. Their folks aren't home; they went to Belle Fouche early this morning. They want you to come out right away," she announced.

Suddenly, the atmosphere changed. The "gong" had sounded. The "juices" began to flow faster, as they had done a few times in the past, and would do many times in the future.

"Tell them I'll be out the minute I get through here. Shouldn't be but another fifteen minutes. Have them round up any that are out and get them penned," I instructed.

Harriet felt my vibrations. Suddenly she had to go to the toilet!

I was through within fifteen minutes, and after placing the dog beside the others and covering her, I turned to Harriet and said, "Guess you'll have to clean up unless you want to just shut the door and leave it until I get back."

"Don't worry, I'll get it straightened up and watch the dogs too. They're doing great and should be okay," she responded, but then asked, "What do you suppose is wrong with those hogs?"

"Beats me, but we'll soon find out. I didn't know there were that many pigs in the county, either."

With that, I rushed out the back door and motioned to Sam, our Boxer, who had been waiting patiently for me to come out. Both of us jumped into the pickup. In less that five minutes, we were headed west, out of town to the Stymus place, a good forty miles away, fifteen miles of which were dirt road. I was there in fifty minutes. As I drove into the yard, one of the kids coming out of the barn waved for me to come over there. When I stopped and got out, he was already talking.

"Got all the live ones in the pen like you said, Doc," he explained. "They look pretty good to me. The two that were sick when I called were dead by the time I got home."

He led me through the barn to a pen outside at the back. Two other kids were sitting on the top board of the fence looking first at me and then at the hogs. I judged the hogs weighed a good 200 pounds and were Spotted Poland Chinas or at least had a lot of that breed in them. They were market weight or close to it.

"Let's give them some feed and see what they do with it," I said to the eldest boy who seemed to be in charge. Immediately he went back into the barn and, coming out with a water bucket full of corn, started to climb over the fence to put it in the old wooden trough. "Hold it a minute," I said. "Is this the corn you've been giving them all along or is it something new?" At this point, everything they might have eaten was suspect.

"We've been feeding them corn out of this bin for over two weeks. It's getting kind of low now. Dad is going to get some more in Belle today," the boy replied.

"Okay, give it to them," I ordered, and watched him climb in and spread it out in the trough. They acted like most pigs, jostling one another for a mouthful. "You're right. Doesn't seem to be anything wrong with them," I said turning to the boy. "Where are the dead ones?"

"The last two are between here and the fence yonder," he said, pointing to barbed-wire fence about 300 feet away. "The others are strung out along the fence about a quarter of a mile over the hill."

"Okay. We'll need to open up some of them, I believe, but before we do, we had best drive over and have a look. You can ride with me and open the gate. Will your brothers be all right here alone?"

"Oh yes, they'll be okay," the oldest boy said, looking at them as they nodded their heads.

After keeping Sam from licking the boy's face when he got in, we started, went through a wire gate, and headed over a rough road to the far fence. The boy told me he was half afraid that when his father found out, he might think it was something they, the kids, had done.

"What time will your folks be back?" I asked, thinking that if I was still here, my presence might diminish any scolding.

"They should be back now," he answered. Then as we got close to the fence he pointed. "There's two of them."

I had already observed them and drove over, getting out after I made sure the windows were open enough for Sam to have air, but closed enough that he couldn't get out. The flies had already started to work on the hogs, and they were beginning to bloat.

"When's the last time you saw them alive?" I asked.

"Last night about five o'clock when I fed them," he answered. "They always come in about that time, and they are usually around early in the morning, too. The only ones here this morning were the ten you saw in the pen. Nobody thought anything about it. Dad just told me when they came in to feed them. When three of us kids came over this way to play horses, we found them."

"Let's walk up the fence line and look at the rest of them," I said, seeing more dead ones strung out along the barbed-wire fence. As Tim and I walked along, I kept looking for any evidence that might have led to this disaster: poisonous plants, a dump with paint cans, anything! Of course, it could always be an infectious disease, but the suddenness of onset and number of deaths made that possibility remote. As we got close to the last one, I happened to look across the fence to the pasture beyond. My eyes came to rest on what looked like the hind quarter of a small beef or something that size about 150 feet away. Stopping and pointing, I turned to Tim and asked, "Have you butchered lately and thrown some of the meat away?"

"No sir," came Tim's reply as he looked in the direction I was pointing. "We only butcher in the fall, and we don't throw anything away."

"We better go see what that is, then," I responded, starting to climb through the fence as Tim helped hold the wires apart. After he got through, too, we walked hurriedly over to the object. Sure enough, it was a piece of meat—the hind quarter of an animal the size of a calf or a colt. It was quite fresh, too, not like meat that had been lying around. A fair amount had been eaten. Puzzled at finding anything like that "out in the middle of nowhere," I looked at Tim. "Where do you suppose this came from?" I asked.

"I don't know. What is it?" he answered.

I told him what it was and what animals it could be from. As we headed back to the pickup, I heard the noise of an engine and saw an old Ford pickup come bouncing over the hill toward my pickup, the dust flying from the rear. "That's Dad now!" exclaimed Tim, "The way he's driving, he could be mad, too."

We all got to the truck at the same time. Mr. Stymus barely got his rig stopped before he was out of it. The other two boys jumped out too, as well as an old dog that was riding in the back. The dog sniffed and urinated on the wheels of my pickup, while Sam, who had been sitting quietly and watching, suddenly "went ape!"

"God, Doc, we just got back from Belle, and the kids here told me about the dead pigs, and where you and Tim were. Have you found anything out yet?" he shot out, while Tim and the two boys stood a little way off as if expecting to be seared by a flame.

"Well, I haven't conducted a post-mortem examination on any of them yet, so I don't know for sure what it is. But Tim and I just found a partially eaten hind quarter of a calf or colt over there in the pasture," I answered as I turned and pointed toward the object. "Whatever it is that's killed them could well be associated with that meat. Have you thrown anything like that away within the last day or tow?"

"Sure haven't," he said, climbing through the fence and heading toward the remains. While Tim and I tried to keep up with him, the two boys and the dog ran after us.

"Better get hold of your dog, Tim," I commanded. "Don't want him to get that meat before we know for sure it's not poisoned." Tim called the old fella to him, slipped off his belt, made a noose of it, and slipped it around the dog's neck.

After we reached the meat, Mr. Stymus peered down at it intently for a few seconds. Everyone was silent. Suddenly, he looked over at me with an expression on his face as if he just recalled something. "By God, Doc, this looks like the kind of meat trappers use to poison coyotes. Come to think of it, just a week ago, I met a trapper on the road, and he asked me for permission to place some of that poison on my land because coyotes had been killing some of the neighbor's sheep. He wanted to get enough spread out to get them all. I told him to go ahead. Never saw him when he placed it, though. He must have come while we were gone. It never dawned on me he would place the stuff so close to the house. Hell, even the old dog or the cats could have gotten into it."

Turning to Tim and the boys I asked, "What did the two hogs look like that were still alive when you called me but later died?"

"At first they were real wild. Ran in circles. One of them threw up. They finally went down on their sides, paddled their legs like crazy, all the time squealing like they do when you catch them. They twitched a lot, too, then died. I'd say they were dead about fifteen minutes after we noticed them acting funny." The other boys nodded their heads.

"Well, it has all the signs of sodium fluoroacetate or 1080 poisoning." I said. "That's what they use on coyotes. I'll take some samples from the last two pigs that died as well as a piece of this meat, just to make sure. It will take a week to ten days to get a report from the lab. In the mean time, keep the live pigs penned up until you can bury all the rest of this carcass. Better get that done today because of the dog and other animals. You may want to get hold of the trapper, too, to see if he did place the bait here."

Mr. Stymus was certain he knew what had happened and felt he was probably as much at fault as the trapper for not making sure he knew exactly where the poison would be placed.

The lab report confirmed the diagnosis. The unusual calls that marked our summer practice had begun.

THE CHICKEN DINNER

All in all, it had not been a very good week. First off, a client had brought in an old, fat, female dog to be spayed. I had seen the senior surgeon at school operate on several, and it didn't look much more complicated than doing the technique on the normal, young, growing bitch. Unhappily, I was wrong. What ordinarily took a maximum of one-half hour took two hours. What normally was a relaxed and enjoyable procedure (when Harriet and I had a chance to talk in private while I was doing the surgery and she was assisting) turned into a battle with fat and a tug-of-war with the ovaries and horns of the uterus—getting them up through the incision where they could be removed. Hence, before it was over, my composure was reduced, and as a result, Harriet's good disposition was shattered.

Later in the week, a grizzly-faced rancher, all of six-feet-four inches tall, came into the drugstore and asked to talk to the vet. When Harriet introduced me, I could see a look of doubt cross his face. After all, I was only five feet five inches tall with my new boots on and had not been out of school long enough to even have a tan on my face. After talking to him about his lame bull, which had what sounded like a bacterial disease of the hoof we called necrotic pododermatitis, or foot rot, I left him waiting while I went to the shelves in the veterinary section to get some medicine. Harriet told me afterward that when I left, he turned to one of the girls working at the soda fountain and said, "Hell, he'll never make a vet; he is too small and his arms are too short to reach inside an old cow to get a calf out of her!" A real confidence builder, after what happened in the surgery!

Saturday of that week, an old friend of Harriet's insisted we have Sunday dinner with her, her husband Willy and her elderly mother. Since we had not been away from the demands of the store or practice since our arrival in Sundance two months before, we gratefully accepted the invitation.

It turned out to be an especially hot day in August, with not a whisper of wind—unusual for that country. We had to drive about thirty miles before arriving at an old, unpainted weather-beaten house, surrounded by equally weather-beaten and partially dilapidated outbuildings, sheds, and barn. A few chickens scratched in the yard as we went through a rusty iron gate and up a dirt path to the front steps. There, Harriet was greeted with much jubilation since she had not seen her friend or her mother for some years. At one time they had been quite close. As for me and Willy, we were sort of outsiders to the reminiscence, so we just talked among ourselves while the women visited. The room we were ushered into at the front of the house was small and the sun beat in unmercifully. A few scraggly ferns and geraniums sat on the ledge in front of the window. The cacophony of the voices plus the heat and closeness were about to do me in when finally the old woman announced that dinner was ready.

We were shown into what, at one time, must have been a near elegant dining room off the kitchen. The slop bucket was in full view of where I was to be seated, the curtains were faded, and the sideboard and other furniture were covered with dust. The dishes on the long table looked clean, but at that point I was not too sure. The food consisted of boiled potatoes, green beans, thick gravy, and fried chicken. I believe there was also some homemade bread and home-churned butter on the table. Later we would get some iced tea and apple pie.

Chicken was not my favorite form of meat protein at that time. I had an aversion to it as a result of some of experiences in the army, and the only way I could handle it at all was to have it fried or baked to a crisp. In no way could I enjoy any that showed the slightest amount of under-cooking. Thus, when I bit into a piece of gelatinous thigh, I had to "gag it down," as they would say out there. The rest of the meal was pure hell, but I managed to make it through by thinking of pleasanter things, like taking castor oil when I was a kid.

Once the meal was completed, and the women were gathering up the dishes while continuing to talk, Willy turned to me and said, "You're a vetinary, maybe you can tell me what is wrong with the chickens. Some of them haven't been acting too good lately. Seem to get thinner all the time, then I find them dead. Can't get any flesh on them either, even though I buy feed for them."

"Let's go out and take a look," I said, glad for the chance to go outside way from the heat, the dust, the dirt, and the noise of the voices reverberating off the old walls. Willy and I went out past the barn to one of the old sheds where some laying boxes hung on the wall. A chicken sitting on the dirt floor by the door was squatting down and didn't move. Very unusual behavior.

"See, Doc, that's how they act before they die. Just sit around for three or four days. Won't eat or drink. Get a film over their eyeballs, too."

When I reached down to pick her up, she offered no resistance. I felt her breast muscles, and they were almost absent. Only the breast bone was prominent.

"Best I conduct a post-mortem examination on her," I said turning to the quizzical husband. "I'll need a butcher knife or something to open her up with. I didn't bring any instruments with me." Whereupon Willy left to go to the house. "Bring me a bucket of warm water, too!" I hollered after him.

By the time he returned, I found two more that might as well be "posted" to give me a good picture of the disease or whatever. I noticed, too, that many of the chickens were probably three to four years old—typical of a farm flock where people raised their own chickens. It didn't take long to discover the cause of illness. Each one was very thin, and the livers were covered with pustules the diameter of lead in a pencil. Cutting into them was like running the blade through sand. It could be only one thing: TB (tuberculosis)!

All the while I was conducting the exam, Willy was telling me they ate only the ones that looked healthy. "No sir, wouldn't eat any that acted funny," he assured me.

"Problem with that is, TB is in them a long time before they start acting funny," I responded. "Fortunately, the kind of TB chickens have seldom is transmitted to man. There are reports of it, however. A fella better not take a chance by eating any more of them, no matter what they look like."

"How does a man get rid of it?"

"You need to kill them all and burn or bury them. Disinfect the shed and laying boxes, then don't get any new ones for at least a year."

On the way home, I told Harriet what had happened. For awhile she just sat there dumfounded. Finally she said, "What should we do? Do we need to take some medicine or something?"

"Well, if you didn't eat any more chicken than I did, we probably don't have anything to worry about. I didn't see or eat any liver that I know of, unless it was in the gravy. If there was anything wrong with it, they probably threw it out, anyway," I answered hopefully.

After a long silence Hattie turned to me, half-smiling. "Guess I know what not to serve you—for awhile, at least," she said.

"That's right," I responded. "My appetite for chicken has just returned to my army days."

Forever afterward, I would always wince a little when, after "gagging down" a meal in unkempt surroundings, someone would turn to me and begin, "Say, Doc, you're a vetinary.... ."

SANDY

Sandy Blake was my pilot the first two years I was in private veterinary practice. He was a rancher when he wasn't flying me or someone else around the country. He obviously loved flying more than ranching for there were few times when I called that he put me off.

He had a flight instructor's rating and license, and for a time I took lessons from him. In fact, the cushion I sat on to see over the instrument panel, when taxiing or taking off, still smoldered in the back seat of the little plane when Harriet and I arrived at the scene of the crash, after they had removed him and taken him to the mortuary.

I never did know his real first name, or at least not well enough to remember it now. I learned to know him the first fall in practice in Sundance, that little town nestled between the Sundance Mountain and the Bearlodge, a short range of mountains that I always thought of as the beginning of the Black Hills of South Dakota.

I had been called to the Blake ranch, about 15 southwest of town, to treat about 150 calves. This ranch was a three-family operation, Sandy being the son who worked with his dad and his brother-in-law. He was taller than I, probably about five-foot-eight, and much more heavy-set and muscular. Outgoing but serious, his bearing was one of confidence without braggadocio. We were probably close to the same age, twenty-eight or twenty-nine.

While we were putting the calves through the chute to treat them, Sandy and I visited. That's when I learned he was a pilot and would be willing to take me on calls that didn't interfere with the ranching operations or his other activities.

One thing that impressed me forcefully that first summer and fall in practice was the distance necessary to get to a call. It wasn't unusual to go twenty-five, fifty, or sixty miles one way to attend to a sick animal. The frequency of that changed five years later after we moved to Gillette and built a large- and small-animal clinic. Before that, however, I traveled to ninety-five percent of my calls.

In those days, Wyoming had a seventy-five-mile-an-hour speed limit, which was about as fast as cars were safe to run anyway. I tried to average a mile a minute, from the time I left the office until I arrived at my destination. Since a good third of the distance to most calls consisted of dirt or gravel roads, I had to move right along on the hardtop. Even then, it took a half-hour to an hour, or more, to get to a bloated animal or one in the last stages of milk fever, or some other emergency. Being trained in veterinary school (in the Midwest) that such cases should be treated within ten to fifteen minutes created an obvious frustration. I was seeking a faster mode of transportation, and Sandy was like the "answer to a maiden's prayer."

His only airplane at the time was a small, two-seat, sixty-horsepower Aeronica Coupe, with seats placed in tandem rather than side by side. The bright yellow canvas-covered frame was very light. Later, he also owned a four-seat Cessna.

The runway at the ranch was in a meadow below the buildings. Most times, depending upon wind direction, the landing approach was a little tricky because of a hill and a set of high tension electric lines. I know about them because he had me practice landings and takeoffs there. It was those wires that got him!

The runway at Sundance, one mile east of town and the Sundance mountain, was a level piece of ground owned by a rancher and used as a bull pasture, in the bulls' "offseason!" There was a five-foot-high, barbed-wire fence to cross either when landing or taking off. The runway was plenty long on takeoff when there wasn't too much weight in the plane, and likewise, on landing, unless you came in too fast!

One time four friends from Michigan stopped to stay with us overnight. They landed their twin-engine in the pasture (after I chased the bulls to one side) and nearly went through the fence before getting stopped. On takeoff the next morning, we had to place fence posts in front of the wheels to keep the plane from moving until the engines were revved up so high, the tail started to lift off the ground. Then, on signal, Harriet and I pulled them out, but even then, they barely cleared the fence.

Anyway, it served as a runway and was all we had. The closest airport was thirty miles away, and to travel back and forth to it each time I needed Sandy would have defeated the purpose. Besides, if ever I was to fly well enough to use a plane in practice, I must learn how to get in and out of tighter places than this!

The first time I called Sandy, shortly after we met, we flew to a ranch some eighty-five miles south of Sundance to treat calves that got sick after they were weaned with the same disease his calves had had. The call came in around eleven o'clock. I had not been to the place before and getting the directions well enough to recognize it from the air was not easy. As I've mentioned, the old crank telephone on the wall, together with the condition of the private telephone system in Sundance, left a lot to be desired in terms of clarity.

After hanging up the receiver, I called Sandy's home; his wife answered. "This is Doc Baldwin, Rena. Is Sandy there? I need him to take me on a call, if he can."

"Just a minute. He just now walked in the door for lunch," she responded. I could hear her tell him I was on the line.

"Hi, Doc, what can I do for you?" Sandy greeted me.

"I have a call about twenty-five miles south of Newcastle and wonder if you can take me. If all goes well, we should be back by four or five."

"Just a minute, Doc, got to talk to Rena." Pretty soon he came back on the line. "Okay, I'll grab a bite to eat and meet you at the runway in town about noon. Get the bulls off the strip if they're in the pasture."

"That's swell. I'll be there." With that, I hung up and made preparations for the trip.

Bill Bently had said he had about 20 sick calves out of 120 he was weaning. I gathered the drugs and equipment I felt would be needed and put them in the trunk of the little green Studebaker. (We had not yet traded it for the pickup.)

Harriet had prepared lunch, and we discussed the trip as we ate. It was our first experience in the use of an airplane in practice, let alone a single-engine one. Sandy had a reputation of being an excellent pilot, though, and more and more ranchers using planes in their operations. It should be safe.

Harriet took me to the pasture, and we got there just in time to see the "yellow bird" coming past the Sundance Mountain and approaching the airstrip. Looking around quickly, I saw the bulls lying under a few trees to the left of the runway, chewing their cuds and switching at flies. Thank goodness!

Sandy landed, taxied up to the barbed-wire gate, and got out, leaving the engine running. We took only about two minutes to load. Before leaving, he said to Harriet, "If it doesn't look like we'll make it back by dark, we'll call you. Then you can call Rena if you will; otherwise she'll worry."

"I'll be glad to do that," Harriet responded. She went on, "How will I know when to come after you, when you get back?"

"Just keep your ears open. We'll buzz the store," he answered matter-of-factly.

She didn't look too pleased. Evidently, it just dawned on her that flying in the bush had the limitation of being able to travel only during daylight.

I got in the back seat and put on the seat belt. The back seat had a stick and a set of rudder pedals the same as the front. Sandy climbed in, closed the door, and hardly had his seat belt hooked by the time we were taxiing toward the east fence. A good breeze was blowing from the west, and we needed to head into it to get all of the lift we could. I had taken quite a few drugs and Sandy said we had about all the weight the plane could safely stand.

Just before we reached the fence, he spun the plane 180 degrees and pushed the throttle forward, all the way. I still remember the noise and vibration inside the fuselage as the tires and undercarriage hit the clods of dirt and brush, and the engine roared. I still remember, too, looking down at Hattie as we passed to the left of her, not thirty feet off the ground. She was waving, but I couldn't. I was too busy with each hand, hanging on to the frame tubing that ran on each side of the seat!

As we got further aloft, the engine sounded as if it was running fast enough to fly to pieces, until Sandy throttled it back and started to crank a lever over his head. Then it got a little quieter and the vibration diminished, but I felt perceptible up drafts and down drafts as we passed the mountain. I began to wonder if all this had been such a good idea.

About that time, Sandy turned his head and started talking over the noise of the now cruising coupe. I released my grip a little on the tubing, since the muscles in both arms were quivering. However, I was able to relax only somewhat, only as long as I looked straight ahead and not down. When I was thinking how great it would be to travel this way, I had not reckoned with the fact I was afraid of heights.

We got to Bill Bently's about 1:45 p.m. and landed on a divide about two miles from the corrals. The landing was uneventful except for the noise of the sagebrush hitting the undercarriage. Again, I thought the whole bottom was being torn off the plane.

Bill was waiting for us in an old Jeep (with no top on it) and took us to the cattle. On the way over, he gave me more details about how the calves acted and when it all began. When I got a look at them, it was pretty apparent they had shipping fever (even though they hadn't been shipped anywhere), a respiratory now called Bovine Respiratory Disease Complex. Sandy recognized they had the same signs as the ones he was treating at home. Therefore, he knew what to do and when, so he pitched right in, and it wasn't long before we were through treating the sick ones. It then remained for us only to look over the others and leave directions along with enough medicine to treat them, before heading back to the plane. Since it was not quite 4 p.m., we could make it home before dark with maybe fifteen minutes to spare.

Riding seemed a little better on the way back. A few times I even let go of the frame tubing and looked down. The countryside was really interesting with the buttes, sagebrush, and pine forests. We even saw a couple of herds of grazing antelope that raised their heads and ran when the shadow of the plane passed through them. Soon the Sundance Mountain came into view and fifteen minutes later, we were buzzing the store. We didn't wait to see if anyone waved in acknowledgment, we just headed on down to the bull pasture. By the time we landed, and got unloaded, I could hear the car coming down the lane. Sandy had already closed the door and was taxiing for the takeoff. Time wise, everything turned out just right.

As we drove back to the store and office, I told Harriet about the trip. After the initial shock, I was convinced flying was the way to get to those calls a long distance away. Her silence told me she wasn't that sure. However, we did use Sandy many times after that, and I even began to take flying lessons from him.

We had some strange experiences together in our all-too-brief acquaintance. One time, in Montana, we got lost and had to land on a dirt road in front of a lone ranch house to get directions. After we landed, we taxied up to the front door. I wish you could have seen the look on those people's faces when they came to the door and saw an airplane in their yard! Even the dog looked amazed. We were about ten miles off course. Taxiing back to the road, we made our takeoff midst much barking and waving.

Another time that spring, I was called out beyond the Devils Tower Store. Since that was the last telephone to the northwest of Sundance for fifty miles, we had an arrangement with the store owner to place a red flag on a pole in his yard if Harriet had called him and wanted me to call home. That day, the flag was out!

"You've got to go right out to Bessy Smith's at Oshoto." Harriet's instructions came faintly through the receiver, yet I knew she was likely hollering at the top of her lungs. "She's got a heifer in trouble. She said you can't get in there by pickup so I've called Sandy. He said he will take you when you are ready. You've got two more calving calls when you get through there."

I thought for a minute about the thirty-mile drive back to the bull pasture in Sundance, and the time it would take versus having Sandy pick me up close to where I was. The only place that came to mind that was flat and smooth enough for landing was a stretch of Highway 14 between Sundance and the Devils Tower Junction, known locally as the Sunny Divide. That time of year there was very little traffic, and certainly no tourists. Anyway, I envisioned that if Sandy landed midway on the stretch, anyone coming over the brink from either way would see the plane and have plenty of time to stop or get off the road!

"Call Sandy and ask him if he can land on the highway on top of the Sunny Divide. If he can, have him come right along because I can be there by the time he is. I'll wait for you to call me back."

"I think it's risky," Harriet responded, "but I'll call him."

With that, she rang off and I hung up the receiver, walked over to the candy counter and picked up a Milky Way. As I waited, I talked with the store owner about the weather and recent events in the community. Soon Harriet called back.

"Sandy says he knows the piece of road, and it will be okay. He wants you to have everything ready to throw in when he gets down because of what might be coming, and he doesn't want to get off the road. He says he'll fly over it once to see if a car is coming from either direction, then he'll set her down."

"Okay, I'll get there as soon as I can and I'll be ready." It was a good six miles to the rendezvous.

"You guys be careful, now!" Harriet urged. "I'll have supper ready when you get back and before you go on the next call." I acknowledged the messages and hung up, hearing the familiar ring-off.

I arrived on the Divide just in time to see the "Yellow Bird" coming over the trees to the southeast. The highway ran pretty much east and west at this point. When I got to what I felt was a good safe midpoint, I pulled of the road onto the sod between the fence and the "hardtop."(Out there, it's called the bar pit or bar-rowpit.) Sandy flew past about the time I stopped. Quickly, I got out the Pandora bag, calf-puller, stainless steel bucket, OB suit, and a few other things I might need. I heard the plane coming in for a landing, so evidently Sandy found the road clear in both directions. When I turned away from the pickup with all my gear, the plane was getting close. Sandy had the door open, too. The minute the plane stopped, I ducked under the wing, pulled the rear seat as far forward as I could, and placed the equipment behind it securely while Sandy and I exchanged a few words of greeting.

As I climbed in, Sandy revved the engine. I hadn't yet fastened the seat belt when he had closed the door and we were moving. It was only then that I noticed that the highway was not very level at the point chosen. In fact, we were heading somewhat uphill. The top of the rise was not too far ahead. A car coming over the hill about now would have trouble stopping, I thought as the little plane roared westward down the highway with its tail lifting off the ground, just before Sandy would "pull her up!"

Just as we were airborne, a car appeared at the top of the rise. We were headed toward one another! Sandy pulled back on the stick, and his feet worked the rudder pedals like a pianist playing a fast crescendo. The little plane responded, and lifted right up and over that car. I'd say we cleared it a good ten to twelve feet! I looked back just in time to see the car heading into the bar pit.

"That was a close one!" Sandy hollered above the roar of the engine and the vibration noise. "I don't know where that car came from; the road was clear when I looked before landing."

Bessy met us above the ranch house and barn on a pasture field where she had the heifer tied to her pickup. The heifer was half-wild, so it was a good thing Sandy was along to help. Within an hour we were back in the plane taking off for the pickup, where we arrived at nearly four o'clock. This time, Sandy circled a couple of times before landing, after which I removed the equipment, and he took off without incident.

Yes, Sandy died in that little plane. About six months after our trip to Bessy's, he was on his way home at dusk from a teaching lesson he had given another rancher. As she related later, Rena was becoming apprehensive. He always said that landing at dusk was the most dangerous time. Suddenly, when the lights in the house went out, she began to cry out. She knew!

The tragedy ended any further desire on my part to become a pilot and have an airplane for practice. In a way, I'm sorry it did, for the greatest tribute I could have paid Sandy would have been to carry out those plans we talked about so often. He even had a good safe plane in mind for me to consider buying. It was a single-engine, sixty-horsepower job ... and was bright yellow!

J.B. STORTS: A WELL-DRESSED COWBOY

Known around the area as J.B., he was the cattle foreman for a 300-cow outfit along the Belle Fouche River. Quite a lot of farming went on out there, too, but J.B. didn't have much to do with that except as it related to feeding cattle in the fall and winter. He knew how to drive a tractor and run some of the equipment, but after he became cattle foreman, he wasn't much inclined to acknowledge it. Folks get that way sometimes when they've worked themselves up to a better job. They don't want anyone to know they'd done the scut jobs, kept their nose clean, and succeeded through good works to get where they are. Instead, they want to think, and have others believe, they were born to their current high station in life. J.B. somewhat reminded me of such a person.

The first time I met him, I really thought he was the owner of the spread, and he didn't give me any reason to think otherwise. Two weeks later, however, I met the owner himself when he came into the store to pay for a call I'd made to treat a sick cow on the ranch. Even today, from the standpoints of dress and mannerisms, I believe they could more appropriately have exchanged roles.

About the last of June, right after Harriet and I had arrived in Sundance, J.B. called in from the Devils Tower Store to see if I could go out to look at what he called "an old cow whose bag(udder) and nose is all blistered and peelin'." That year a heavy snowstorm the middle of June had covered the grass for about a week. The only feed most of the range animals could get had to be at least eight inches high. Not finding that, some ate the new leaves off the scrub oaks and died, or got scoured "awful bad," as they said out there. As J.B. talked on, I thought the problem might be after-effects of sunburn, too. The reflection of bright sun off the white snow onto the pink nose and udder of a "white-face" or Hereford cow will do this.

"Is the cow a Hereford or something else?" I shouted into the mouthpiece of the old wall phone.

"She's a white-face," came the response.

"Is she the only one that looks like that?"

"Yep, the only one I found, and I got a good count on all of them."

After getting the directions to the ranch, I told him I would be there about one o'clock.

It must be something other than sunburn, I thought, because it isn't likely that only one out of three hundred would be affected. So before I left, I got out the books and read up on everything related to blistered, peeling skin in the bovine. There wasn't much.

Two or three dogs met me at the place, jumping and barking at the car. When I pulled up in front of the open doors of a three-bay machinery and repair garage, a young fellow directed me around a set of buildings and down to the corrals a quarter of a mile away. He said J.B. had told him I was coming and he would be waiting for me down there.

After two more gates that I had to open and close, I arrived at the corral, located in a little grove of trees. A good-looking setup, I thought. About that time, I saw a real typey Palomino quarter horse tied to one of the corral poles about halfway along the chute leading to the metal head catch. He had on one of those fancy padded saddles with all the silver trimmings you see cowboys riding in a parade. I pulled up about twenty-five feet behind him. A well-dressed cowboy came around the front of the head catch and walked toward the car. By well dressed, I mean he had on what looked like a whole new outfit from his broad-brimmed hat down to his shiny boots. When he got to me, I could see they were not new, just immaculately kept. As he approached, he pulled off a rich-looking buckskin glove and extended his hand in greeting.

"You must be the new vet," he said, smiling warmly as he looked me square in the eyes. "Hope you can figure this one out. I can't, that's for sure."

Shaking his hand I responded, "Yes, I'm the guy you talked to on the phone. Hope I can do you some good, too." I liked this man right away. The firm handshake, the pleasant smile, the air of confidence, and the clean well-matched clothes reminded me of a trim sailing vessel.

"Got her right there in the catch-pen, ready for you to look at," he said, pulling his glove on and heading back the way he'd come.

That's when I heard a jingling sound and looked down at his boots to see a set of rowels, the size of silver dollars, forming the end of his spurs. He stepped along at a lively pace, like a man in a hurry. I followed as best I could, using the ring of the rowels for cadence. Then I noticed the chaps, made of heavy leather and light tan in color, pretty much the natural color of a Hereford hide. They had been worn a lot, but I could tell by the back of the legs that they had been well taken care of, too. The areas that would meet parts of the saddle were smooth and glistening, clean and oiled. They, too, had what looked like silver mountings.

Arriving at the catch pen, we both peered through the poles at the sick cow and her calf. Sure enough, the skin if her muzzle and udder were blistered. More evident, however, was the peeling and cracked appearance of the skin over her neck, and down along her shoulders. That looked like a reaction to a hot brand.

"Let's get her in the chute," I said to J.B. "I need a better look."

I went to the front to operate the head catch, while J.B. climbed over the poles and got behind her to urge her up the chute. Halfway up she stopped and tried to back out. J.B. hollered and shouted and at the same time placed a short pole across the chute to prevent her from escaping. She backed into it and wouldn't move forward again until J.B. got hold of her tail and began to twist it, with one gloved hand, amid much shouting. After awhile he got her in, but not before those gloves and the front of those pretty chaps had taken on some manure. While I was taking her temperature and otherwise examining her, I noticed J.B. go over to the fence where the grass was tallest and rub his gloves as clean as possible. Then he took them off, got out his pocket knife and carefully scraped his chaps. By the time I got through, he looked as pretty as a picture!

Mentally ruling out Hoof and Mouth Disease, Vesicular Stomatitis, and some of those other foreign or rare disease drilled into our minds at veterinary school, I turned to J.B., who, while busy with his grooming, had been jabbering about the snowstorm and how much stock had been lost. "Looks like photosensitization to me," I said.

Suddenly, he stopped running off at the mouth (as they say in the South), looked at me quizzically, and said, "By golly Doc, that's just what I thought it might be."

Photosensitization is a known, but fairly uncommon, disease of sheep or cattle. The animal becomes hypersensitive to light as a result of ingesting a photodynamic agent such as certain plants or, in some cases, drugs. Usually, only the white-colored areas of the body show the effects.

Off and on over the years when I worked with J.B., he always manifested the same apparent cocksure attitude about his knowledge of cattle and their ailments. He always gabbed, and the larger the audience, the more voluminous the voice. He was always impeccably dressed for a working cowboy, and didn't touch anything about a cow, especially her tail, unless he had on his buckskin gloves.

A couple of years later, about the same time of year, J.B. called about "an old cow he'd picked up in the brush that morning that had only the tail of a calf sticking out." Before he hung up, I knew what I'd be facing; however, I didn't have any idea how bad it really would be or the fun I would have with an otherwise unpleasant job.

I got to the corral right after lunch, about one-thirty in the afternoon. The day was unseasonably hot, and the flies were already working. J.B. was waiting for me as usual, and the minute I turned off the pickup motor he was telling me about the time he had finding her and getting her in. Before he finished the story, I had gotten out all the gear I felt I would need and had put on my black OB (obstetrical) suit. That done, we moved over to the catch pen where the cow was standing quietly. J.B. had already haltered her. As usual in such cases, while all my equipment was clean, I gave her an epidural anesthesia (something like a spinal in humans) to prevent or reduce her ability to strain against my arms, and an injection of penicillin to reduce chances of infection.

Normally, in calving cases I got the tail out of the way, too, by using a piece of baler twine to tie it about her neck. This time, however, I asked J.B. to hold it until I examined her, and then I planned to tie it around her neck. He appeared a little reluctant to take on the task, but did so after "gloving up." Before long I understood his initial hesitancy. The examination revealed the cow had an emphysematous (dead and deteriorating) fetus retained inside her uterus. Further, it was coming "upside down and backwards," as the cowboys would say. I judged the calf had been dead for over a week.

Now, in such cases, the odor can be quite overwhelming, and this was no exception. I became so interested in the challenge to my skills in removing the calf, I forgot about the chore I had assigned J.B. It wasn't until he stopped telling me a story and began to groan, "Golly, Doc, ain't it awful!" that I realized he was still holding onto the tail.

With one hand and arm still inside of the cow, I glanced over at J.B. He was as far away from the animal as he could get and still hanging on to the tail, and had his face turned away, but was seemingly gasping for air. Suddenly he dropped the tail, went over to one side of the pen and threw up. I stopped my work to go see how he was getting on. When he could speak, he said again, "Golly, Doc, ain't it awful?"

"Sure is. Been a long time since I had one this bad," I responded, whereupon I returned to the animal and started the task of removing bits and pieces of the calf. J.B. was recovering nicely and the tail was getting in my way, so I urged him to get hold of it again. Being somewhat embarrassed, something like a father who fainted at the sight of his wife giving birth, he reached at arm's length for the switch and held it, keeping his face turned away from the scene and the odor as much as possible. Before long, however, he dropped the tail again and headed to the fence. He didn't have anything else to lose, so this time he just retched. This happened about four times, and each time I waited for him to finish so he could return to his job of holding the tail out of my way.

When finally I finished, J.B. stood quietly watching me clean my gear. I could never remember him being so quiet. His face was white and drawn, but at last he said, "By Golly, Doc, wasn't that awful?"

SLEEPING SICKNESS: THE FIRST EXPERIENCE

It was late July during the second year of practice when the call came in. I was close to the phone, so I answered it.

"That you, Doc?" came an anxious sounding voice I recognized as Sam Dunn's.

"Yes, Sam, what's the trouble?"

"Just came in from riding the fence line, and the old horse is acting funny. Noticed it a little this morning when I saddled up, but I thought whatever it was, he might warm out of it."

"How's he acting?" I asked in a loud voice, trying to overcome the noise on the line.

"Well, this morning he had his head down when I went into the corral to get him. Didn't look up and snort like he usually does. After we got going, he didn't act too chipper, and he stumbled from time to time. I didn't like that too much 'cause we had to go around the rim of the canyon. It's quite a way to the bottom if a fella went over there. Anyway, we made it. Then we ran across an old cow that was lame. I took down the rope to catch her, and when I urged the horse to get after her, he started pretty good, but stumbled again. That's when I knew for sure something was really wrong 'cause he never does that when he's getting after a critter. Funny thing, too, when we got back, he just stuck his nose down in the water tank, but he didn't drink."

"Well, I can't tell what it might be until I see him. I can come out right now if you want me to."

"Hell, Doc, sure I want you to see him! Just come on. I'll be here. I'll have Betty get some lunch. You should be gettin' here by that time, the way you drive."

"That'll be fine," I laughed. "See you in about an hour."

The place I had to go to was Moskee, an old ghost town close to the South Dakota/Wyoming border. This had been a lumber town, but when the timber was cut over fifteen or twenty years earlier, the company just moved out, leaving a dozen houses (shacks is a better word) and some other buildings vacant.

Sam, his wife Betty, and their two boys spent summers in one of the better houses since he was hired by the grazing association to tend cattle that members had on pasture there. This was part of the national forest that ranchers leased for grazing purposes. The country was too rough for a vehicle, so Sam kept a little string of horses there to carry out his job.

When I hung up the receiver, I went to the office and told Harriet where I was going and when I expected to be home. Before I left, however, I stopped long enough to get out the textbook on infectious diseases of livestock. I read the chapter on rabies. Next, I turned to the section describing equine encephalomyelitis: "sleeping sickness." I hoped the horse had neither, but the signs Sam mentioned sounded suspiciously like the latter.

I got there in a little over an hour. Had to travel about twenty miles east on the blacktop, then nearly fifteen miles on some very rough red clay roads—the closer to Moskee, the rougher the roads were. It was easy to find the house where Sam and Betty lived. I drove up the only street in town until I saw a house with kids and a border collie dog playing in the front. Sam came out the screen door as I drove in the driveway behind his pickup.

"Ya made it in good time, Doc," he greeted me.

"Not too bad. Where have you got the horse?"

"He's over in the shed where they used to keep work teams when this place was running." He pointed back the way I had come. "Better eat a bite before we get started, though. Betty's got it ready."

As we started into the house, the boys and the dog came racing up, but Sam intercepted them.

"You kids go out to the well and wash before you come in. Your mother's got enough to do without carrying water for you. Want you to be quiet at the table, too, while Doc and I talk."

I knew by looking at them it would be a tall order, but then I remembered as a kid watching the veterinarian treat some sick goats my Dad had gotten for my brother and me. We were real quiet, watched his every move, and listened to his every word. Couldn't figure out how he knew what to do, but the goats got well! "Maybe the same thing will happen with these youngsters," I said to myself.

When we entered the house, Betty had just finished setting the table. "You can wash up over at the basin," she said pointing to a wooden counter-top where a bucket and old aluminum wash basin sat. "There's some hot water on the stove, too, if you want that."

"Hope you didn't go to any bother on my account. I don't eat too much at noon."

"Well, we don't have much in the way of vegetables, but we always have plenty of meat."

I looked over to the stove. There must have been at least two fried chickens as well as a platter full of chicken fried steaks. Probably venison. I groaned to myself.

We finally sat down after we had washed and Betty had put the food on the table. As he passed the dishes around, Sam started to talk. "Something else I noticed after unsaddling my horse. His lower lip was drooping down. I never saw him do that before. Does that mean anything more, Doc?"

"Yes, it could," I responded. "I'll know a little bit more after I examine him." I thought that this might be as good a time as any to tell them all what two diseases it could possibly be. Betty and the kids thought the world and all of the old horse. They could help Sam share the burden if it turned out to be either disease, for he would be sick. His favorite horse.

"Right now it sounds like one of two conditions, rabies or sleeping sickness. If it's rabies, he won't last too long. The only way to tell for sure is to conduct laboratory tests on his brain if he dies. If it's sleeping sickness, he's got a fifty percent chance to make it, but it's a long road to recovery. The reason I'm telling you all about this is because man can get both diseases. Rabies can be gotten directly from the saliva; therefore, Sam should be the only one to go near him. I'll tell him how to protect himself. Sleeping sickness is transmitted to people and horses from mosquitoes that have contracted the virus from birds. Not likely anyone could get it from a horse directly, but until a few years ago a lot of experts thought they could."

Everyone was very quiet for some time after I finished. Finally, Sam looked at the boys. "You heard what the Doc said. Don't go near the corral. Keep the dog up here at the house, too. I don't want to hear tell of any of ya going down there! Do you hear what I'm tellin' ya?"

The boys nodded their heads in unison. Looked like they had heard their Dad's admonitions before. Betty looked over at me. "You don't sound very encouraging, Doc. That's Sam's best horse, too. Sure hope it isn't either of those things you talked about." She then got up for the coffee.

Maybe I should have waited until I looked at the horse before saying anything, I thought. A man's favorite horse, the milk cow, and the family dog are just about as important as anything can be, short of the wife and the kids. *Should have been more sensitive.*

Years later, after leaving rural practice, I missed these kinds of calls. Now I know why. In very personal, stressful situations, a special kind of bond was established between the family members and me as the veterinarian. This can occur in the office setting, also, but somehow not to the same degree as sitting at a man's table with his wife and kids.

There you get the whole load—the eyes, the changed facial expressions, the shuffling of the feet, the reprimand of a kid who really hasn't done anything wrong, the sudden passing of the meat and the bread and potatoes, even though it is obvious no one wants more. All those things happen over and over again in a country practice, and you become a real part of that family for years to come. You're no longer just the vet. You have a stake in that family's life, and they have a piece of yours!

Sam and I left the house and went down to the corral, which wouldn't have held anything that wanted out very badly. It was made of pine poles in the last stages of rotting. One of the two pens that made the corral had an old shed off to the right. A sorrel, or reddish brown horse with a blaze face and four white stockings, stood in the doorway with his head down. The other pen had three horses, standing there switching flies.

"That's him over there in the door, Doc." Sam motioned toward the shed.

"Well, let's see what we got." I got out of the pickup and walked toward the gate. By the time I got to it, Sam had opened it and was waiting for me to go through. As we approached, I could see the horse was a gelding, not that it mattered much, as sick as he looked. For about three minutes, I just stood and watched him.

At first, he raised his head a little and looked at me, then Sam. He nickered a little, then dropped his head.

"He wouldn't do that if he was feelin' good," Sam offered. "He'd be lookin' for a handout."

I didn't say anything, just watched him. He was standing with his legs apart, like a sawhorse. His lower lip was hanging down, as Sam had indicated, and his eyelids were droopy. All this would be very uncharacteristic of the horse a cowboy would call his best. You might have seen an old wagon horse like this in a city many years ago—one that had to wait for long periods while the driver delivered coal or ice, or tried to sell a garment to some woman in an apartment.

While we watched, the horse yawned. When he finished, he began to grind his teeth but showed no signs of aggressive behavior.

"Get me a bucket of water, will you, Sam? I want to see if he will take a drink."

Sam grabbed a bucket from the shed, went to a watering tank located between the fence separating the two pens, and returned in a few minutes.

Taking the bucket, I held it so the horse's lips were immersed in the water. He started to make drinking movements, then pushed his nose down into the bucket until the water ran out. Although he acted as if he was swallowing, the water level in the bucket remained the same.

"You're right about him not being able to swallow," I said to Sam. "He sure is thirsty, though. I'm going to give him some water with the stomach tube and pump. If I don't, he'll soon be very dehydrated, especially since he worked all morning, too."

I went out the gate to my pickup, where I got out the eight-foot rubber stomach tube and the chrome-plated stomach pump. I also got a pair of rubber gloves from the Pandora bag. (Nowadays, plastic disposable gloves are available for such procedures.)

When I returned to the horse, Sam had already refilled one water bucket and added another, in anticipation of what I would want. I pulled on the gloves, turned to Sam and said, "I am still not sure what we're dealing with here, so I'm going to use these gloves to be on the safe side. I'll leave them with you after we're through. Any time you do anything about him, put them on, then rinse them off in "Clorox" water after you finish. Finally, wash your hands real good with soap and water. Use a different watering tank for those other horses, too."

"What about my boots and clothes, Doc? Can I carry anything up to the house on them?" Sam asked.

"I really think this is a case of 'sleeping sickness,' in which case, all these precautions are for naught," I responded. "But even if it's rabies, there is only a very remote chance of anyone catching it from clothing. It's caught by getting a bite from the rabid animal or by exposure to saliva from the infected animal, especially, if you have open wounds or scratches. That's what a fella has to be concerned about. That's why the rubber gloves."

I looked at Sam, who was examining his hands. "Hell, Doc, I bridled him this morning and unbridled him when we got back. Been around him most all day so far, except for eatin'. Suppose I could be in trouble already?"

"Like I said, it looks for all the world like 'sleeping sickness' so don't worry unduly. We should know within the next five to seven days if you need to take shots for rabies or not."

Sam seemed relieved for the moment, but I was sure that night he wouldn't get any sleep. It was always a hellava spot to put a man in, but it couldn't be helped.

Before passing the stomach tube, I instructed Sam how to operate the pump. When I started one end of the tube into the left nostril of the horse, he offered none of the common resistance. I pushed the tube gently and knew it was passing down the esophagus because of the rippling effect on the skin. I had learned that in the clinics course at school.

When I believed that the tube had entered the stomach, I put the outside end to my ear and listened. I heard gurgling sounds but not inhaling or exhaling.

"I'm in the right spot," I said to myself. If breathing sounds had been evident, it would mean the tube was in the lungs.

"Okay, Sam, start pumping," I said, watching the reaction of the horse to those first few strokes of the pump.

The sorrel stood there with no evidence of pain or discomfort. Soon the bucket was empty.

"Let's give him that other bucket full," I said. So Sam switched the pump to the other pail and pumped until it was empty. Then I withdrew the tube, wiped it off, and rolled it up.

"That will do for now," I said, taking the pump and starting to the pickup. "He'll either be better by morning or much worse."

As I placed the equipment back in the truck, I thought more about the instructions I should leave with Sam. "If he should die, I want the head to send to the laboratory. They can tell us pretty accurately whether or not the horse had rabies. If it isn't that, we'll figure it's sleeping sickness."

"Okay, Doc. I'll let you know first thing in the morning how he's gettin' on," Sam said as I got into the pickup to leave.

All the way back to Sundance, I kept trying to think of what else we could be dealing with. I had never seen either a case of rabies or sleeping sickness, but it was the right time of year for both diseases to occur. However, rabies had not been reported in Wyoming for over twenty-five years.

Arriving back at the store, I walked into the office and got out the book again. I reread the sections about each disease. It just had to be equine encephalomyelitis.

An early morning call to treat a sick cow the next day prevented my talking with Sam when he called in. But Harriet, who was always on duty in our drugstore, received his call and later related their conversation to me.

The old-time crank telephone, so much a part of our country practice, was located in view of customers shopping or enjoying treats at the fountain in the store. When the phone rang midmorning, Harriet strained to hear the far-away voice at the other end of the line.

The store was a noisy place that morning, full of tourists. The store was located halfway between Spearfish, South Dakota, thirty miles east, and the Devils Tower National Monument in Wyoming to the west.

The noise and poor line transmission required Harriet to shout to Sam, "Speak louder!"

"Doc told me to save the head if the horse died. Well, he did last night! The trouble is, I don't know how far down on the neck he wants me to cut it off."

Harriet thought a few seconds, then shouted into the mouthpiece, "Cut the head off right behind the ears!"

The store suddenly became silent as a tomb. Only the shuffle of feet could be heard as Harriet turned away from the phone and looked out over the staring eyes and gaping mouths of the customers.

The next few moments must have been the "highlight" of the trip for our tourist-visitors from the East, for Sam asked Harriet what he should use to remove the head.

"Use a sharp axe!" she screamed into the mouthpiece. Sam asked her to repeat that.

"Use a sharp axe!" Harriet bellowed even louder.

The result of all this shouting was a mass exodus of the entire store population. Harriet was apologetic as she related the story. Sorry that the image of veterinary practice in the West might have been misunderstood and sorry she had caused the evacuation and the loss of dollars for our mortgaged drugstore.

Sam delivered the now famous head in the afternoon, and I prepared it for shipment to the laboratory in Laramie that evening. In those days, we had to pack specimens in dry ice and send them by mail. Later, a procedure was established so that rabies suspect heads were sent by state police relay.

A week later, the lab called reporting no sign of rabies. The pathology slides looked more like encephalitis.

It didn't take long for word to get around that there was "sleeping sickness" in the country. Soon we were besieged with calls. Folks wanted their horses vaccinated.

To get the best immunity, an animal had to be injected twice, ten to fourteen days apart. The scheduling became a nightmare until we arranged to cover one community a day. For a solid month I injected horses, gentle ones and wild ones alike. By in large, kids' ponies behaved the poorest. The injection would sting as it had to be given between the layers of the skin. During the first shot the horse's behavior was not too bad, but the second one could cause hoofs to fly, or teeth to bare at whoever was handy! One cowboy suffered a broken leg when he was kicked by a range mare protecting her foal.

Still, today, I realize how much I learned concerning people's behavior and their attitude toward their horses, not to mention how hearing about chopping off a horse's head can spoil a good ice cream soda.

NUCLEAR FALLOUT/ NOEATUS

This was one of these nasty spring mornings that occurred every once in awhile. By nasty, I mean there was a heavy fog, it was damp and cold, and the snow was beginning to melt so the ground had bare spots here and there. The wind "cut right through you," as they say.

Although it was not yet eight o'clock in the morning, I already had two calving calls—in opposite directions, a good thirty-five miles apart. Just as I was going out the back door of the store, Harriet answered the telephone again and hollered quickly, "Bob, hold on a minute, it's for you!" She held the receiver in one hand and had the other over the mouthpiece of the old crank telephone hanging on the wall. "This guy is calling from the Aladdin Store. Something about sheep and fallout. You better talk to him so you can get the story straight." She handed me the receiver.

"Yes, this is Doctor Baldwin. What can I do for you?" I asked.

"Doc, you don't know me, but my name is Rufus Banard. I live in the Bearlodge, between Alva and Aladdin, and I've got some sick sheep. They've been sick ever since they set off that atomic blast in Nevada. (That happened at least six months previously, I believe.) Can you come out and look at them? Don't suppose you can do anything, but the banker is getting kind of worried, so I have to do all I can."

This was the first time I had encountered such a reason for animal deaths, so I was intrigued. "How do I get to your place, Mr. Banard?" I asked, without making the usual inquiries about how many were lost, and how the sick ones were acting.

He responded by telling me where to turn off the hardtop onto the dirt road, after leaving Aladdin. His road ended ten miles from the hardtop.

"How's the road in there?" I asked, knowing that at that time of year there was no bottom to many of the dirt roads because the ground was thawing and the mud was deep.

"Well, it isn't too good. I got out early this morning while the mud was still froze a little on top; otherwise, I might not have made it. What time will it be before you can get here?"

"It will be at least two and maybe three o'clock. I have two heifers I have to attend to first. If all goes well, I should be there about then." Then came the kicker.

"You won't be able to drive all the way to the place. The mud will be too bad by then. I'll leave a saddle horse tied to a tree near the road, where there's a trail through the woods to the house. It's only about a mile and a half. Just give the horse his head. He knows the way."

If all didn't go well, I could just imagine the headlines in the local weekly the next week: "Massive Manhunt To Find Vet Missing In Bearlodge For A Week! (Rancher said horse he left for him to ride should have known his way home.)"

"I'll have to carry a bag in with me. Is the horse gentle enough to stand for that, do you think?" I asked, knowing full well what a horse might do under strange circumstances.

"He's 'plumb gentle,' Doc. He may act up a little when you first get on, but after that, he'll be okay."

This response was not too comforting, knowing what masters of understatement these ranchers could be. "Look for me then by three-thirty," I said.

After hanging up the receiver, I went into the office where Harriet was already getting the end-of-the-month bills out. I told her what had transpired on the phone, and ended by instructing her to tell anyone who called that it would be at least six o'clock before I could get to them. I would call in from the Aladdin Store, if I ever got back to it!

"I'll have a good supper ready when you get back," was her response. "You're going to need it."

About one o'clock I turned off the hardtop onto the dirt road. Things had gone well all morning: I got two live calves out of the heifers I attended. I finished with the last one about 11:30, and the rancher invited me to the house for a "bite of lunch." Some bite! Venison steak, mashed potatoes, string beans, hot home-made rolls, and what I used to call the "third vegetable," a thick white gravy. The kitchen was clean, too. The slop bucket, where one threw the dirty wash water, potato peelings, coffee grounds, and other kitchen wastes, was under the sink, out of sight of the table. Indeed, it had been a real good morning!

When I pulled off the road, I stopped and studied the road ahead. Two ruts about twelve inches deep were located right in the middle. They were still well formed, meaning no one had been up the road in the last four hours at least, because that's about when things began to thaw. Although the half-ton red pickup I was driving, had nobbies with thick tread on the rear, I decided to put on the chains just to be sure. Better to put them on before I got stuck, I had learned the hard way.

That was a good lesson to have learned, because the little truck had ground through both mud and snow before I got to where the horse was tied to a scrub oak. It had taken at least an hour. At times like this, I felt more like a truck-driver than a veterinarian.

I pulled the truck off the road into a little brush area and got out. The horse watched me intently as I got out a small bag and placed post-mortem instruments into it: a butcher knife, a steel for sharpening it, and a stainless steel saw. Then I added rubber post-mortem gloves, and plastic bags for specimens. "That should be all I need," I mumbled to myself, as I closed the doors of the box on the back of the truck and turned toward the horse.

He was a bay gelding with two white stockings on front and a white streak down his face. From a distance, I judged he wasn't more that a four-year old, although he was thin enough to be twenty-five. When I approached him, he showed the white of his eyes and snorted, just a little.

"Easy boy," I said quietly. "You and I have got to get along 'cause we're both in this together." I went on talking to him as I untied the halter rope from the tree and reached over to pat him on the neck. "That's a good boy. Don't be afraid," I jabbered.

I always thought there was something animals like about a man chattering. Seems to make them less afraid, if you're a stranger, and reassures those you own or know well. I never ran a controlled study on it though; maybe it does something for me instead.

I removed the bridle from the saddle horn where it was hanging and placed it on his head. When I was ready to mount, I took the black bag from the tailgate of the pickup and held it in my right hand while with the left hand I held the reins and grabbed hold of the saddle horn. Placing my left foot in the stirrup, I started to swing into the saddle. But that didn't work. He didn't like that black bag; he kept moving away from me. After trying a couple of more times and yakking to him all the time, I finally decided the equipment could be carried in the pocket of my coveralls and coat. Then things went smoothly. In twenty minutes, we entered the clearing around the log shack and barn. A whinny came from the direction of the barn, and the horse I was riding nickered in response. A thin black and white dog, somewhat like a border collie, met us. He didn't bark but, in typical fashion, stayed off a little distance, crouched down, and watched intently. As I rode in, I noticed a man coming out of the barn.

From a distance, I could see he must be all of six-feet-four or five inches, even though he was somewhat stooped. His clothes were loose fitting and his face had a full beard. When I got to him, the thing I remember most was a pair of brown penetrating eyes peering out of very deep sockets. They reminded me slightly of the picture of the Dachau and Buchenwald prisoners.

"Good afternoon, Doctor," a voice with a pleasant resonance came out of the beard. "Did you have any trouble getting in?"

"You must be Mr. Banard," I said, extending my hand after dismounting. "Had a little trouble getting the horse to stand while I got on, until I got rid of the black bag. After that he was all right," I answered.

I looked at the surroundings for a minute. In short order, you can tell a lot about the management of a place. This was not the typical sheep outfit with painted buildings and a picket fence, well-kept yard, and well-kept machinery under cover. This outfit looked like something you'd expect to see in the Ozarks. A rundown log house and barn made of pine slabs. A dozen or so chickens and a rooster, in different shades of browns and whites, scratched on bare spots in front of the cabin door. A wood pile, not over three feet high and six feet in diameter, consisted mostly of old dead pieces that had fallen from the surrounding scrub oak. Over in the field, away from the barn, was a sulky rake, half covered with snow and rust. Just beyond that was the flock of sheep. They were spread out over most of two or three acres of snow-covered ground. Snow-covered, that is, except where they had pawed away the snow in search of a few blades of grass or old vegetation. I could not see any hay or any evidence that they had been fed that day. Near the left side of the barn, in a snow bank, lay five dead sheep. I assumed these were the ones upon which I would perform the post-mortems.

My course in pathology had been taught by a very dynamic, opinionated professor with a religious bent. In addition to thinking that drinking and smoking were bad, he also looked askance at women in the veterinary profession. Nevertheless, for me, he made dead tissue and organs live. He always said a post-mortem examination was a message from the dead to the living—that is, if you had the knowledge to interpret the signs.

Mr. Banard took the reins from me and led the horse into the barn. I followed. The dog came as far as the door, then crouched down and watched every move. I needed to relieve my bladder at that point, so I went over to one corner. Looking around, I could count no more than about fifty bales of hay. I saw no evidence of grain or protein supplement called "cake," a compressed form of grain about in inch square, fed to sheep by most stockmen in the area.

As Mr. Banard came out of the stall after tying the horse next to another one, which also had a saddle on, I asked him to tell me more about the problem he was having.

"Well, Doctor, I bought this band a year ago last fall. There were 250, and all had good mouths. No broken teeth or anything like that. They wintered good last year and had close to a hundred and ten percent lamb crop in the spring. Only lost half a dozen all year. That's not bad for sheep, you know. Well, sir, along about this December, I noticed some starting to loose their bloom, then get thin and finally die.

"I looked in the veterinary book I got and figured it might be worms, so I got some worm medicine in Belle Fourche and wormed them all. A fella can't afford to have a veterinarian out every time there's something wrong with sheep. Anyway, it didn't do any good, for they continued to sort of wither up and die. Like I told you on the phone, we've lost fifty, at least.

"I was reading in the paper the other night about them setting off another atomic blast in Nevada and got to wondering if some of that fallout might be causing the problem. They say sheep are real susceptible to it, and they started getting sick about the time it would take for that stuff to get over here. We're in a canyon and the wind currents could easily have settled it out."

He paused and looked at me in what I took to be a request for a sign of concurrence with his theory.

"Are those five dead ones outside the ones you have for me to 'post'?" I asked, not indicating one way or another whether his thesis was plausible, and wanting to get on with the investigation so I could leave before darkness settled in.

"Yes, Doctor, they died yesterday. They should be fresh enough to see something, if any special changes take place with that condition. They've been lying right there in that pile of snow since I brought them in."

This fellow is no ordinary dude, I thought as I headed out the door to the dead animals. He must be well read or have been around enough to know the sooner after death an animal is 'posted', the easier it is to see the pathognomonic or characteristic lesions of a known disease.

"I'll need a bucket of water to wash in when I'm through," I instructed, as I proceeded to lay out the instruments and plastic specimen bags on a piece of pine board I found close to the barn. Immediately, he went back to the barn, got an old galvanized pail, went over to a rusty watering trough just outside the door, and dipped out a bucket of water. "What I wouldn't give for lots of hot water," I muttered to myself, remembering wistfully the nice warm dairy cattle barns with plenty of hot running water in Michigan where I took my training. By the time he returned and set the bucket in the snow, I had already started to open one ewe.

Before that, however, I had looked at all five and noted their emaciated, or excessively thin, wasted condition. The wool was drier than usual and looked less oily, too. I had parted their lips, and like Mr. Banard had said, they all had a full, unbroken set of lower incisors. Normally, this meant they would be somewhere between three and five years of age, so I ruled out old age as a causative factor. Also, like cattle and other ruminants, they had no upper incisors, and the dental pad used in place of them looked normal.

A proper post-mortem examination, like any medical exam, requires following certain procedures in order that it be complete, and that significant findings be exposed. Thus, I went through each organ system according to the methods I had been taught, taking specimens for laboratory analysis, and making observations of any gross pathology or abnormalities.

My first observation, about the dryness of the wool, was confirmed as I opened each animal. The skin was also dry and leathery and I had to stop often and whet the knife with the steel.

"How much and what kind of feed are they getting?" I asked Mr. Banard, not stopping, but listening intently for the answer; these animals were not carrying one ounce of fat. Furthermore, two showed fluid in the tissue beneath the jaw (commonly called "bottle jaw"), and all had excess fluid in the abdominal cavity—signs of protein deficiency. None showed any other significant lesion, not even evidence of worms. Unless the lab tests showed something different the evidence was adding up to starvation: "Noeatus," some locals called it.

"Well, I've been giving them ten bales of hay a day since the middle of November. That's when the snow got deep enough so they couldn't graze," Mr. Banard answered.

"Is that hay in the barn what you've been using?"

"Yes, it's the last I have. Going to have to buy some this week if the banker sees fit to advance me more money." His voice had a real question about what the banker would do.

The hay was coarse-stemmed native grass. Sheep at this stage of pregnancy should be getting good clover or alfalfa hay, and in addition, should also get some grain or grain supplement. Further, they should have been fed at lease twenty to twenty-five bales of hay a day, just for maintenance.

"Let's ride out and look at the flock," I said, after rinsing off the instruments and gloves, putting my jacket back on, and gathering up the plastic bags with the specimens in them. "I'll need a burlap sack to carry everything in, if you've got one."

"There's one in the barn. We can get it when we get the horses," he added as he turned and headed toward the door. I followed, taking one more look around for evidence of cake or grain. There was none.

He untied the horses and led them outside. He held the horse by the bridle until I mounted, then handed me the sack. This time, the horse stood quietly with none of the dancing around that occurred at the pickup. "We can ride on through them and then go right to the road, since it will be on the way anyhow," he offered.

"That's good because it's getting late, and I would like to make it to the hard-top by dark." With that, we rode toward the biggest bunch of sheep about 500 feet away. The dog followed a little off to the left.

As we approached, the sheep looked up from their pawing through the snow and began to run toward us, bleating.

"They think they're going to get something more to eat!" Mr. Banard shouted to me above the noise. "They always clean up what I give them." His comment sounded like boasting, I thought, as if he was feeding them just the right amount.

Most ranchers would have said it differently. "I give them all they will clean up without wasting much."

There was no waste here! In fact, it would be hard to tell they'd been given any hay at all that morning, except for some holes in the eight-inch, hard-packed snow, down to the mud underneath, indicating where he probably threw out a flake from the bales here and there.

What I saw among those sheep was pitiful. Every last one of them was nothing but "a rack of bones," a favorite expression in the West. If they had been old, they would have been called "shells." Their eyes—those beautiful eyes of a normal sheep that always remind me of the eyes of a girl in love for the first time—were dull and lifeless, sunk back in their sockets.

As they ran toward us, some staggered, fell in the snow, and just lay there for a time before getting up. Pointing to one of them, Mr. Banard shouted, "They do that for a couple of days, then I find them dead!"

I had seen all I needed or wanted. I reined the horse away from them, toward the trail opening at the edge of the woods. We could still hear the plaintive bleating until we were deep in the woods. Finally, it grew quiet enough for me to talk as we rode along.

"I can't tell from what I saw whether this is associated with atomic fallout or not. What I do know is those sheep are getting less that half enough feed to maintain themselves.

"When I get back, I'm going to send these specimens to the state lab in Laramie, then I'll get in touch with the veterinarian in charge of animal testing at the Atomic Energy Commission Laboratory at Oak Ridge, Tennessee. He will be able to send me some data on the signs and pathology of atomic radiation in sheep since they have conducted studies there on sheep, specifically. Fortunately, we won't have to guess or speculate. When I get it all pulled together, I'll send word to you, or you can call me in two weeks if you haven't heard from me.

"In the meantime, you've got to get more feed into those animals. You should at least double the amount of hay you're feeding now. When you buy some, make sure it includes a lot of clover or alfalfa. Then, you need to get some grain or range cake and feed the amount recommended by the feed mill operator. It will vary according to the percentage of protein in it. You should do that first thing in the morning because they can't stand much more."

"Golly, Doctor, it will cost a fortune to feed them that much. Don't think the banker will advance me the money. I know the feed mill won't give me any more credit. It'll have to be cash for them."

"Well, you tell the banker to call me if he wants any information. I'll be glad to tell him you both will lose if those sheep aren't fed more, and soon. More are going to die before this is over, anyway. And you'll be lucky to wean a seventy-five percent lamb crop this fall, since many will be born weak, and the ewes won't give much milk for awhile. You can't expect to reverse a process like this overnight."

By the time we had reached the mud-covered pickup, the sun was beginning to set and I was more than ready to leave the tragedy I had witnessed. What had started out as a good day had turned into a gloomy one. That night, at supper, I told Harriet about it.

"I can't believe anyone in this part of the country would not know how much feed to give their livestock," she commented. "Do you think their condition might be associated with radiation, in addition to the 'Noeatus' syndrome?"

"Don't know this minute, but as soon as I talk to that veterinarian at Oak Ridge, I'll have a good idea. I just can't believe fallout would end up in just one canyon. We haven't had any calls about unusual death losses in other flocks around here, either," I answered. Then as an afterthought I added, "Can you just imagine the amount of money the government would have to pay if it turns out to be true? Everybody between here and Nevada would stake a claim for every animal and relative they lost since last fall!"

"Quit being facetious. You've got another calving call to go to," Harriet retorted, as she got up from the table with a handful of dishes and went into the tiny kitchen.

Because of the time difference, it was ten o'clock the next morning before I could reach anyone at Oak Ridge. By then, we had customers in the store, so I made the call from our bedroom in order not to be overheard. No need to have anything like this get out into the country at this stage. When the call was completed, I pretty well knew we were not dealing with atomic radiation, but to make sure, I had the veterinarian send me a copy of the data they had, plus some picture of animals in various stage of the poisoning. I'd wait for the reports from Laramie, too, before giving Mr. Banard a final diagnosis. This one had too much potential for a lawsuit; I needed to be more than right.

Ten days later, I had received the Oak Ridge material and had gotten a phone call from Laramie. It definitely was not radiation poisoning, and the state lab found no pathogenic bacteria or pathology in the specimens that pointed to any known disease of sheep.

Before I had a chance to get a letter off to Mr. Banard, he came to the store to see if I had found out anything. I took him into the office and closed the door, not sure how he would take the news. I motioned for him to sit on the couch and after getting the manila envelope that I had received from Oak Ridge, I sat down beside him and handed him the letter and photos. He studied them for awhile, then turned to me and said, "My sheep never looked like these."

"I got a call from Laramie day before yesterday, and they couldn't find anything in the specimens that wasn't normal, either," I said.

I waited anxiously to see how he would respond. Because of his beard, I was not able to see a change of facial expression, had there been one. He did fidget a little, however, and dropped his head. Staring at the floor he mumbled, "I guessed it wasn't fallout after I got them some better feed and did as you suggested. It took only a couple of days for them to start looking better. Haven't lost any for a week now. Guess I knew all along what might be wrong, but a fella hates to think of the worst. Besides, I didn't figure the banker would give me any more on my loan. Turned out, he wasn't too bad."

He handed me the papers, got to his feet, pulled out a checkbook, and said, "What do I owe you, Doctor?"

I hesitated. The bill was high, considering the telephone calls and all. I always hated to charge a normal fee when the client's loss was so great. "Thirty-five dollars will cover it all," I answered, as I got up.

He wrote the check and handed it to me. "Fair enough, Doctor. If I had spent this money for feed in the first place, I probably wouldn't have needed you. Thanks, anyway."

With that, Mr. Banard opened the door, and with his old, beat-up, dirty felt hat in hand, he walked through the store and out the front door. The last time I ever saw him, he was placing the hat on his head and settling himself in an equally old, beat-up, mud-covered pickup.

MRS. HENRY

Harriet and I were about to finish supper when the phone rang in our apartment above the store. I went into the bedroom to answer it as Harriet started to clear the dishes from the table and serve up the chocolate cake.

"Doctor, is that you?" a very demanding feminine voice asked.

"Yes, this is Doctor Baldwin," I replied.

"Well, Doctor, this is Mrs. Henry. We have a cow in bad shape that needs attention. Will you come right out?"

"What seems to be the matter with her?"

"Well, Doctor, if I must say, she has 'come apart at the seams'!" I thought I could detect a slight embarrassment in her response.

"I see. I am just about to have piece of cake, then I'll be right out. Should be there in about thirty minutes."

I was thinking that was a real good response time to a non-emergency that could easily wait until morning. The ranch was about fifteen minutes away. Three of those miles on country road included two wire gates to open and close. But it was my first summer in practice, and I wanted to make sure folks knew I was interested in my work. Besides, we needed all the income we could get after five years in veterinary school.

I was taken aback, therefore, when she responded to my statement by saying, "Doctor! we want you to come right away. If you need something to eat after you get through, we'll be glad to feed you. The animal needs attention; that's why we called you!" The voice became intimidating.

"Okay. Get her in the chute and I'll be right out," I ended, glad to be through with that conversation.

When I returned to the little dining room, the cake was already on the table, along with a glass of milk. Harriet had started hers, not knowing when I would be through on the telephone, and having enough experience by now to know our mealtimes would frequently be interrupted. Besides, she had to go back downstairs to the store and allow one of the hired girls to go home.

"Just set the cake back and put the milk in the refridge. That was Mrs. Henry. She wants me to get right out there, and you know what that means," I said to

Harriet as I reached for my hat and started toward the stairs leading down to the store.

Indeed, Harriet did know what that meant. Her brother, and her father before him, were both veterinarians and had done work for the Henry ranch. The idiosyncrasies of all members of the family were well known. Now that the old man was dead and the daughter was married, the workload was left to Mrs. Henry and son James. She was sixty or more, and everyone said she was getting funnier all the time, apparently meaning more set in her ways.

Harriet looked up from her plate and said, "What time do you think you'll be back?"

"Probably in a couple of hours. The cow has an everted vagina and it shouldn't be too bad, knowing how they look after their stock."

"Okay, I've got an order to mark and place on the shelves. I should be nearly through by then, and I can help you spay the dog you planned to work on after supper."

By that time, I was heading down the stairs. "That'll be great!" I hollered over my shoulder.

I knew I had all the needed drugs and instruments in the trunk so I headed right out the back door to the car. As I headed out of town to the west, I mentally went through the procedure to repair the malady as I had been taught in school. When I arrived at the ranch a few minutes later, I was thus quite prepared to get on with the surgery. James met me at the last gate, and we went directly to the corral where the cow was standing in the chute as I had asked. Mrs. Henry was not in sight. As I finished the job of replacing the vagina, James said he had another cow in the barn he wanted me to look at. He said she had been lame for about two weeks and he had treated her for foot rot, an infection that usually located in the soft tissue between the two claws. She had not responded very well to the treatment, so he wanted to see if there was anything else to do.

After cleaning up and placing the instruments back in the car, we let the cow out of the chute and went into the barn. In one of the big box stalls a registered cow stood, principally on three feet—she was holding up the right rear foot so the toe barely touched the dirt floor. She was thinner than most of the cows at the Henry ranch, and James said she didn't eat much because she lay down a lot. The pain would make her do that. I had only to take one look to know the infection was located in a joint of the right claw.

"How many times have you treated her?" I asked, turning toward James.

"I gave her drugs for three days last week and again this week. She seems better when she is on them, but the day after I finish, she's right back to where she was before."

I knew the medication he used, because he purchased it at the drugstore. It was the best there was at the time.

"Well, there is no use giving her any more medicine," I said. "The only thing that will help her now is to remove that claw with the infection in it; otherwise, she will keep going downhill until you have to shoot her. Of course, you could take her to the sale yard and get a little something out of her, too."

James looked down at the floor and shuffled his feet as if in deep thought. "Well, she's Mother's cow so you'll have to talk to her about it. If she was mine, I'd take her out and shoot her and put her out of her misery right now. Hate to watch an animal suffer. Besides, I have to feed and carry water to her every day. It's getting to be a real chore." With that, we left the barn, got in my car, and drove up to the house.

Mrs. Henry was standing by the stove in the kitchen when we entered. After the greeting James said, "I had Doctor Baldwin look at your cow in the barn, and he has something to tell you about her."

She stood straight as a ramrod, even though she was only about five-foot-three and on the pudgy side, and looked at me intently as I told her the diagnosis and the prognosis I had given James at the barn. At that point, James looked at his mother and gave his opinion on the matter. With hardly a change in facial expression, she returned her eyes to mine.

"Have you performed this operation before, Doctor?" she asked, watching me earnestly.

"Well, no, I haven't," I answered, looking directly into her eyes, "but I saw it done at the clinics at college, and did the aftercare, so I know how animals respond to the surgery. I have no doubt about the procedure or the outcome."

Without acknowledging what I said, she asked, "What will it cost?"

I hesitated a minute as I quickly calculated the time it would take plus the drugs and supplies for the operation and aftercare. "About thirty-five dollars, if I figured the drugs right. Close to it anyway."

Evidently, James knew his mother well enough to know she was about to accept the plan of treatment. He was dead set against it. "I'm not going to have a thing to do with this if you are planning to go ahead," he said as he looked directly at his mother, almost as a challenge. "It means fooling around with her, changing bandages and all, then you don't know for sure it will work. We're trying to finish combining the wheat. There's just so many hours in the day to do all this." With that, he pulled on his hat and stormed out the door.

Mrs. Henry asked one more question. "When can you do it?"

Not to be caught appearing indecisive, I answered, "Tomorrow morning at eight, if that's not too early."

Thus, the next morning it happened. When I drove up to the house to get a cream can full of water before going to the corral, Mrs. Henry greeted me alone. Neither James nor Sid, the hired man, was in sight. She had on bib overalls over what I assumed was a gingham dress, since that was the kind she always wore when I saw her at the ranch. She had a kerchief over her hair. She was the only help I was to have to throw the animal to the ground and hold the leg steady during the surgery.

Once the 1000-pound cow struggled to get loose. It seemed they always did when you kept them down long. As I grabbed the instrument tray to keep it from getting kicked over or full of dirt, Mrs. Henry sat back on the leg to keep the animal from getting much slack in the rope holding the leg and hoof. I was very glad, then, that she was packing enough weight to get the job done!

Even though the operation was bloody, and certainly had to be unsightly to her uninitiated eye, she chatted about her husband and how pleasant the ranch was when he was still alive. When I needed an instrument or dressing material, she was quick to get it for me. In short, she was undaunted by the whole procedure, pitching right in to help. "That is some old lady," I would tell Harriet that evening, when we had a chance to talk of the day's work before going to bed.

Just as we were letting the cow get to her feet, after completing the surgery and the extensive packing and bandaging to the wound, James drove up in the pickup. He didn't say hello, how are you, go to h—or anything. He just sat looking out the open window at the heavily bandaged hoof. Of course the infected claw was gone, so she stood on the remaining claw. I knew what he was thinking. When she puts much weight on it, it will break off. An animal that size needs two claws on each hoof. If God had meant them to have one, like the horse, he'd have made them that way!

Mrs. Henry looked over at him and said, "See, James, she's putting weight on it already. Doctor was telling me we need only to change the bandage a couple of times. Sid and I can do it since I know how to now."

James still didn't say anything. He just started the pickup and drove back toward the field.

When I was at the ranch a couple of weeks later, testing bulls for brucellosis before they were sold, I looked in the barn for the cow. I didn't see her.

"What happened to our surgical patient?" I asked Mrs. Henry, in some appre-hension, since I told them to keep her in for at least a month to watch her and make sure the maggots didn't get into the wound.

"Oh, Doctor," came the reply, "she's doing so well, we let her out into the lit-tle pasture every day. She still limps some on that leg, but she's filling up and gaining weight. That was sure a wonderful thing you did for the poor thing. She suffered so much pain before that."

That evening I told Harriet again, "She is some old lady." As I think of her now, some fifty years later, I can say, in the idiom of today, "She was one *neat* lady."

THE FOXY TERRIERS

A number of humorous things happened during our four and one-half years in Sundance. One had to do with a dog. Sooner or later, some such event happens to every veterinarian and it always seems to happen when you are sure everything is under control. In short, a time when you know it just *can't* happen!

Shortly after we arrived in Sundance from veterinary school and were living in that four-room apartment over the drugstore we owned with Harriet's brother and his wife, it became apparent we needed dog runs where animals could be confined before and after surgery. So we purchased enough metal five-foot chain link fencing panels for two pens, and we erected them on a wooden platform. The platform was to prevent an animal from digging underneath the fencing and escaping. We didn't put a cover over the top, figuring the height too great for any animal to jump over. Besides, the occupants of the cages were to be surgical patients, and we wouldn't keep them longer than overnight. (You've heard of the best laid plans of mice and men, I presume?)

One day two female fox terriers—a mother and her daughter—were brought in to be spayed. Like most full grown-fox terriers, they stood only about a foot and a half off the ground. Since the mother was very excitable, we placed both bitches in the same run, thinking to ally mother's fears. My usual custom then was to spay animals after 10 p.m., when Harriet could help me after the store closed.

A large room that served for both examination and surgery was located behind one section of the store. Early in our practice we did surgery any time it appeared the store would not need Harriet's attention, but we soon learned that this arrangement was unworkable. It seemed never to fail that no sooner would we get underway than something would interrupt—more often than not, at a critical point in the surgery. The ether we used to anesthetize cats was also a problem. It was amazing how fast the fumes spread throughout the store, and how objectionable they were to many people—especially, if they were drinking a malted milkshake!

The morning after surgery on the two terriers I left early to make a country call, planning not to return until noon. Before leaving, I took the dogs from their inside cages and placed them together in one of the outside runs. I noticed the old bitch had not calmed down much, in spite of the surgery.

Harriet will check them once she gets the store open, I thought. Nothing can happen to them, anyway.

On my return when I pulled into the driveway, I noticed only the young female in the run. What could have happened to the other one? I wondered as I headed for the office.

When I entered, it was apparent some sort of crisis had occurred. Instead of sitting at the desk, Harriet lay back in the rocking chair fanning herself with a newspaper. Her face was "beet red," and being nearly eight months pregnant with our first child, her belly protruded noticeably.

"What in the world happened to you?" I asked anxiously, going in to look at her more closely.

"I just got through getting that old dog in the cage inside the garage. She's been loose since at least nine o'clock. We have been chasing her all over town. When I went to look at them after you left, she was just climbing over the top of the run. She put her paws and legs through those links and used them like steps. I tried to catch her then, but she ran down the alley toward the courthouse. I chased her on foot all over the courthouse lawn, then she took off toward the creek. That's when I gave up and came back and got the Jeep.

"By that time, Larry, (the operator of the garage next door) came along, and we both started after her. We saw her once or twice along the creek, but she wouldn't come when we called. We finally came back a few minutes ago, and there she was out by the run with her daughter. She was tired enough by then she let me pick her up. What a hellava morning!"

I went out to check the dog's stitches, and to see if she was all right otherwise. Other than being thirsty, she looked no worse for the experience.

The next day, I installed corrugated steel sheeting over the two outside runs. This served to shade the runs and prevent further escapes, at least, from over the top!

As for Harriet, months later, folks still laughed about witnessing the spectacle of her running up the alley and around the courthouse in a "family way" with her wrap-around skirt flying open at the back. Harriet would even laugh, too—after awhile.

FRANK HASELTON

Shortly after arriving in Sundance, I got to know Frank Haselton, a truly old-time cowboy. I had met him briefly when Harriet and I made a trip to Wyoming the summer after we were married. This was a special kind of trip because Harriet's family and friends out there had not yet met me. Frank was one of the many I met at that time, and it was only later that I would get to know him better.

He was about five-foot-ten inches tall and as thin as a bean pole. His prominent handlebar mustache accentuated his rather long nose and hid deeply hollowed cheeks. Dark, penetrating eyes conveyed his normally somber demeanor. Maybe that was because he was going blind with cataracts, though I doubted it, as he appeared to have always been of a serious nature.

Sitting in his favorite chair, he crossed his legs in a fitting manner and his ankle-high cowboy boots were always shined to perfection. He walked with a forward stoop and a little shuffle, the results of having been bucked off many broncs in his lifetime.

I remember him as a perfect gentleman, always rising and offering his chair when a woman came into the room. When outside, he courteously tipped his Stetson hat. I never heard him swear, either, though stories told about his eventful life revealed that on occasion he was known to utter many an oath!

I considered myself lucky to have him ride with me from time to time that first summer and fall I was in practice in Sundance. He told me may things about that part of the country I wouldn't have heard otherwise. I remember one story about how homesteaders from the East were placed on the land described in the paper they held from the government.

According to Frank, he worked for the bank as a field man. A field man needed to know the layout of the country and about management of livestock. His job included counting the number and kinds of livestock a rancher had before the bank gave him a loan, and periodically recounting them to see they were all still there!

The homesteaders would arrive without any idea where their land might be. Unknown to them, neither did the county officials or the bank know, since most of the land had not yet been officially surveyed. Some way or other, it became

Frank's job to take these folks to what they thought was their 160 acres. He would chuckle as he told me he simply took one family in one direction and one in the other. When he got to a place he knew had no other family close by, he told them this was their land!

He always made sure they were not within sight or hearing distance of one another. He would add that he always wondered how the folks ever got their land straightened out after the official survey was done some years later. To give credence to the story, I once talked to a lawyer about it, and he told me he could become a millionaire challenging property rights in that part of the country because land descriptions and ownership were so fouled up. That is, he could become a millionaire if he wasn't "dry-gulched" first.

For a number of years, Frank drove the stage between Sundance and Moorcroft. Since Moorcroft was on the railroad, mail and freight were dropped off there for distribution. At first he used a four-horse hitch to get through the hills and over the sagebrush flats. Later, he learned to drive a Model T Ford truck and used that. The distance between points was about forty miles with horses, and nearly fifty miles by auto.

During the time he drove teams, a ranch called the halfway house was located about midway between towns. He stopped there each way to let any passengers freshen up and to rest the horses or get different ones. Since he "had a way" with horses, he would sometimes be asked to "green-break" a team. The process would start and end at the halfway house.

A green-broke team has just a little of the edge taken off. That means it has been harnessed and hitched, and perhaps been used a time or two. The team has not worked long enough or often enough to know how to pull together. (Maybe something like newlyweds!) They have had only one or a few lessons in responding to either voice or rein command. Most of them are not too trustworthy, and if you were to leave them unattended they would probably be gone when you returned.

Well, when Frank green broke them, he would have the owner meet him at the halfway house with enough cowboys to get them harnessed and hooked to the stage. He always drove his best lead team on those mornings, and it mattered not whether he had passengers. The green team was hooked next to the pole and the wheels while the leaders were hooked in front of them. He used the mostly flat stretch between the halfway house and Moorcroft where he had room to maneuver rather than the hilly stretch between Sundance and the halfway house, which had many places to tip over or run off into a canyon.

Usually, harnessing and hooking these frightened animals took quite a bit of time. Heels and dust would fly, and before it was over, someone could be kicked or bitten. Frank would get in the middle of the seat and when they handed him the reins, he would brace his feet against the footrest and holler at the leaders. From there on, for at least five miles, it was anybody's guess in which direction they'd be headed when they finally stopped the first time for a rest. Sometimes, one of the green horses would fall and want to remain there. But Frank and the lead horses would not allow that! By the time the forty-mile round-trip was completed, the new team was green broke, though not necessarily "gentle broke," and Frank was able to collect his ten or fifteen dollar fee from owners who seemed pleased not to have the pains and danger of doing the job.

Folks that knew him well said he had a really bad temper. Nan, his wife, liked to tell about one time after he bought his Model T Ford truck, he got stuck in the mud for the fourth time on his run between Moorcroft and Sundance. He became so angry that although darkness was coming on, he jumped out of the truck and beat both headlights to a pulp with the truck crank handle.

The last time we saw Frank, he was sitting in his favorite rocking chair with his legs crossed in the usual manner and his boots as shiny as ever. Although he tried to see us, he couldn't because the cataracts had finally blinded him. Today, that would not happen, which once again confirms the saying: "The good part of the good old days is that they're gone."

THE MULE

After we had been in Sundance some months, I had noticed that not all our rancher clients had "American" names like Blake or Cabot or Lodge. Some had names like Perino, Mitich, Pzinski, or Lissolo. I noted, too, that many of the ranchers with those kind of names lived mostly in one locality, an area called Four Corners, between Sundance and Newcastle.

That part of the country was quite flat, and the soil was just right for growing wheat. And indeed, that is what these folks did best. They raised some cattle, too, but their main source of livelihood was wheat. On that basis, I would say they were more farmers than ranchers.

Since I was born and brought up in the Northeast, where "non-American" names were commonplace, I naturally wondered how these people got to northeastern Wyoming (just as you maybe wondering, at this point, what I have said so far has anything to do with the title of this story).

Well, the city of Newcastle is located on a railroad. In the old days, when the locomotives were powered by steam, coal was the source of heat to make the steam. Just north of Newcastle, toward Sundance, was a coal mine called the Cambria. The people with these foreign-sounding names were brought in to dig the coal. And this is where the mule came in. Mules were used to pull the coal cars out of the mine shaft.

It happened that while these folks were digging out the coal, the government opened much of the land in the West to homesteading. The word was not long in getting around, and soon these miners filed claims on the land in the vicinity.

To "prove-up" on a claim, the owner was required to build a house of some sort on the land. This was most often referred to as a "homestead shack." Another requirement was that someone live in the shack for a specified number of months each year. With the entrepreneurial spirit that made this country great, the men built the shacks and placed their wives and kids in them ... and to work the land. Now, back to the mule!

One day, when I was at a horse sale in Gillette, conducting health inspections on the animals consigned, I noticed one of my clients from the Four Corners area studying a mule that had been unloaded. This good-looking jack appeared to have a gentle manner. When the client saw me looking at the mule, he said, "Doc, do you see that mule's ears a wigglin'? When a mule does that, he's figurin'. I worked them in the Cambria in my younger days, and I can tell you they'll be good to you for five years just to get to kick you in the belly once!"

Although I didn't have occasion to treat many mules during my years in practice, I always remembered that story told to me by Vic Lissolo, one of those persons with a "foreign-sounding" name.

TAKING MOTHER-IN-LAW
FOR A RIDE

One cool July morning in 1951, my mother-in-law and I took off for Recluse, Wyoming in a little bullet-nosed Studebaker. The coolness of the morning portended a day that would turn out to be 105 degrees in the shade. A heat that would add another dimension to what would prove to be a most thought provoking and, in the early stages, a most baffling problem.

A telephone call had come into the office-drugstore in Sundance the previous afternoon. I happened to be there and took the call.

"Doc, we got cows dying all over the place up here and need someone to come tell us what's doing it," the caller reported.

"How many have you lost?" I inquired.

"About fifteen head that we could find."

"How many head do you have?"

"Somewhere about 250."

"Have you seen any sick ones?"

"Nope, Just find them dead."

Even though I had been out of vet school hardly a month, I knew that I had an interesting diagnostic problem on my hands.

"Where do you live?" I asked.

"Recluse."

"How far is that from Sundance?"

"It's about 110 or 115 miles north and west of you. I called the vets in Sheridan but they are too busy to come out so I thought I'd try you."

"Give me directions to get to you," I said.

"Take highway 14-16 through Gillette, then about thirty miles out of Gillette toward Sheridan you'll see a road to the right with a sign pointing to Recluse. That is, if it wasn't pushed down by a snow plow this spring. Take that road and come up to the store. It's about three miles." Then he added, "It's the country store."

I thought to myself, "H—, that's going to cost him at least fifty dollars just for the trip, let alone any drugs I might use or laboratory expenses!" Aloud I asked, "It's pretty late today to get there and see anything before dark. How about if I come up first thing in the morning?"

"Fine. Tell me what time you expect to be at the store and I'll meet you. I live another ten miles up the road and this is the closest telephone to the ranch."

"If I leave here around six in the morning I should be there around seven-thirty or eight o'clock. That is if I don't get lost."

"Well they've been dying now for about two weeks, so I don't guess any half hour or so will make much difference."

Not to you maybe, I thought, but it will to me if I have to do a post-mortem in the heat of the day on a several-day old cow!

"Who am I talking to?" I asked.

"Sam Clark. Doc Port knows me. I'd like to have him come too if he can."

Dr. Port was my brother-in-law who also practiced veterinary medicine. He had a ranch west of Sundance and was busy haying this time of year.

"I'll ask him," I said, "but he's heavy into haying and I don't expect he can get away. I'll see you around seven-thirty or eight in the morning."

Hanging up the receiver on the old wall hand-crank telephone, I turned to Harriet and asked her if she thought her mother would like to take a ride with me in the morning. She had been staying with us for a week or so and hadn't gotten out much since Harriet had to manage the drugstore. Harriet had heard my side of the conversation, along with everyone else in the store.

"I don't know, let's go upstairs and ask her," Harriet suggested.

Arriving upstairs we told Mother Port about the call and asked her if she would care to go along on the trip. Since she at one time had accompanied her husband, also a veterinarian, and was familiar with the work as well as the area, she thought it would be a great adventure.

That night I talked with Dr. Port and told him about the call I was making the next morning. We thought it possible there was a poisonous plant problem but the season didn't exactly fit the problem. Newly out of school, I thought about Anthrax or a foreign animal disease. In addition to discussing a possible diagnosis, Dr. Port gave me more detailed directions to Recluse.

Harriet got breakfast in the morning around five o'clock and waved her mother and me off about quarter of six. Averaging sixty miles an hour, we figured to be at our destination before the day's heat descended.

We reached Upton around 6:16, twenty-eight miles from Sundance and right on time!! Then came Moorcroft, another twenty-five minutes, and finally Gillette, all of seventy-five miles. The time was now 7 a.m.

Heading northwest out of Gillette, we began to see more and more wheat fields, and fewer and fewer houses, and I began to watch the speedometer. I had noted the mileage on the instrument when we left Gillette, and now that we were meeting no traffic to speak of, I was afraid we might miss the thirty-mile marker that was supposed to be located to the right. The ranch buildings we did see were far off the road in the distance so there was little chance to ask anyone directions, even if we had wanted to.

Finally, in the distance and to the right we spotted a line of flying dust and then the sign appeared to the right, a welcome sight.

Turning up the dirt road about five minutes later, we saw some buildings ahead. As we approached we saw cars and pickups parked on the road and in the adjacent yard, and we thought that this surely must be the Recluse country store and post office.

Men were standing around talking and joking with one another as I got out and went into the store. Inside, three or four more men were talking to one another. I asked for a rancher by the name of Sam Clark.

"I'm Sam Clark," answered a rotund, pot-bellied, pleasant looking older man. "Are you the vet from Sundance?"

"I'm the one. My name is Baldwin," I replied, extending my hand to him. He shook my hand and came right to the point.

"Okay, Doc. Why don't you follow me and when we get up to where the cattle are you can leave your car and come with me in the pickup. The ground is too rough for your car."

With that, we took off. Soon, a check in the rearview mirror revealed a whole caravan of cars and pickups following us. It was only then that I realized that all the "traffic" at the store had been there out of curiosity to learn what the trouble was at the Clark ranch. After all, what affected one rancher's cattle could affect another!!!

I told Mother Port the plan and she said not to worry about her, she would just rest while I was gone.

At the first stop, I dressed in coveralls and got out the post-mortem equipment, consisting of an axe, post-mortem knife, a steel, scissors, rubber gloves, rubber boots, specimen containers, and a ten-gallon milk can of water. I also carried a bottle of disinfectant soap. I placed all these items in the back of Sam's pickup and we took off across the sagebrush flats to the cow that had died yester-day.

As we were driving, I was looking at the terrain and vegetation for plants that could be considered poisonous, and the living cattle for any signs of illness. There were not too many grazing cattle before we arrived at the dead one. Then I remembered it took twenty-five to thirty-five acres of land to maintain one cow and calf, and so you wouldn't expect to see very many in one place—except per-haps at a water hole.

As we pulled up to the dead cow I noticed that she was bloated a little. The ground under her legs was somewhat churned up, as if she had struggled for awhile before expiring. There was a small amount of blood running from her nos-trils and of course the flies were already working on all of the body orifices.

"Doc, that cow was all right the day before yesterday when I rode, but she was missing yesterday morning and I found her dead last evening." Sam volunteered.

"Have you seen any of them sick?" I asked as I put on my boots and gloves and prepared to conduct the post-mortem.

"Nope, just find them grazing or otherwise acting normal, and dead."

By this time the entourage had arrived.

"Anyone else around here having this kind of trouble?" I asked.

"Not that I know of," replied Sam, and turning to the group, he asked, "Any of you fellows losing cattle?"

They all shook their heads except one who volunteered he'd lost a calf to what he figured was post-castration infection back in June and an old cow that had "cast her withers" at calving. Other that that, nothing more was volunteered.

"Where is the water from here?" I asked, looking around.

"Just over the hill there," Sam said pointing to the south.

"Okay," I said to Sam, "how about you and your hired man grabbing a leg and rolling this critter onto her back and I'll begin. I don't think these other fel-lows should help in case it turns out to be a disease. They wouldn't want to be carrying anything back to their stock."

With that, I went through the procedure of conducting a post-mortem, observing signs of pathology and taking specimens for laboratory analysis as nec-essary. Coming to the end of the procedure, I knew that this was going to be a tough one—everything looked normal except for a little irritation in the small intestine. I grabbed a sample of ingesta from the first compartment of the stom-ach, placed it in an uncovered coffee can and turned to Sam.

"Where is the next one?" I asked.

"Just over the hill, yonder," he said pointing east.

"Okay, let's see what she looks like," I said trying not to show my disappointment with the findings from the cow just "posted." "Before I forget to tell you, you should dig a hole and bury these animals or bring out some oil and wood and burn the carcasses," I added.

"Going to be tough digging this ground," Sam said shaking his head, "and it's going to take a lot of wood and oil to burn all that I got. But we'll try something."

As we drove to the next carcass I noticed some of the pickups that had first accompanied us were taking off toward the road, and when we approached this cow, Sam told me she had died about two days earlier. He really didn't need to have said a word—she was so badly bloated her legs were sticking straight out from her body and extending into the air.

"There won't be much to see that is normal in that cow," I stated. "She's been gone too long. But I'll take some sample of paunch content for poison analysis."

The time at this point was near ten-thirty and the sun was beginning to make itself felt. The flies were thick on the carcass and I was beginning to wonder if I'd missed my calling, a question I'd ask myself many times in the years to come.

When I ran the knife through the skin and into the paunch, pent-up gas and ingesta came spewing skyward like a miniature volcanic explosion. The stench was indescribable.

"Golly, Doc!" exclaimed Sam as he jumped backward and grabbed for his handkerchief.

"It's pretty bad," I responded and reached for the paunch material to place in the can. Then I set about washing the knife and my gloves.

"Those are the only two around this water hole," Sam explained. "There are some more about a mile from here near a reservoir."

"Have they all died around water holes or reservoirs?" I asked, thinking I might have the first clue.

"That's right."

When we got back to my car, Mother Port had climbed into the back seat and had the doors open in order to get away from some of the heat that had built up. I took the specimen containers out of the Sam's truck and placed them in the trunk of the car. The paunch contents in the cans had become even more fetid than when collected and gasses were beginning to bubble out of the mess.

"Mother Port, we're going to follow Sam up the road to where there are some other cows," I explained. "I hope it isn't getting too hot for you."

"Don't worry," she said. "I'm enjoying the quiet and looking out on the land. It reminds me of where Harriet's father and I homesteaded twenty years ago."

Driving down the road, I noticed some distance away an old homestead shack and a shed in the pasture to the left. The buildings looked as if they were ready to fall down; the windows had long since been broken out and one of the outside walls had fallen away.

Sam slowed down suddenly and turned onto a road to the right. I followed cautiously, since the car was low slung and I was afraid of becoming "high centered." We had proceeded on a short way when we came upon two dead animals not fifty feet apart. It was obvious that they had been dead for some time; they were no longer swelling and their sides were collapsing inward toward their stomach and intestines revealing the rib cage.

"Boy! This is going to be sweet smelling," I said to Mother Port.

She laughed and said, "Now aren't you sorry you chose to become a veterinarian?" Having had a husband, a brother-in-law, and a son who were veterinarians, with a son currently in vet school, she knew how to pronounce the word and didn't have to resort to the term "vet."

"No. I like what I do," I responded. "We could have stayed in the Midwest or gone back East with the Public Health Service but my farm background wouldn't let me."

After pulling the car up near one of the carcasses, I got out and spoke to Sam, who was standing nearby. "I'll take rumen samples from these two animals, just like I did from the last one. There's just no use doing a complete post-mortem on them. They are too decomposed," I told him. "After we take these samples I'd just like to drive around over the range and look. There might be something I haven't seen so far."

Collecting the two samples didn't take long. There were no "sightseers" to ask time-squandering questions. At this stage of the game, all had had enough, or were already heading home out of the encroaching heat. In this heat a cool glass of water would prove more interesting than standing around watching someone plunging a knife into a stinking, fly-covered carcass, then reaching in to remove putrid ground-up grass!

"Let me pull the car up under the tree at that old homestead shack we passed," I said to Sam. "It will provide a little shade for Mother Port while we ride around a bit."

We followed the faint road leading to the old shack and came to a halt under the only tree in sight for miles. "I'm going to open the trunk and set those specimens out on the ground until we return. Hope you'll be cooler here," I said to Mother Port.

"It's cooler already," she replied and watched me as I bailed out of the car and emptied the specimens out of the trunk.

There's something poignant, I thought, about an abandoned homestead shack. Most of the time they represented the beginning and the end of at least one dream a young couple had shared. Hopefully, they had moved on to something better: a bigger house, more productive land, a better way of making a dollar. Grubbing out a living on this arid land would be no joke. It would be interesting to learn the particulars of these abandoned dreams if one only could find the time.

After I joined Sam and his hired man in the pickup, I asked if there were any other old building or building sites in the pasture.

"Not that I know of," he responded. "I just bought this place about three years ago and there's several sections of land in this pasture, so I couldn't be sure. Do you know of any others besides these?" Sam asked his hired man, Jim. "You've been around here longer than most."

"No, that's the only set of buildings in this pasture, but there's another one over in the winter pasture," Jim noted.

Driving over the hill to the north of the shack we came upon another water hole. There were two more dead animals there lying face away from the water. There were quite a few live ones around this hole drinking water and licking on a block of mineral salt that had been placed there for them. They looked normal. The vegetation also looked normal.

"Do you have coyotes out here?" I asked. Perhaps, I thought, cyanide bombs had been placed strategically around the water holes in order to "gas" curious coyotes coming or going from water.

"Haven't been bothered with them for a number of years now," Jim offered. "Hasn't been many sheep up this way for the last ten years. Last time I can remember anyone poisoning anything around here was about twenty years ago when the government was in here trying to stop the grasshoppers. Now that was somethin'."

"How did they manage that under range conditions?" I inquired, all the while looking at the range grasses for any clue of poisonous plants. My spirits were falling and I was becoming more and more disappointed that something more definite was not becoming apparent.

"Well, I tell ya, Doc, they had some white dope in barrels that they brought out here and mixed with bags of bran. Then they would scatter it on the ground ahead of the "hoppers." You could hear them things crunching the grass half a mile away. The idea was when they ate the grass with the bran and dope in it, it would stop 'em dead. And it damn sure did until some more come along. Then it had to all be done again. When it was all over, everybody around here got a bag of that stuff from them government fellows and had it on hand in case the "hoppers" come back."

"How did they keep the chemical?"

"Oh, most of us just tied the bag up to a rafter in a barn so nothin' could get it."

"Was that homestead shack and shed occupied when the crickets came through?"

"Yep, folks by the name of Johnson lived there. Came out here from Iowa, proved up on the land, but when the draught came along during the '30s they had to sell back to the government in order to make enough money to go back to Iowa. Lots of folks did the same thing."

"Let's go back to those buildings and have a look around that shack and shed, Sam. It's getting pretty warm and I need to get the tissue specimens from that first cow into some dry ice before too long or they'll be useless to the lab folk. The paunch samples are okay. They're just about as bad as they'll ever be."

"I believe that!" Sam laughed and lit another cigarette.

We returned to the shack and began a search of the buildings. It was obvious from the amount and consistency of the cow droppings found on the grounds of the buildings, that the cattle had frequently and recently visited the place. The wall caved in on one side of the shack, leaving an opening large enough for cattle to come and go at will. Inspection of the interior revealed nothing extraordinary, just more droppings. We then went to the shed where once the homesteader had kept the milk cow in winter, along with a few chickens and some farm implements. Here, too, it was obvious the cattle had been inside. The first thing that peaked my interest was the remains of a burlap sack, tied at one end and hanging from one of the two remaining rafters. On the ground directly below the burlap fragment, I saw a hole about six inches in depth and two feet across. There was no mounding of dirt around this hole, as if a groundhog or other burrowing animal had dug there. Rather, the hole and an additional area about a foot back from its edge were uniformly smooth. Just as if it had been brushed with a broom.

"This looks suspicious to me," I remarked and thought that this was the first really good evidence I had seen that we might be dealing with a poison. I had no idea what the "white dope" was that Jim had referred to earlier so I couldn't be sure.

"Do you know what the white material was that the government folks mixed in the bran?" I asked Jim.

"Sure don't," he said, "but it sure killed them 'hoppers'."

"Well, I'll find out when I get back to Sundance. That will be no problem. I'm just going to take the rest of that sack as well as a soil sample from around that hole." I pointed to the six-inch deep hole directly under the piece of sack. "The lab can run some analysis on those items as well as the rumen contents in case we might be dealing with a heavy metal poison."

I took the last empty coffee can from the car trunk and told Mother Port to hang in there, we were about to finish. I collected the soil sample, cut the twine holding the burlap fragment to the rafter, and returned to the car. I placed the last two specimens in the trunk and returned those remaining on the ground, washed my hands and boots in the last of the disinfectant water, closed the trunk lid, and turned to Sam. "I'll get these samples off to Laramie this afternoon if I get back in time for the mail. Otherwise, it will be in the morning," I explained. "It will take about two weeks before we receive a written report, but I'll call the lab and ask them to telephone any significant findings before they send the report. In the meantime, you'd better find a way to close the cattle out of both the shack and this shed. It would be a good idea, too, to check the other place in the winter pasture. If the cattle were in that building last winter, you probably should close it up somehow."

As I turned to leave I asked, "How can I get in touch with you by telephone if I find it necessary?"

"Just call the Recluse store and leave a message for me to call you. Someone goes down that way nearly every day and they will be sure to stop," Sam answered.

We said our goodbyes just a little after noon, and Mother Port and I started down the dusty road toward the Gillette-Sheridan highway. Very soon the fermentation odor from the paunch contents in the trunk began to permeate the interior of the car. This, in spite of the fact we had all the windows open and were traveling as fast as the dirt road would allow. Dust was pouring in through the windows, and Mother Port's hair was blowing around her head. But the odor was choking.

"It'll be better once we get to the pavement and can travel a little faster," I said apologetically, hoping that my prediction would prove correct.

"I hope so," came a muffled reply from behind a handkerchief pressed against Mother Port's nose. "It will be quite a trip if this smell stays with us all the way home!"

Once on the highway, I swung the little Studebaker southward toward Gillette. The road was straight and clear so I accelerated rapidly to sixty-five miles an hour hoping the odor would subside. Five, ten, fifteen miles—no change. Ugh! I shifted in my seat and glanced over at Mother Port. She was starring straight ahead, holding her handkerchief over both her nose and mouth.

"Pretty bad!" I yelled over roar of the wind and road. She looked over at me with a glint in her eyes and I knew she was smiling underneath that handkerchief. That knowing smile of past experience.

When we arrived in Gillette, we stopped for gasoline and a cold soda. I asked the attendant if he could direct me to the ice house or somewhere where I could obtain dry ice. He sent me to the creamery on a side street about two blocks off the highway. We found the place easily, and I made my request for dry ice. The owner said they didn't keep dry ice, but they would be happy to order some from Denver for me and it would take about four days to arrive—that is, if it made the right connections at Cheyenne and Lusk. If not, it would take longer.

"Sorry," I said, "that won't do me any good at all. Do you have any plain ice I can buy?" I was dreading the response.

"Got a few pieces left from the milk that came in from Spearfish this morning. You're welcome to them if you want," he offered.

"How much do I owe you?" I asked after obtaining about four fist-sized pieces of rapidly melting ice, which, after I wrapped in newspaper, I had stuffed into the pail holding the tissue samples.

"Nothing. I just hope it does you some good."

"I hope so too."

We were back on the highway in a few minutes and headed east toward Moorcroft and Upton. The soda had refreshed us and we started to talk loudly to one another over the road noise and wind. The smell didn't seem as bad once we were moving again, but still it hovered there like a cat ready to pounce, especially when I slowed down for a curve or a chuckhole in the road.

Mother Port told me that many, many years earlier she and the whole family had come up this way on the way to the Yellowstone. They had an old touring car with plenty of patching material for the tires. She recalled that it was a great trip even though she never cared for living in the out-of-doors. She giggled when she related that a bear messed up their camp one night when it had gotten in and stolen the bacon they had strung on a rope fastened between two trees. She was having a much better time now than several hours earlier sitting under a tree in the heat. Soon, however, I saw the handkerchief again being held to the nose and mouth. We stopped talking and I kept the speedometer needle on the sixty-five mark except when we went through Moorcroft and Upton.

Finally, we pulled into the back yard of the drugstore in Sundance around 4 p.m. The clothing clung to the skin on our back as we tumbled out of the car. Harriet, who had been working on the books at the back of the store, heard us drive in and came out to greet us and to help her mother.

"How did it go?" she asked.

"Pretty good," I responded and hoped I had the answer to the problem in one of the cans in the trunk. "Awful hot, though."

"How are you, Mother?" She gave Mother Port a little pull away from the seat of the car.

"I'll be better," she replied, "when I can get away from the heat and that awful smell. And I'd really like to wash the dust off my face."

"Bob had a miserable job up there, but he did just fine," she continued while walking into the drugstore.

"These specimens need to be put into the refrigerator," I said to Harriet. "Is it filled up with food so that there will be no room for these?" I opened the trunk and pointed to the specimens. She came over to look at the cache while I proceeded to remove them and place them on the ground behind the car. Her next breath was a gasp—she looked at me and said that under no circumstance could those smelly specimens be housed in our refrigerator! It was only after some discussion that she grudgingly agreed to let me use part of the freezing compartment in the refrigerator for the fresh tissue samples. Once we agreed, she turned and climbed the stairs to the apartment where she would make room to house the tissue specimens.

There was not enough time left in the day to prepare the material for the four-thirty mail, but I sealed the paunch material in the cans and placed the cans in a heavy cardboard box, which I wrapped with a twine.

The next morning I composed a letter to the director in charge of the laboratory, packaged the rest of the material, and mailed all of it to the State Laboratory located in Laramie. With that accomplished, I telephoned the laboratory director and told him about the specimens I had just mailed and asked, "By the way, do you know what the government used to stop grasshoppers during the plague some twenty years ago?"

"Yes," he replied. "It was arsenic."

"Wouldn't arsenic deteriorate over a twenty-year period?"

"No, no. Arsenic is very stable and a most difficult chemical to dispose of without risk to other animals. Is arsenic poisoning what you suspect happened to the Clark cattle?"

"It is now, after what you have just told me."

"We don't do any analysis here for heavy metals, but I will send the samples over to the University and have the chemists there run an analysis for you."

"Great! And would you please have them call me immediately if they isolate anything?"

Nearly a week later, a call came from one of the chemists at the University of Wyoming. He told me that a high level of arsenic trioxide was present in all of the paunch samples as well as the soil sample we had taken from the homestead shed and in the remnant piece of burlap sacking. He hoped, also, that we wouldn't send any more such samples. The odor, he said, even before they opened the package, filled the room, and when they opened the box that terrible odor permeated the entire building—a very distressing working condition in a closed building where the material required heating as a part of the analysis procedure.

He also informed me that he understood the odor coming from the package was so bad when it arrived at the Laramie Post Office that the postmaster called the laboratory director and asked him to come pick up the package promptly. He wanted the laboratory director to be aware that he thought there was something dead being shipped through the mail and to inform him in no uncertain terms shipping dead creatures through the mail was not allowed!

The news didn't surprise me; I'd suffered the odor, too. But I thanked him for the information and offered my apologies for their distress caused by the samples and assured him that I would make every effort to avoid sending any such samples in the future.

When I hung up I turned to Harriet and Mother Port, who had heard me and wandered into the room in order to learn the news. "Those cattle of Sam Clark's died from arsenic poisoning," I announced. "I better call the Recluse store at once. Sam will want to know, and I'd like to know if he has lost more cattle. If he's boarded up that shack and shed, he should have no more deaths."

"I'm happy your tentative diagnosis of poison turned out to be correct," Mother Port said with a smile. "But next time you invite me for a ride, please make sure it's a little less long, less hot, and less odiferous!"

HOLLOWTAIL

There are many signs of summer in the West. Not least among them are hot days—maybe 100 degrees—cool nights, down around 60; and, in veterinary practice, decidedly different types of calls.

After calving and branding are over in the spring and early summer, cattle are pushed onto summer range. It might be to pastures owned by the individual rancher or to leased land held by the rancher(s) but owned by the U.S. Government. Anyway, before this change takes place, all routine veterinary service has been completed—for example, the required vaccinations and the testing of bulls for fertility.

When the movement of cattle is completed, veterinary practice consists mainly of treating sick dogs and cats, spaying female pets before they come into season in the fall, and making a few calls to treat an acutely ill horse or cow ... "odd ball" cases, so to speak.

One morning around ten o'clock, Harriet and I were sitting at the soda fountain in the drugstore having a cup of coffee. We were talking about whether we could afford a new pickup for the practice. Our little Studebaker was fast wearing out, and yet, we weren't so flush we could just step out and buy another vehicle without a lot of figuring. We were making payments on an automatic washer and dryer and we pondered the feasibility of increased monthly payments. Payments would be too great, perhaps, if we didn't trade in the little Studebaker, yet trading would leave Harriet "a foot" when I had the pickup. And if we chose to travel any distance, like to a veterinary meeting halfway across the state, a car would be much more convenient and certainly more comfortable.

Suddenly I became aware of "our girl Friday," Mrs. Binny. She was directing a curious looking gentleman our way. "He's sitting right over there," I heard her say.

When I looked up I saw a stranger approaching. That wasn't unusual at the time, as I hadn't really known anyone in the area prior to this, our first summer in practice. The exceptions were the banker, my brother-in-law and his wife, and an old cowboy named Frank Haselton (a friend of Harriet's family) and his wife

Nan. Notwithstanding, I was not to forget this man, though I would never see him again.

"Are you the vet?" he asked as he shuffled up to me.

"Sure am. What can I do for you?" I slipped off the stool. Harriet gathered up the two cups and headed for the sink at the back of fountain.

Close examination revealed to me that this man was not the ordinary rancher—if, in fact, he was a rancher at all. He wore bib overalls as opposed to Levis. His face was sort of pale, indicating he'd not been in the sun much. And he needed a shave. Normally, cowmen in the area were clean-shaven, with heavily tanned faces. This fellow's hat was made of soft cloth and the brim was very uneven, something like a fisherman would wear. It was not a straw Stetson, or similar brand, usually worn by local ranchers and cowboys at this time of year. Looking down at his feet I knew, for sure, this man was no rancher! He had on an old pair of flat-heeled brown shoes with laces, and the heels were badly run over.

Only years later while practicing in Gillette did I see this kind of garb on a gentleman, and he was an FDA inspector from South Dakota who had come into Wyoming to "make a buy" of veterinary prescription drugs. Obviously he was not aware that he stood out like the proverbial sore thumb. It was just because he did that everyone was "real legal" while he stayed around!

When finally this fellow began to tell me why he was there, I knew he had a serious problem. "We've got a milk cow that's been down since yesterday afternoon." he said. "She calved yesterday morning and stayed up only long enough for her calf to suck. Then she went down and she hasn't got up since. At first she sort of moaned and groaned, and would keep her head turned against her side. We knew there was something wrong, so we treated her. This morning she was laying on her side and thrashing about pretty bad. Her eyes are all glazed over, too. How much would you charge to come out of look at her?"

Having listened intently to the description of the malady, I chose to answer, "I can't give you an exact figure without knowing where you live and how many drugs I will have to use. I charge fifty cents a mile, one way, plus drugs for most calls, and, if there's surgery involved, it could cost more."

"I live about twenty miles south of Upton," he replied. "That would make it about twenty-five dollars, wouldn't it? We don't want to loose the cow; she's a good cow and gives lots of milk. When can you come out?"

From the description he'd given me, I surmised what the problem was and knew that there was no time to lose.

"I'll leave right now, just as soon as I get some drugs," I told him.

"Why don't you follow me, then? It might save your getting lost. The place is kind of hard to find."

Although I wasn't often lost, the cow needed immediate attention and as "time was of the essence" I thought it prudent to follow.

On the way back to the treatment room to pick up the drugs I'd need, I made a detour through the front of the store where the candy was kept by the cash register. Harriet was there looking out the window at the client getting into his car.

"I'll miss lunch so I'm going to take a couple of Milky Ways and a Coke," I said, as I reached for the candy bars and turned toward the fountain to gather up the Coke. That's something I did many times those next four years and for which I would pay the price in later years!

"Any idea what time you'll be back?" Harriet asked. "Someone might call and it would be good to know when you'll be available."

"Figure three hours at the earliest," I answered. "I'll call you from Upton on the way back just in case there's something over that way." Then I headed out the back door and to the car.

At the front of the store I drove in behind the client's car, motioned for him to go on, waved to Harriet and followed the car ahead of me. We reached our destination in about an hour and a quarter. There was a beat up old mobile home with a dog tied near the front steps ahead of us when we pulled into park. The dog ran to the end of its chain, barked, jumped around, and carried on in general. A young woman and two or three kids came out of the mobile home as we stopped.

Soon the client came over to my car and as I removed the Pandora bag from the car trunk he pointed and said, "She's up in back near that shed."

The shed looked like a pile of old plywood and boards that where partly stuck together and covered with tarpaper. It was located perhaps a hundred feet behind the trailer and was inside an old woven wire fence. The shed sagged badly, boasting of a supporting post only every twenty feet. The pasture in which it was located was no more that a quarter of an acre and there wasn't a blade of grass anywhere within the fence ... just bare ground. We entered the lot through the gate and the woman and children followed. The cow was stretched out near the shed and as we approached I looked intently for sings of breathing—she was so very quiet I wasn't sure she was alive. Suddenly she sighed and took a deep breath.

"Thank goodness she's still breathing," the woman said. "A couple of times when I came out to look at her, I thought for sure she was gone." She sighed when she looked at her husband.

After depositing my bag, I began an examination of the cow. Her eyes were glassy, sure enough, and she would not respond to my tapping her on the ribs. I took a fever thermometer out of my shirt pocket, removed it from the case, reached for the animal's tail, lifted it, and inserted the thermometer into the rectum. As I did so I noticed a clean, neatly tied white bandage midway down the cow's tail.

"What's this?" I asked, looking first at the man and then his wife.

"Well, Doc, we treated her for hollow tail, yesterday. I told you we had treated her. I remember as a kid seeing my dad treat a cow that looked just like this one. It was for hollow horn or hollow tail, I forget which. That cow got up, but this one hasn't. That's why we got you."

I made no response, but rather just removed the thermometer. Her temperature was subnormal, just as I had suspected it would be, and I needed to hurry along and get an intravenous injection of calcium and dextrose running into her jugular vein. She would need at least a pint, or 500 cc's, maybe more. Her condition was so poor it required the medicine to be given slowly so as not to shock the heart muscle and cause it to spasm. At that time, there was no cure for heart muscle spasm that amounted to much.

After placing a two-and-a-half-inch long, large gauge needle into the cow's vein, I started the medicine running into her through an intravenous catheter. I held the bottle with the tubing attached in my right hand; the left hand I used to hold the bell of my stethoscope over the heart region to monitor the heart beat. At first it was very faint and slow but when the bottle appeared a quarter empty, the heart sounds became strong and regular. As the bottle emptied, her ears began to twitch a little and her eyelids blinked several times. These are all good signs, I thought to myself.

The young ones who'd been standing around watching every move the cow and I made started to jabber and laugh and point to the cow's tail. I thought they were laughing at the bandage but instead, it was because the animal was defecating. This to me was another good sign. (Why do kids always seem to laugh when an animal defecates?)

When the last of the calcium solution had left the bottle and started down into the tubing, I pulled the needle from the vein and placed the equipment near the bag. The cow was still stretched out but was showing encouraging signs of survival. She let out a big sigh, as if she had been holding her breath, then threw her head around to her side and raised herself up on her sternum or breastbone.

Chatter really started at this point—the woman said she know they should have called me yesterday, and the man responded with something about not having the money. The children giggled and patted the cow and talked to her while they tried to get the dirt away from the eye that had been next to the ground.

"Where's the calf?" I asked, looking around the enclosure.

"He's in the shed," the woman stated. "We put him in there yesterday when the cow went down. We have been milking her and feeding the calf the milk from a bottle. We didn't take all of her milk, though. I figured if she had anything like human mothers do once in awhile after having a baby, it wouldn't be good to take all the milk. Isn't that right?" She looked at me.

"It surely is!" I responded enthusiastically, a little uncertain now who I might actually be dealing with. Turning to her I said, "That was exactly the right thing to do. This cow has what we call milk fever. Actually, it's a misnomer because a cow with this condition usually has a subnormal temperature rather than an elevated temperature. It occurs when too much calcium leaves the bloodstream either just before, during, or directly after calving. When this happens, there is an extreme metabolic upset, which causes the animal to go down, gradually lose consciousness, and, finally, more often than not, to die if the condition is untreated.

"Most of the time it takes only that little pint bottle of calcium and dextrose solution to allow survival. In the old days, before they discovered the tie-in with calcium, farmers and veterinarians would treat the disease by pumping air into the udder through the teats. It wasn't uncommon, however, for the animal to survive the calcium deficiency but become acutely ill and die from septic mastitis as a result of pumping contaminated air into the bag. Now, very few cows die if proper treatment is instituted promptly."

The woman nodded and said, "I understand you completely, doctor. I'm a registered nurse. In women, as you probably know, there is a condition called eclampsia, which occurs after childbirth. The patient behaves symptomatically, for all the world, just like that cow did. When I saw her yesterday, it crossed my mind that she could have something similar."

"You surmised correctly," I went on. "Bitches, queens, and mares are also subject to the disease. It is sometimes called Puerperal Tetany."

Turning then to the client I asked, "Is there some warm water around that I might use to clean up a little before leaving? There's a bucket in my car trunk if you need one. While I'm waiting, I just want to have a look under that bandage."

That said, I knelt down behind the cow and untied the knotted bandage. Underneath the bandage was a gauze pad and under the pad was a sight that I shall never forget. There, in an incision that extended for about two inches, I found a generous amount of salt and pepper that had been forced into the wound and under the skin. The wound, however, was only the depth of the skin. Without comment, I used the gauze to wipe away the salt and pepper from the wound. Then I reached into my bag for some antibiotic ointment, which I applied generously to the lesion. When I re-tied the bandage no one present said a word.

By that time, the client had returned with the water, and the cow was acting like she wanted to get on her feet.

"Let's see if she can make it up," I said, grabbing her tail and making sure to avoid the bandaged area. When we both took hold of her, I hollered and kicked her gently with the side of my foot and she raised herself up on her hind legs and then finally upon her front legs. As we steadied her on her feet, I heard the calf bawl. The cow looked toward the shed and headed toward it, half falling first one way and then the other, and all the time the client and I were trying to steady her and "steer" her by the tail.

Everyone began to laugh, the nurse most of all.

"She acts like a drunken sailor!" she cried.

As I cleaned the equipment I had used and washed myself as best I could, I gave instructions on how to care for both the cow and the calf, and advised them that if they had questions or if anything happened they could give me a call on the telephone.

The woman had, after having asked me the cost of the call, written me a check for thirty dollars. I made note that she had signed her name Sara Franklin.

My watch told me it was 12:30 p.m. when I swung out on the road and headed for Upton; my stomach told me it was time for the Coke and candy bars.

By the time I passed the abandoned livestock sale yard in Upton, I was in need of a restroom, and as I had to call back to the drugstore, I decided I could relieve myself and use the telephone at the only gas station in the town. After using the facilities and making the phone call, I stood in the doorway of the station a minute and passed the time of day with the owner. There were no calls waiting, so I felt I could relax a bit.

"By the way," I said, pointing in the direction from which I had just come, "do you know the Franklins who live about twenty miles south of here on a small place?"

"Yea!" the owner responded. "He works as "night hawk" in the oil field for one of the outfits. Just startin' in down there. She's a nurse and works for a doctor in Newcastle. They come from the East somewhere."

"That accounts for what I saw," I said to myself. "Folks from the East rarely know it takes more than five or ten acres to keep a milk cow in the country. (I was beginning to sound like a Westerner!) They'd be money ahead to buy milk from the store rather than to do what they're doing. It cost money to buy feed and all for a cow."

After I got home, Harriet asked my what was wrong with the cow and how had it gone at the call. When I finished telling her the story, she looked at me quizzically and said, "You're pulling my leg!" and searched my face for the telltale signs of jest.

"Now, how could I think up anything that funny?" I protested, grinning all the time. I'm still not sure she believed me. She probably thought that the days of the "hollow horn" and "hollow tail" were long since buried. As I never again had a call to treat either the "hollow tail" or "hollow horn," I'm not so sure she wasn't half right.

A CASE OF FORCED CHARITY—ONE OF SEVERAL

"Bob! Long distance!" Harriet called. "I think he said he was calling from Bay-horse, Montana." I walked over to the old wall, hand-crank telephone and picked up the ear piece, which Harriet had left dangling.

"Is this the vet?" came the question from a faint rather high-pitched voice.

"Yes, this is Dr. Baldwin," I responded in a little louder tone than my greeting. I didn't want to talk so loud that everyone present in the drugstore could hear the conversation.

"Golly, Doc, ya gotta speak up. I can hardly hear ya!" came the reply in full timbre. "This is Joe Altman from up here at Bayhorse. You know, you were up here last month testing and vaccinating cows for the Traub boys. I was helping run the cows through the chute."

Try as I might, I couldn't remember what the man looked like. There were many cowboys around helping and I didn't have any particular reference point to help me remember this person, at least at this time. That comes only after living in a community for awhile and I never was one who could shake a fellow's hand and remember his name forever afterward. It's a mighty good trait, I must admit.

"Okay, what's the problem?" I shouted.

"Well, Doc, something's wrong with the old milk cow!" he shouted into the telephone. "She was a little lame last night when I brought her in. She gave some stringy milk from one of her quarters, but she ate some. This morning she can hardly walk and looks bad out of the eye."

"What kind of a cow is she?" Now I was hollering, hoping his voice would become stronger because the last of his description I was barely able to hear. It really didn't make much difference what the breed of cow if what I suspected was in fact the condition he described, but I always liked to have a picture in my mind of what type of critter I'd be dealing with. Temperament and breed sort of go together.

"She's a white face. Raised her from a calf." His voice now was not so faint.

"Is she gentle?" I asked.

"Yes, she's gentle! I only have to tie her two hind legs together to milk her! What do you think is wrong with her?"

"Sounds like acute mastitis!" I shouted, now aware of folks in the store taking an interest in the one-way conversion. "You might want to get one of the vets out of Sheridan to look at her. Better yet, haul her to one. It would be cheaper."

"No!" he shouted. "I want you if you'll come. This cow needs tendin' right away. I sure don't want to lose her! When can you come?"

All the while we were talking, I was thinking of the distance to Bayhorse, at least 125 miles one way, as I recalled from the previous trip. A good twenty-five to thirty miles of that dirt road. "Do you have a place to land an airplane up there?" I shouted, now unconcerned about who might be listening. I had in mind calling my friend Sandy to take me up. He was the local rancher who flew me on calls when his time and the weather permitted.

"Yes! You could land east of the corral. I can get the cows in the corral so they won't be in your way in the pasture where you'd have to land. What time do you think you'll be here? It'll take me a little bit to get them rounded up and in."

"You just stay there at the post office for a half hour, and if I haven't called by then, you'll know I'm coming by plane and should be there by early afternoon. Early enough so we can get back before dark!"

At that point he said he understood me and it would take him a couple of hours to get the cows in the corral, out of our way. That time period would be about right if I went by plane. If I didn't, it wouldn't make any difference what time I got there.

After I rang off, immediately I cranked up the old phone again and told the operator I wanted to talk to Sandy. It wasn't but a few minutes until he was on the line and I was asking him about taking me on the call.

"Yes, I have time to take you, Doc," Sandy replied, "but it will be about an hour before I can pick you up. I got to gas up the plane and check her out. I'll have to look over the maps for that area, too. Never flown into that country before."

From what I told him about the location, as I remembered it from the ground, he thought it would take about an hour to get there from Sundance. Figuring an hour to land, treat the cow and get off again, we should be back in Sundance in plenty of time for Sandy to get home long before dusk. A bad time for judging landing distances in the bush.

"I'll call Todd to make sure the bulls aren't in the pasture next to the runway," I offered. "If they are, I'll get down there early enough to get them off." With that, I rang off and began making preparations for the trip. As I have said before, the runway at Sundance was on private land owned by a rancher just outside of town. It was land used for a bull pasture in the "off" season. Todd had a son who flew. Also, he was very accommodating and let anyone use the runway.

After a hurried lunch, I packed what drugs I would need in the Pandora bag and with Harriet in tow, headed for the little Studebaker, parked in the back drive. About that time, a cousin of Harriet's drove in. We called him Uncle Lewis. Quickly we told him what was going on and Harriet invited him to go along to see me off. We all piled into the little car and headed to the "Sundance Airport."

As I swung into the lane, leading to the runway, I looked toward the Sundance Mountain and saw the little yellow plane heading in our direction. We arrived at the airstrip in time to see that there were no bulls in sight, and Sandy was coming right in without making an overpass. At the gate where we would enter the field, we watched the little plane land, its wheels just bobbing and hopping as they ran over the hard-packed ground.

Sandy turned the plane around quickly and taxied to the barbed-wire gate. I was ready and waiting as he came to a stop. He jumped from the plane, leaving the engine idling. Producing a map from his pocket, he asked me to locate about where I thought the ranch was. Soon I located the spot and we figured it wouldn't be too difficult to find the place since there would be cattle in the corral and the house nearby. At any rate, if we got lost we could always drop down at a ranch house and get directions. We had done that before.

We were ready to depart; Sandy grabbed the bag and the two of us headed for the little plane. When we got to the door, Sandy lifted the bag a little as if weighing it.

"This bag is pretty heavy," he said with a worried look on his face. "Are you sure there isn't something in there we can leave here?" Then he explained how hot the ground was and that the more ground heat there was the less lift an airplane had.

"I can get rid of about ten pounds," I said.

"Well, that's not much, but every little bit will help," he responded.

I took the bag, went back to the gate, opened the bag, unloaded what I could, and gave it to Harriet and Uncle Lewis. All the while I told them what Sandy had just said to me. Neither of them said anything. However, Uncle Lewis told me at a later date that he was thinking at the time that if ten pounds was going to make a difference, he questioned the safety of that mode of transportation!

Sandy stowed the bag behind my seat, located behind the pilot's seat, and we both boarded. He taxied the plane to the far end of the pasture and approached the fence as close as was safe. Then he stopped, tromped down hard on both brakes, and revved the little eighty-five-horsepower engine to a fevered pitch. Finally I could feel the tail begin to lift and as it did, he released the brakes and we catapulted down the pasture, bumping and jiggling, toward the gate where Harriet and Uncle Lewis were standing. All the while, Sandy was rapidly working his feet up and down and teasing back and forth on the wheel with his right hand. With his left hand, he was holding the throttle all the way forward. Looking around him I saw the fence getting closer and closer. My heart was in my mouth when suddenly the plane lifted and the rumbling noise ceased, though the roar of the engine increased. The plane rose steadily then and looking ahead I saw that we had just barely cleared the fence and the car! Harriet and Uncle Lewis were standing like two pieces of petrified wood, mouths hanging wide open.

Sandy swung the plane around and we headed north toward Montana. Uncle Lewis told me one day that when we were banking in the turn, it looked as if the plane had lost all forward motion and was just suspended in the air—sure to fall.

It took some time to get leveled off toward our destination, but in the process I just enjoyed the view of the Bear Lodge, a mountain range behind Sundance. Far in the distance I spotted the little town of Alva nestled among the hills. The engine noise prevented Sandy and I from making any conversation, so we just settled down and enjoyed the sights: a herd of antelope grazing or running; here and there, the occasional lone ranch house and set of outbuildings; an abandoned homestead shack; Herefords spread out grazing over large areas; and, of course, flocks of sheep gathered around water holes, this being the time of day that sheep go to water.

Occasionally Sandy would reach up and turn a little crank located on the ceiling of the plane. This adjusted the plane's "trim." Otherwise he just kept the machine flying north.

When we approached the spot I had designated on the map as Bayhorse, he told me to start watching. He indicated he couldn't see any evidence of a town. I responded by holding up one finger and shouting, "There's only one house and some outbuildings at Bayhorse!"

Sandy nodded and soon pointed his finger downward; he had found the spot. With that he turned northwest and followed the road leading toward the spot. I poked him on the shoulder and pointed to another road leading away from Bayhorse. That road led to Joe's place. He banked the plane in that direction and soon we caught sight of a house with a set of corrals nearby. A closer inspection revealed a corral full of Hereford cattle, with Joe outside the gate waving his hat.

When Sandy saw him he began to look first one way and then the other, searching for a place to land. I, too, was searching, and as Joe had promised, there was an open space just east of the corral. What Joe hadn't said to me was that the field wasn't level ground. In fact, it was on about a twenty-five percent grade heading upward away from the corral. That would mean landing on an upward incline and taking off on a downward incline! With no other suitable place in sight, Sandy banked the little plane and brought her around to make his approach.

"Hang on!" he yelled. "It might be a rough one!"

After tightening my seat belt, I leaned back as hard as I could and took a good grip on the two pieces of the air frame that ran through the cabin. As we crossed the corral, I looked down just in time to see one end of the log structure give way and cattle spew in all directions. We finally got on the ground and taxied to the corral. The only creatures left inside the structure were Joe and the cow to be treated. She was too sick to move out.

When Joe approached us he acted a little perturbed about the cattle bursting out of the corral. "I'd have directed you to a field about two miles from here if I'd knowed them fool critters was going to knock the side out of the corral," he said gruffly as he surveyed the wreckage.

Sandy too allowed as how it might have been easier to land, and he knew darn well it would a better place from which to take off.

We entered the corral and walked toward the cow. She tried to get up, but after a couple of feeble attempts she laid back down with her back pressed against the poles of the corral.

"When did this happen?" I asked Joe.

"Well, about a week ago, I took a couple of calves off her when we decided to dry her up. She gave enough milk for them and the house, too. She's due to calve in about a month. I figured she needed the rest until then. Leastwise, that's what my vet book says to do. I milked her out a couple of times after that, then just turned her out with the range cows. She come up missing about three days ago. When I went lookin' for her, there she was layin' in the water down at the creek. She got up when I urged her to, but when she started to walk, she acted lame in the right hind leg. Her foot wasn't swollen but when I got her to the house and in the chute, I noticed her bag was swollen right bad ... 'specially the right rear quarter and tit. I rubbed coal oil on it, but it wasn't gettin' any better. That's when I called you."

When I knelt down and felt the quarter it was cold and looked bluish black in color.

Joe and Sandy had struck up a conversation by this time, talking about the weather and the price of cattle. Those two topics are always safe for ranchers anywhere in the world.

When I stood up and shook my head, Sandy and Joe stopped talking. They probably weren't listening to each other anyway.

"Gangrene!" I exclaimed. "She's got gangrene!"

"Figured it had to be somethin' pretty bad," Joe sighed, "else she'd been long gone outta here by now. Anything you can do for her, Doc?"

"The teat on the right hind quarter must be removed, for sure. That will get some drainage going. The left quarter still has some heat in it but it is affected too. I won't take the teat off that quarter but it will likely be blind—that is, if she lives. If we had her at a clinic where I could do some clean surgery, I'd want to remove the right hind quarter entirely. It's too risky out here, though."

Surgery hadn't entered my mind when Joe called and now as I looked at my watch I felt some urgency to get on with the task. It shouldn't take too long, I figured. It wouldn't be necessary to anesthetize the area around the teat and I wouldn't have to disinfect any instruments—the tissue was dead and completely devoid of feeling. Contamination of the wound was not a factor.

"Will you get me some warm water, please?" I asked Joe as I opened my bag to get out the necessary equipment. While he was fetching the water I ran a sulfonamide solution into her jugular vein, and by the time he returned I had also given her some penicillin in the muscle of the hind leg. That done, I laid out on a clean towel my scalpel, two pair of hemostats, and a sharp bistoury. Then I washed my hands with a disinfectant soap and scattered some around the area of the incision. A few strokes of the scalpel and the teat was off. Some black-looking blood oozed from the wound, but there was no pus or other matter.

Deftly I worked one finger into the wound and made as big a cavity in the quarter as I could. I didn't want to rupture any of the larger blood vessels that I felt within. The goal was to establish as much drainage as possible so that the body would slough out the dead and rotten tissue rather than absorb it. Absorbing it would poison her entire system further. The operation took only about five minutes, and after completing it I sprayed the area with a fly repellent and left the remainder with Joe. In addition I gave him penicillin and sulfa pills, enough for four additional days of therapy.

"She'll be a lot better in four days or she won't be here," I said.

As we walked back to the plane Joe said, "I'm a little short of cash right now, Doc, but you send me a bill and I'll see you get the money right away. Sure glad you could get out here."

Sandy and I said our goodbyes and climbed into the little plane for the return trip. The takeoff didn't bother me at first; logical thinking told me we could get up to speed faster going downhill compared to level ground. Wrong!! What I hadn't factored in was the tree-covered hill on the other side of the corral. When we came in I really hadn't noticed it because we had swung away from it. Now, as Sandy swung the tail around and taxied to the top of the knoll, I could see it straight in front of us. The corral was this side of the copse.

This time Sandy didn't have to holler to me to hang on. I had a death grip on the air frame—you couldn't have torn me free.

Sandy revved up the machine and let her go. We hurtled downward toward the corral and at the very last minute, he jerked back on the stick and we cleared it in good shape. Immediately, he heeled the left wing to the left and I swear I could count the number of pinecones on one of the trees!

When we straightened out I looked back and saw Joe waving his hat. I didn't give up my grip on the frame tubing to return the wave.

Our return trip was uneventful and as we passed over the drugstore, Sandy buzzed the engine so that Harriet would know she should meet us at the Sundance Airport. We were back in time for Sandy to make his home landing before dusk.

While driving back to the store, I told Harriet and Uncle Lewis about the landing and takeoff at Joe's place and just what I found wrong with the cow. Neither said too much, though I knew they were doing a good deal of wondering.

Nearly two months later, I saw Joe at the saleyard in Gillette and asked him how the cow got along. "Got along just fine, Doc," he responded. "I sold her here at the sale a couple of weeks before she calved. I'm going to send you the money for that call as soon as I get home. I just used my last check to buy some feed."

Six months later as Harriet was preparing statements to be sent to clients, I was sitting reading the latest veterinary journal. "You know that trip you made to Bayhorse, Montana to treat the sick milk cow?" she asked.

"Ya, I remember."

"Well, old boy, you've been snookered," she said with a grin. "This is the eighth statement we've sent to him, and I bet my bottom dollar he won't pay this one either. Looks like this will be a charity case."

When the first of the year rolled around and we still hadn't received payment, we took it off our income tax as a bad debt. It wouldn't be the last one, but it hurt a little every time it happened—and not just financially, either.

But we made sure that Sandy was paid his $35 out of our own pocket. After all, he did get me in and out of there alive.

EUTHANASIA

Those unusual and unforgettable one-time events from those early years in private practice are still pristinely clear in my memory. One such event occurred on a Monday morning.

I had just finished breakfast and was sitting at the table mentally preparing for the first call of the day: the removal of a cancerous eye from a cow owned by a rancher who lived some ten miles west of Sundance. Medically, this surgical procedure was called "enucleation of the eyeball." The nature of the procedure was such that it was difficult for me to classify it as surgery, though technically it was. Perhaps that is why I was just sitting at the table preparing myself mentally.

"Bob, there is someone down here to see you!" Harriet called up the stairway to the apartment from the drugstore below. "She's got a dog she wants 'put to sleep.' I told her you were getting ready to go on a call but that you might see her before leaving."

I removed myself from the table and went to the head of the stairs to reply. "Okay, have her take the dog into the treatment room. I'll be right along." I returned to the table, drank the rest of the coffee in my cup, grabbed my hat, and descended the stairs.

A short, coarse-looking woman was leading a shaggy, rough coated collie through the front door of the store. I motioned to her to lead the dog around the front of the U-shaped fountain and through to the back of the store where the examination/treatment room was located.

When I stepped around the back of the fountain on my way to the treatment room, I greeted Marlene, one of the fountain girls, and Mrs. Binney, our sixty-plus-year-old "girl Friday." Marlene was preparing the fountain for the day's operation and Mrs. Binney was sitting on a stool at the end of the fountain, tearing covers from outdated magazines. These were to be returned to the broker for credit.

Suddenly the lady who was escorting the dog through the store started to speak. She said that the animal was not too friendly and she was afraid it would bite someone. Besides that, both she and her husband worked and didn't have time to take care of the dog.

In those days no such thing as an SPCA existed in Sundance—probably still doesn't—and the closest one was 90 to 100 miles away. In no way would this lady have considered that alternative.

"Have you tried giving the dog to a rancher or someone who might be able to care for him?" I inquired.

"We got him from a rancher who couldn't have him around because he chased the livestock," she replied curtly.

"He hasn't bitten anyone lately, has he? If he has, we must hold him for ten days in order to observe him for signs of rabies. Only after that time could he be euthanized."

"No, he hasn't bitten anyone since we've had him, but he snarls and acts like he would. Besides, he had a rabies shot last year, before we moved up here."

"Okay, let's get him on the table. It won't take long," I said, going around the table to where the dog was sitting. Suddenly the dog jumped to his feet, snarled, and acted as though he were about to lunge and bite.

"See what I mean?" the client said and jerked back on the leash. She seemed rather pleased that the dog had verified her claims.

In a short time the deed was done and I placed the animal in the kennel out back of the store. I would dispose of the body later in the day when I had more time.

Euthanizing a healthy animal and disposing of the remains was always an anathema to me. Our desire has always been to use our training and skills to alleviate the pain and suffering of dumb animals. Euthanasia was always an alternative in critically ill animals with little hope of recovery, even if heroic measures were employed. To euthanize a perfectly normal, healthy animal, however, was quite another thing.

"What a way to start a day," I muttered to myself as I was driving out of town to care for the cancer-eyed cow.

Ben Janson was standing outside the yard gate waiting for me when I arrived at his ranch house. He wanted to ride with me so that he could save me from having to get out of the pickup twice in order to open the two gates that led to the squeeze chute where the cow was located.

"Morning, Doc," he greeted me. "Looks like it's going to be a good day for some haying. Guess I'll put a little up as soon as we get done with the old cow."

"Morning, Ben," I responded. "It didn't start out too good for me. Sure hope it gets better." Then I told him about having to put the dog to sleep.

"If you don't mind my asking, what do you charge for a job like that?"

"Seven-fifty." Actually, I did mind the question.

We ran the cow into the chute and with the use of a halter, pulled her head around at a right angle to the chute. While Ben kept the position of her head I "prepped" the site: clipped the hair, washed the skin, infiltrated the periorbital region with an anesthesia and sutured the eyelid closed. While the anesthesia was deadening the area, I lit a cigarette and listened to Ben tell a story about a feed salesman who worked the country before the days a graduate veterinarian was located in the area. The salesman would remove "cancer eyes" from cows for no cost, so long as the rancher bought mineral and supplement from him.

Curious as to how a layperson would perform such an operation I looked at Ben and asked, "What did he do to deaden the pain and what did he use for instruments?"

"Well, I tell ya, Doc. A couple of cowboys would 'head and heel' the old cow and stretch her out, keeping the bad eye upward. Then, they'd lay a plank across her neck and one guy would get on one end of the plank and another guy on the other end of the plank. That way they could hold her head still. That's when the salesman got the red-hot poker out of the fire he'd built and go to work burning the eye out of the cow's head. It was really awful!" He shook his head at the memory.

"They say one year, old Charley Lentz had ten or twelve cows with bad eyes that he corralled for this salesman to treat. After the first one, he couldn't stand the sight he saw and hollered to his cowboys to turn 'em out. He said he'd rather have them suffer with bad eyes than to watch any more of that—what with the critter bellering, the stink and smoke of burning flesh, an' all. Havin' something to kill the pain is sure a great thing!"

He repeated, "sure a great thing," as he watched me shroud the cow's head, except for the immediate area around the affected eye, and make the first incision. The animal didn't move or show any signs of pain.

There was always something about the work we performed and our presence that seemed to provoke recollections for the men watching. Most of the time the stories were fun to hear, not like the gruesome details Ben had just recalled. That kind of story I would never encourage.

The operation finished, I cleaned up the instruments and prepared to leave. "Here," I said, handing Ben a bottle of fly repellent, "I want you to get her in every other day and put this around the incision. It's late in the season to be doing this and we don't want it to be undone by flies getting in the wound."

Ben took the bottle and said, "I'll be in town tomorrow and stop by to pay you. Forgot the checkbook when I left the house. I need to get right on with the haying as soon as I let you through the gates. Don't want to take time to go back to the house."

Late that afternoon I was in the office at the back of the store, reading one of the latest veterinary journals. Harriet had been at the front of the store marking an order and placing the items on the shelves. Suddenly she appeared at the door.

"There's a man out here who acts really angry—wants to know where his dog is," she half-whispered in a frightened tone.

"What dog could that be?" I asked as I rose from the chair. "The only dog we have in the kennel is the one I euthanized this morning. I was planning to cart it off a bit later. Send him in. I'll talk to him."

A ruddy-faced man a little over six-feet tall entered the office door and growled, "Where's my dog? When I got home he was gone! I asked a neighbor if he'd seen him—my wife was still working. My neighbor said that she had taken him to you this morning to have him put to sleep. He's my dog, not hers!! You better not have put him to sleep!" He appeared quite distraught and not a little menacing.

"Come in and sit down," I said and motioned toward a chair near the desk.

"Sit down, h—!," he roared. "All I want is my dog!"

Afraid the loud voice would alert all the customers in the store to listen in on our conversation, I said, "Let's go out to the kennel. It's right this way." I headed out the back door hoping he would follow; he did. Once outside, I stopped, turned to him and described the morning events that led to the death of his dog. "The dog," I said, "is still wrapped in a sack lying in the kennel."

Suddenly he lost his belligerence and asked to see his dog. Once inside the kennel he poured out his side of the story. It appeared that from the time he married, some three years earlier, he'd wanted a dog. He'd had one as a youngster that had been killed by a car. His parents refused to allow him another and now his wife didn't want one either. She thought they were too messy around the house: hair, barking, flatus, one other mouth to feed. Well, he'd gotten one, anyway, one a rancher was going to shoot because it chased his livestock instead of being a herd dog. Over the weekend he said that he and his misses had argued about the dog. She'd threatened to have it put to sleep but he really didn't think she'd do such a thing. "I was wrong!" he said.

"So sorry this happened," I offered, "but you know, when someone brings a dog to me for euthanasia, I assume right up front it belongs to them. My only concerns, most of the time, are whether it has had rabies shots within the year, and whether it's bitten anyone in the past ten days. If it is normal and healthy, I always like to try and find a home for it but after that I get on with the chore—not a task I enjoy, you know."

"Mind if I take him out and bury him? He growled once in awhile and acted mean, but he was my dog and he liked me." He walked to the sack, bent down, and gently picked up his dead dog. Holding the bundle in his arms he walked around the store building to the street where he had parked his car.

"What a tragedy," I muttered to myself, "and what a way to start the week."

The next day my first act of the day was to order "Release" forms from a veterinary supply house. One of the items on the form was a question concerning ownership. I wanted to make certain that the bearer of the animal was, indeed, its owner before I took any action. And the owner had to sign the form, too.

THE SNOWSTORM AND
THE ACTORS

For two hours I had worked on a heifer performing an embryotomy. The heifer had been down on her side unable to rise. She had been in labor for some time and the rancher who owned her had been trying unsuccessfully to help her deliver. Such cases call for an embryotomy: cutting up the fetus while still in the mother's womb and removing a piece at a time.

In this case, the fetus was dead before I began the procedure, probably due to too much pressure placed on it by the pulling and hauling done by the rancher. As usual in these cases, the fetus was dry; normally it would be moist and slick. The birth canal was swollen from excessive trauma.

Purposely I had worked with great caution, lubricating my hands and arms thoroughly before each insertion into the birth canal to keep from tearing the swollen and fragile tissue. Most of the time, I was lying on my stomach. At other times I raised up on my knees. This cautious approach required a much longer than usual period of time to sever and remove both the front legs before the rest of the fetus could be extracted from the heifer.

When I had completed the task, I left the barn to go to my pickup to procure some extra rags, which I needed to help me clean up and dry my equipment. Boy, what a shock I received when I stepped out of the barn door. It was snowing! There was at least eighteen inches of snow on the ground and it was snowing so hard it was difficult to locate my pickup, which was parked just fifty feet away. There had been no snow on the ground when I arrived here at dusk and the sky had been clear. I had driven sixty or seventy miles an hour on dry roads the entire distance to the ranch.

As I worked on the heifer, Bert the rancher, was as intent as I was on the progress. He, too, had been unaware of the event taking place outside the log barn as he held the lantern and told me stories about the "old days" … the days before graduate veterinarians were in the area.

"Golly, Doc, you better figure on stayin' the night. It'll be h—driving in this stuff. Besides, you could run off the road and no one would find you 'til spring."

"Thanks for the offer," I said, "but I really have to get back if I possibly can. I might have another call and Harriet will be real worried if she doesn't hear from me. If I can make it as far as the Tower Store, and I figure it's too bad to go on, I can at least call her and let her know where I am. That's only fifteen miles from here. Maybe the plows will be out by the time I leave." I continued to wash and dry my equipment and prepare my gear for loading back into the pickup.

The clean instruments I stowed in my Pandora bag and removed from it a bottle of penicillin and a syringe. I put 5 cc. of penicillin into the syringe and then gave the heifer a shot in the muscle of her right hind leg. When she felt the needle, she raised up on her sternum and started to look around. "Have you got any water handy?" I asked as I turned to Bert. "I'd like to see her drink some before I take my leave. I hope she will."

"There's some out in the stock tank in the corral, if I can find my way to it!" he laughed. He took down a bucket that hung on a peg over his head and left. Five minutes later he returned with a bucket full of watery slush. There appeared to be an inch of snow on his head and shoulders.

"Pretty bad, Doc! Sure you won't think again about stayin'?" he inquired. He seemed seriously concerned.

"With my new knobby tires and the added weight of the equipment box in the pickup bed, I should be able to get through," I assured him and proceeded to offer the bucket of slushy water to the heifer.

Though she was still down on the ground, she smelled the water for a moment and then began to drink A good sign!

"You give her the rest of the penicillin in the morning," I said, handing him the extra one. "Give her 5 cc. a day for two additional days, too. We don't want any infection to get ahead of us."

The heifer had finished drinking and was nuzzling some of the straw in front of her.

"Let's see if we can get her up," I said to Bert, grabbing her tail. He took hold of the tail and we both hollered, hoping to "scare her up," a favorite saying out there. She gave a heave and got her hind legs under her. Again we hollered, steadying her hind quarters, and she rose on her front legs and stood there—wobbly and shaky, but she was up. Another good sign!

"I'll get some good green looking hay before I go to the house," Bert said. "I might even bring her a bucket of warm water from the house—that is, if I can find my way to and from in this storm!" He wasn't laughing when he said that.

"How much do I owe you, Doc?" he asked as he reached into his shirt pocket for his checkbook.

"Let me see," I said and then paused to add up the call and drugs in my mind. "With the penicillin and all, thirty-five dollars should do it."

"If this one bounces, I got another one just like it." Bert was grinning as he handed the check to me. I knew then that he felt good about the heifer and the hackneyed joke was his way of showing it.

We stepped out into the snow, he carrying some of the gear, and, with his help, I stowed it away in the box in the bed of the pickup. By that time, there was a good two feet of snow on the ground and it was still snowing. "Let me know how she gets along!" I shouted out of the window and revved up the engine to get a running start up the snow-covered incline ahead.

"You take care, Doc," was his farewell.

It was now 9 p.m. I had been gone three hours.

There was no telephone service in that part of the county at that time, and only in the previous year had the REA run electric lines through the area. Bert's ranch was fifteen miles to the closest telephone and Sundance was another twenty-five miles further east.

It so happened that Sundance had just had a group of actors perform a play in the high school auditorium that evening. The players were itinerants who came from Deadwood or Spearfish, South Dakota, I forget just which, and they were scheduled to play in Sheridan the following evening. Harriet and I had planned to attend the play when I returned from the call on the heifer. It wasn't the first or last time we had our plans disappear in smoke because of an emergency, real or manufactured.

Leaving Bert's yard, I swung left onto the canyon road leading to Hulett, ten miles away. I could just barely see the outlines of the dirt road and made sure to stay in the middle, where I seemed to get along with out any trouble. I was certainly happy that I had had new knobby snow tires mounted on my pickup not long before this trip. My hope was that I wouldn't have to get out to put on chains. That's not a fun job in the dark with the wind blowing in your face as you lay under the vehicle trying to fasten the inside links!!

The windshield wipers, going at full speed, were successful in removing the snow from the windshield; they made a racket as they did so. The heater and defroster fan made the only other noise in the frozen night. Once in awhile I would feel the truck slowing down and would quickly downshift into second gear so as not to lose momentum. Only then did I hear the engine. So far, so good! In fact, it was kind of pretty ... just the snow and shadows reflecting off the headlights. I turned the radio on, hoping to get a weather report, but all I could hear was static. Some time later, about forty-five minutes I guessed, a few very dim lights appeared far ahead.

That has to be Hulett, I thought. Suddenly I caught sight of the Hulett sign. I had already entered the town and didn't even know it.

As I eased past the gas station and only store, both closed, the storm seemed to be abating, but even so, the pickup was pushing snow with the bumper. There still were no tracks in the road as I headed out of town toward the Tower Store, and I continued to watch the edge of the road for landmarks.

Twice it was necessary to stop and back into the middle of the road; gusts of wind blowing great clouds of snow had blinded my vision and I had driven toward the barrow pit. Only when I became aware of a feeling of roughness and of hearing a slight rumbling noise over the noise of the wiper and heater fan did I realize something was amiss. Then I pulled to a stop and took a look before going on. Both times the pickup was on the edge of the road, heading into the barrow pit.

The snowfall had decreased a great deal by the time I reached the Tower Store; it was falling only about a quarter as much as it had been falling at Bert's. The store, of course, was closed long since and there were no lights at the storekeeper's house located next door. It would be a shame to waken them, I thought, and decided to plow on toward home. The snow was still over the front bumper, but it was so soft that the truck was able to push it aside with little trouble. Those new knobbies were doing a great job! I had purchased the kind that contained sawdust interspersed with the rubber, a kind I hadn't seen in years.

When I passed the store, I pushed down on the gas pedal because, even though I could not see it, I knew from experience that there was a fairly steep incline coming up; it was a place where one wouldn't wish to become immobile. Once past this particular spot there still were two fairly good-sized hills to pass over before getting into Sundance, twenty miles away.

When the snow stopped the wind picked up, a common condition in that area. Little skiffs at first, then finally a continuous wind, all of which made the road ahead a veritable moving target. The edges of the road were harder and harder to discern, especially between the Tower Junction and the foot of Odin Hill. Once there, however, I could see much better. It probably was because from the foot of Odin Hill to the top of the rise, the terrain formed a kind of canyon that was protected from the wind. Arriving at the top, however, I was greeted full force by a ground blizzard, raging like a stormy sea.

There was less snow on the road now, so the pickup did not have to labor as much. The wind, however, was increasing in strength and pushing the vehicle toward the left side of the road. Occasionally it was necessary to downshift and accelerate in order to return to the center of the road. It continued this way for two or three miles, until I started down the other side of the divide toward Houston Creek. In that area there was protection from the wind for a few miles.

It was now after 10 p.m. and I was beginning to feel tired; there was still another ten miles and Rupp Hill to cross. It was a short hill but rather steep and winding. The ground blizzard proceeded to worsen as I climbed upward. I had to shift down into third gear to make the last mile to the top. Just over the crest, the road curved sharply to the left and then to the right, not really a "hairpin" turn, but sharp and slanted enough to make it easy to slip off either edge of the pavement. I knew this, of course, even though it was hard to see any part of the road at that point. The wind had reduced visibility to approximately twenty feet maximum.

Suddenly, just off the left front fender, a set of lights appeared. Quickly I let up on the gas pedal and started to pump the brakes. The pickup came to a halt beside what looked like an outline of an automobile. When I wound down the window, I saw the car lying on its side at about a forty-five-degree angle. Fortunately, it was on the upper side of the road. If it had been the lower side, it would have slid into a deep draw and likely not been seen for weeks.

Leaving the engine running and the lights on, I set the brake, pulled on my jumper and mittens, grabbed the flashlight, and got out of the pickup. I landed in two feet of snow. The car was only about twenty-five feet away, but it was difficult walking to it in the deep snow and howling wind. By the time I arrived, someone inside was trying to force the left front door open. I grabbed the outside handle and started to pull. Between the two of us, we managed to get the door far enough open for me to see inside. There were four people, two men and two women, inside.

"Are we ever glad to see you!" they shouted in unison.

"Is anyone hurt?" I yelled against the wind.

"We're nearly frozen but not hurt," the driver responded. "We've been here since about nine-thirty this evening."

Following much effort, the two people in the front seat were able to climb out onto the highway. Those in the back then climbed over the front seat and were able to make their exit. They helped each other through the snow to the idling pickup. None had overshoes and they were wearing dress shoes, not boots; the women wore only dress jackets and short skirts; the men wore lightweight suits.

The cab of my 1953, half-ton Ford pickup wasn't made large enough to carry more than three people—even with three it was tight quarters. Now we were five

... but we had to find a way to make do! Fortunately it was only about three miles into town. One of the men opened the right hand door, looked in, and said, "Going to be a tight squeeze, but we'll make it. Jim, you sit in the middle and I'll sit beside you and the girls can sit on our laps." I had already gotten behind the wheel and picked my obstetrical suit up off the floor and placed it behind the seat and out of the way. It was nice and dry and warm when I picked it up off the floor.

As I was tending to this housekeeping chore I glanced over at the man holding the door and giving instructions. What a shock! He must have weighed 300 pounds if he weighed on ounce. Peeking at the other man I realized he was no lightweight slouch, either. Still, we were all in the cab in a few minutes—uncomfortable, but all okay.

Soon the windows steamed up and it was necessary to roll down the window enough to clear the windshield. Then we got underway.

"How did you happen to be out on the road on such a night as this?" I asked.

The big fellow responded that they just had to be in Sheridan for a performance the following evening and that when they left Sundance it was snowing very little. Unfortunately, they had missed the road to Upton—a longer but straighter route. By the time they realized their mistake, there was no place to turn around, and shortly, without the protection of snow tires, their car had slid off the road.

"We thought about trying to walk back to Sundance, but I've always heard a person is much better off staying with the car," the leader continued. "This time it really paid off."

"What are you doing out on the road this time of night and in this kind of weather?" one of the girls asked.

"I'm a veterinarian on my way home from a call," I informed them.

By that time we had reached the edge of town. The few lights we saw were a welcome sight, and when I pulled in front of the only hotel in town, they thanked me profusely.

I never saw or heard from them again. The next day when I returned from that direction after making an early morning call, their car had been removed from the snow bank and was gone.

Oh, yes! Bert's heifer recovered beautifully. "Didn't miss a meal," Bert told me some weeks later when he was in town. His check didn't bounce either!

HAZARDS OF THE TRADE

One of the reasons veterinary medicine is unique among the medical professions is that a practitioner is constantly exposed to the self-protective measures of his patients. Daily he must be on guard against being clawed, bitten, kicked, pawed, jumped on, run over, charged, knocked down, etc., by one of the various animals he encounters on his rounds. In addition to those kinds of hazards, there is always the breakdown at critical moments of restraints, such as chutes, stanchions, ropes, or other mechanical devices, plus those "helpers" who are in the wrong place at the right time when an animal becomes fractious. Physical threats to life and limb are very real, and few practitioners escape entirely.

Exposure to diseases of animals that are transmissible to man also constitute a very real concern for practitioners. These diseases include rabies, undulant fever, leptospirosis, histoplasmosis, and psitticosis, to name just a few.

Fortunately, in the fourteen years of my clinical practice I escaped without a broken bone, and not too many bites or scratches. Of course I had my share of being micturated and defected upon, hissed and growled at, and on occasion scented upon. But all in all, I was luckier than some of my colleagues, though I didn't entirely escape the "fickle finger of fate."

One extremely cold day in February I met my Waterloo. It came one afternoon about four o'clock during the last call of the day. I was vaccinating heifer calves against brucellosis. There was a great deal of snow on the ground. In fact, I had parked my pickup on the county road a mile away from the ranch house. The rancher had met and taken me to the ranch on a sled pulled by a team of horses, the only means of access to the ranch. There were only twenty head of cattle to vaccinate so the task shouldn't have required a lot of time, but the chute was half full of snow and the head catch was not working well. For each animal entering the catch it required several attempts to close and fasten the latch securely; all this activity required time. Because it was so cold and because I was pushing to finish the work before dark, I started to vaccinate one of the heifers before her head was securely caught in the head catch. When I pulled the skin out on the heifer's shoulder with my left hand and started to insert the needle under that skin, the calf reared back and her head hit my hand holding the syringe. The next thing I knew the needle was sticking into the fleshy portion of my left middle finger. My hands were not gloved.

There was no pain particularly, but I remember as if it was yesterday; the sinking feeling in the pit of my stomach. I had just vaccinated myself with brucellosis! I stopped and stared at my hand for a moment and then pulled the needle from my finger. The rancher who was running the head catch noticed the difference in my actions and said, "What's the matter, Doc, something happen to your outfit?" Maybe he thought the needle or syringe had broken.

"Nothing wrong except I just vaccinated myself instead of the heifer," came my reply.

"What'll we do now?" he asked and came around to the side of the chute toward where I was perched.

"Not much we can do here. Just let's finish the last few heifers, then I'll call the doctor in Newcastle when I get back to town. He'll probably get me going on some antibiotics or some other medicine."

It seemed to take forever to finish the last two or three heifers, but we did finally finish and headed back to the pickup. It was a cold, slow ride on the horse-drawn sled and it was nearly dark.

"Sure sorry you got hurt, Doc," Bill said solicitously. "Is there any chance you will get something from the shot?" All the while he was urging the team to a faster pace.

"Depends on how much vaccine went into the finger. It can give a person a dose of undulant fever, especially if he doesn't have any immunity built up against it. I've worked around cattle most of my life, so hopefully I can ward off the disease."

As we neared the truck, the sun dropped over the horizon and the air took on an additional chill—at least I thought it did.

Bill stopped the team, jumped off the sled, and stowed my gear in the box I carried in the bed of the pickup.

"Damn! Doc, I sure hate it you got hurt. You promise to call me as soon as the doctor tells you anything. Sure hope you don't end up getting the Bang's."

"I'll let you know tomorrow how I'm getting along," I promised. "Can't get down for too long, though. I've got a lot more heifers to vaccinate before spring." I'd started the pickup engine and was ready to start home by the time I finished the sentence. It's doubtful that Bill heard the sentence or I'm quite sure he would have told me what to do with those heifers!

It was a good twenty-five miles back to Sundance and it was pitch dark when I walked into the office in the back of the drugstore. My finger was beginning to swell and throb. The pain wasn't acute.

Harriet informed me when I walked through the door that I had a calving call to make thirty-five miles south of Newcastle, about sixty miles south of Sundance.

"Your supper is ready, so I want you to eat before you leave," she stated emphatically. This, before I reached for a bottle of coke and a Milky Way candy bar—my usual fare on short-notice calls. She looked at me intently and said, "You look a little 'white around the gills'. Are you sick?"

"I stuck myself with a needle a couple of hours ago and it's beginning to hurt a little," I admitted.

"Let me see it," she demanded, looking first at one and then the other.

When I extended my hand to show her where the needle had penetrated, the area was already beginning to swell.

"I'll call Ben and tell him you can't possibly come and ask him to get someone out of Lusk to come treat his cow," she announced firmly. "You're going to stay home and soak that hand. I'll call the doctors in Newcastle and see what can be done tonight, then we'll go over in the morning and have them look at it." A no-ifs-ands-or-buts-about-it statement. However, in those days she didn't always have the last say! Before she could reach for the phone to call Ben, I interfered.

"Now then, let's have supper and talk this over," I suggested. "Then we'll decide what's best. You know that it takes several hours before infection sets in after a puncture wound. If the doctors will prescribe some antibiotics now, at least a contaminant might be controlled. If I got a dose of the vaccine, then it's going to take a week at least for undulant fever to develop, and maybe, just maybe, the antibiotics will prevent that occurring, too."

Seeing that Harriet wasn't looking too convinced, I continued, "Why wouldn't it be best if I went on the call and on the way back stop in Newcastle to see one of the doctors? That way we can kill two birds with one stone."

At that point she must have known that she wasn't going to change my mind.

"Okay, but I'm going with you," she insisted. "We'll let one of the girls close the store. I'll bundle up the baby and we'll all go together."

The matter settled, we finished supper, stacked the dishes, gave the girls in the drugstore their instruction, called one of the doctors in Newcastle to ask him to meet us at the hospital emergency room and started on our trip. It was around 8 p.m.

When we arrived at the hospital the doctor was waiting. He proceeded with a normal work-up: getting the history of the accident, taking my temperature, and drawing a blood sample. He prescribed the antibiotic, his choice for treatment of undulant fever. "Soak that hand every two hours," he instructed. "Stay in touch. It might be necessary to alter the treatment if this doesn't do the job."

Harriet seemed somewhat satisfied, so we headed on south to deliver the calf. It took a good little while to travel the thirty-five miles further south, and even more time to deliver the calf. By the time the delivery was completed, my finger was beginning to scream at me. The throbbing was intense and I was glad that it was dark in the cab on our return trip home, dark enough so that Harriet couldn't see my face or she probably should have made me stop at the hospital and stay there rather than return on home. Before we got home, however, she realized I was experiencing great pain because I was driving with one hand and the silence was broken by my occasional groan.

When we arrived at home, I let Harriet and the baby out at the front door and continued to the back of the store. There I garaged the pickup where it would stay for the next two weeks. My hand had swelled to twice its normal size, and the pain was excruciating. The doctor had prescribed Codeine for the pain, but even that gave little relief and the drug made me nauseous. The hot wet soaks Harriet administered every two hours were a nightmare to me. The only relief I seemed to obtain was when I held the hand up in the air at a right angle to the bed; then the pain was just bearable. It was a good week before I could stand without agony.

We kept in contact with the doctor daily. He called me into his office the second week of my illness and drew blood for another blood test to determine whether or not I had contracted undulant fever. Fortunately, the results of the test were negative and the doctor felt fairly certain that I had not contracted it.

The final determination was that I had suffered from an extremely painful tendonitis. When the swelling finally subsided the hand felt normal and there was no loss of function.

Meanwhile, my clients had become anxious for my attention. Many calls had been placed on hold, but the emergencies had had to seek help from other sources. A single-person practice has its drawbacks in that there is no system in place for clients' emergencies. In many instances, great distances created too large an expense for ranchers to use a veterinarian from another location. The results were that ranchers who couldn't adequately handle the situation themselves, or with the help of a neighbor, would shoot the animal rather than tolerate its suffering.

Fortunately, my illnesses were few and far between in the ensuing years, and they never were so severe that I was confined to my bed. Never did I suffer from another injury. Perhaps it's like the old sage: "You know how many times you've been kicked by a horse, but only God knows how many times you haven't been."

THE MOVE

In the fall of 1955 we were offered a satisfactory price for our half of the drugstore and decided to move out of Sundance forthwith.

We had journeyed to Gillette one weekend in search of a suitable house and lot. We hoped to purchase a house situated on enough acres to accommodate a large-animal clinic, which we hoped to build in the not too distant future.

The moving date was set for the day before Thanksgiving and that time was approaching rapidly. Therefore, one day when I passed through Gillette on my return to Sundance, I decided it would be wise to contact the realtor and see if he had had any success in finding a location. We had asked him to do so on a previous occasion. Fortunately, he had located a site and we went together to have a look from a distance. Harriet had not seen the inside of the house but I had, on another trip. I knew she would love it, so I contracted for its purchase on the spot. The ten-acre parcel of land was located on the very edge of town, with the house, garage, and quasi-barn/storage building situated in the center of the lot.

When moving day arrived, we decided that Harriet would stay in Sundance to oversee the furniture loaded into the moving van, then lock the Sundance house and follow the truck and furniture to Gillette. There I was to meet her early in the afternoon at the new house; I was to vaccinate calves that morning.

As often happens, there was a glitch or two in carrying out our well laid out plans. First, the single trucker in Sundance (Bill) owned only one truck—a diesel tractor-trailer at least ten years old. He used it most of the time to haul livestock, but in the offseason, like at that time of year, any kind of hauling was welcome. He had been recommended to us as adequate to haul what little furniture we had to move.

As it happened, the day before our move Bill had been called to carry a late shipment of lambs to market in St. Onze, South Dakota. It was only a fifty-mile haul but his truck had broken down and it had required most of the day to get it moving again. As a result, he arrived home late in the evening and the lambs had been in his truck for at least six hours.

Harriet became anxious when Bill didn't show up at the designated hour of 9 a.m., so she decided to give him a call. When she found that he was still in bed, she knew immediately that she was in for a bad day. Finally at ten o'clock he arrived in his old rig and said he was ready to go. Harriet went outside to direct the trailer as it backed to the door from which the furniture was to be loaded onto the truck. Once in place, Bill raised the tailgate and what a sight! It was obvious that he had not cleaned away the sheep manure from yesterday's haul, or perhaps even from before then! Just as bad, he had not removed the double-deck platform, either. The platform, made up of 2" x 12" x 7' planks, was arranged in channel iron that ran the full length of the trailer, about halfway up its side. This allowed for carrying twice the number of animals as would otherwise be possible; it also made it impossible to load anything over three feet in height.

There was nothing to do but get rid of the platform and as much manure as possible, since it was too late to get another mover out of Spearfish, South Dakota, some thirty miles away. Loading was finally finished about two o'clock in the afternoon and the old tractor departed for Gillette, belching black smoke from both its stacks.

Harriet was to follow with our two-year-old son Harry and our Boxer dog Sam. As I had the pickup in Gillette, she had to drive the old second-hand Jeep we had purchased from the REA some months earlier. The Jeep wasn't too road worthy; the heater didn't work well, and the floorboards were in such poor condition that one could see the road passing underneath the vehicle. The cold weather was great for consolidating the sheep droppings in the moving truck, but was miserable for Harriet and a child and short-haired dog. Nevertheless, she made the trip in good shape, and for her a memorable one.

It was also later than planned when I drove up to the new house that afternoon. Harriet and Bill were already there unloading the trailer. A neighbor lady, Jean Hadley, who with her husband, Dr. Frank Hadley, and family became lifelong friends, greeted us and took Harry into her home while we unloaded. While Bill and I lugged the furniture in, Harriet stood inside the door and wiped the manure off the legs of chairs and tables before we placed them on the floor. We finished just as darkness descended.

After Bill left, and we had Harry settled in for the night, we had a good chance to walk around and examine our "little house on the prairie." This was the first time Harriet had really seen the inside and it was only my second inspection. We liked what we saw, and Thanksgiving Day found us happy and thankful for our blessings.

Even though we did some remodeling to the house in the nine and one half years we lived there, we still loved it when we left Gillette.

PART II
THE GILLETTE YEARS

GILLETTE: THE SCENE

So Harriet and I, our son Harry, and our Boxer dog Sam had arrived that day before Thanksgiving, 1955. At that time, our ten acres included a white bungalow with green trim, a white stucco, a detached garage, and a red shed further up the hill to the west that once held a horse or a pony. We were located just outside the city limits of Gillette on what is called the 4J Road, named after a ranch further down the country.

Gillette, named after a surveyor who helped lay out the railroad through that country, probably had a population of close to 5,000 or better souls when we moved there. It is the county seat of Campbell County, which covers 120 miles north to south and 60 miles east to west. The county had several post offices at the time, but Gillette was the only town or city. Recluse, Spotted Horse, Wildcat, Rozet, Rocky Point, and Weston, on the Little Powder River Road, are but a few of the places that had post offices, sometimes with a general store and/or a gas station and a schoolhouse.

Cattle and sheep ranching and the services associated with them provided the main income for the area. Thus, the Gillette Livestock Exchange, operated by Homer and DeLoss Hockett, and the Chicago, Burlington, and Quincy Railroad were integral parts of the community, since one sold much of the livestock produced and the other hauled them away, mostly to eastern markets. Gillette then was basically a "cow town." The discovery of oil, the prospecting for uranium, and the expansion of coal mining in the county would bring tremendous changes a few years down the road.

Building a clinic to accommodate both small and large animals was one of the conditions Harriet and I set for ourselves when we decided to move to Gillette from Sundance. With only a couple in the state at that time, it seemed the way to go. In addition, four and one-half years of fighting the roads at Sundance provided the resolve! For the first spring of our practice at Gillette we wanted something ready to handle cows and heifers having difficulty calving. We reasoned, correctly, that during the spring calving season I could in no way cover the whole county plus parts of three other counties. The next closest veterinary practice was 60 miles to the west, at Buffalo, 75 miles to the east, at Sundance, 100 miles or more to the south, at Casper, and Miles City, Montana, to the north. In my judgment, calving cases could be hauled to a clinic without undue stress or harm, and at the clinic I could do a better job than in ranch settings. That judgment proved correct, too, with few exceptions. Such exceptions included wild or fractious patients and, of course, "downer" animals, worked on so long they couldn't get up by themselves but had to be loaded on a truck with a tractor.

Lining up financing for our clinic was our initial challenge. The only lending agencies at the time—The Stockmen's Bank at Gillette and a savings and loan at Sheridan where we got our loan for the house and land—either weren't chartered to make loans for such a facility or didn't have the money. We were stumped for awhile until we talked to our builder, who later became our great and good friend, and our first employee, Pete Bertoncelj.

"Why don't you go down and talk with Bill and Sally Underwood at the lumber yard?" Pete suggested after we revealed our dilemma to him. "I'll bet they can find someone to 'stake' you. Hell, maybe they will themselves. They know how bad this town and county have been trying to get a vet to locate here!"

After a visit to the yard and a little palaver, we struck a deal whereby they would supply the building materials so long as we paid something on the bill, no interest. As it turned out, they gave us a ten percent discount if we paid something on the bill each month. The only thing we had to cover then was the day wages for Pete and whoever he needed to help. We figured we "couldn't beat that deal with a stick!" We surely didn't make out that well in the many years that followed.

Anyway, the foundation was poured by the end of January, in spite of some pretty cold weather, and we held an open house on March 17, 1956 (St. Patrick's Day). We made it in time for the first spring calving season and, boy oh boy did we ever need it! I don't think I made a dozen ranch calls between mid-March and the end of May, at least not to handle dystocias. The ranching community responded to the service as if had always been there. Harriet and I had fulfilled another dream.

At that time, Gillette had been in existence only about sixty-four years, by our reckoning, the first post office opening in 1891. Thus, in relative age to say, Virginia or Massachusetts, in one sense Gillette wasn't even a teen-ager, though it had some of their ways! Quite a few of the older people in the area could remember when that part of the country was "opened up." And, as far as I could tell from talking with them, I was the first graduate veterinarian to settle in the town and county. Some laymen had helped out in emergencies, and at least one graduate veterinarian who was stationed there worked for the federal government. But he was soon transferred. Then, of course, veterinarians from Sheridan, Casper, or Sundance serviced the area when called. Because of the distances and costs, folks themselves usually took care of all but the most important aspects of animal health and care. Veterinarians in general were in short supply with only thirty-three in the entire State of Wyoming!

By law, the saleyard was required to have a veterinarian present at every sale. That had been handled by my brother-in-law, Dr. Rodney Port, who lived in Sundance, with other vets filling in as necessary. Since various livestock and farming groups in the county had been actively seeking a veterinarian to locate there permanently, Harriet and I were received with the utmost welcome and we never had reason to regret the move.

Because of the location of the clinic (about a hundred feet away from the house, up the hill to the west), the difference in terrain and the difference in ranching operations from what we had been used to at Sundance, many of our experiences were different, also. Our daughter Jen was born in Gillette, and she and our son Harry got a lot of their formative training there. Through their antics, their parents got some training as well!

We stayed in Campbell County nine and one-half years. During that time, we added onto the house and the clinic, and employed another full-time veterinarian, first Dr. Deloyd Anderson, now in Afton, Wyoming, then Dr. Donald Dunbar, who owned the clinic for several years before selling it. (I understand it's still operating today as part of a larger service, by the way.) Also, during that time, I was appointed to the Campbell County Memorial Hospital Board and elected to the Campbell County High School Board. We were active in Holy Trinity Episcopal Church. At the state level, I was first a member and then Chairman of the Wyoming State Board of Veterinary Medical Examiners.

We left Gillette the summer of 1964 for me to attend Colorado State University, where I earned a Masters Degree and then went on to a whole different aspect of veterinary medicine with the U.S. Food and Drug Administration. For Harriet and me, however, the Gillette years were some of our happiest and most memorable times, even with its ups and downs. To be sure, there were many more ups than downs!

WITH FRIENDS LIKE THAT

This story is about Bill Hartley, a well-known livestock trader in the Gillette area. Veterinarians have a lot of contact with livestock traders because many of the animals that are bought and sold must be inspected or tested before they are moved from one state to another.

I first met Bill when I was a substitute saleyard veterinarian while Harriet and I still lived in Sundance. After we moved to Gillette, he was one of our first clients. Bill was of medium height (maybe six-feet tall) with a big belly and a fat face, and like most traders, he always greeted me with a quip. But more so than most, he loved to make and play jokes. Even when things should have been serious, he would make light of it. Harriet and I had not been in town more than two weeks when we had occasion to feel the effect of his jest.

Unknown to us initially, our Boxer dog Sam started running over to town, about a half-mile away. He'd sneak off when we weren't looking, and for awhile we didn't know where he had gone. Before long, however, it became abundantly clear.

"Doctor, this is the Reverend Stanley," the caller announced. "I have a little dog that just got his leg broken. Can I bring it right out?"

"Sure, bring him along and we'll see what we can do," I responded. At that time, I was examining and treating small animal patients in the basement of our house, using the washer and dryer tops as an examination table. When I hung up and told Harriet what was coming, she suggested, "Better get Sam tied up. You know how he acts when there's a strange dog around."

I immediately went out to do it but Sam wasn't there. Neither did he come when I called. I didn't think much about it except for the thought that at least he wouldn't be around when the minister arrived with his dog.

As it turned out, the little dachshund had a simple fracture of the right rear leg that wouldn't take long to fix, once I got him under anesthesia. "How did it happen?" I asked the preacher, who was not very talkative for a "man of the cloth."

"I don't know for sure," he said. "About an hour ago, we let him out to run a little and when he came back, he was hurt like this. Maybe he was hit by a car; I don't know."

The fracture reduced very nicely, and I had a splint just the right size, so we were loading the sleepy dog back in the car within forty-five minutes.

"Keep him covered up well until you get home, then place him near some heat—the furnace would be good if you have one," I answered. "He should be awake in a couple of hours. If anything concerns you, call back; otherwise bring him back in a month for a checkup. Maybe we can take the cast off then, too."

"Okay, Doctor, how much do I owe you?" the minister asked as he reached for his pocketbook.

"Ten dollars will do." Normally I charged at least fifteen dollars, but I gave the reverend a "professional discount."

Less than an hour later, Reverend Stanley called back. "I just got through talking with my neighbor, Bill Hartley. He said he was looking out the window when my dog got hurt, and he said it was your dog that did it," he claimed.

I didn't know just how to respond to this news, but Harriet said afterward that I babbled something like "Dogs will be dogs." Whatever I said did not satisfy Mr. Stanley.

"What do you intend to do about it?" he asked with some hostility in his voice.

Again, I don't know what I said, but it must not have satisfied him because it took a good five years before he ever spoke anything more than a cursory word or two whenever we met. Within a couple of days, however, I got the full story of what Bill told the preacher.

Bill had driven out to our house to get me to go to the railroad yards to look at a shipment of calves he had purchased to send to Iowa. As he was ready to leave, he started to laugh. "Say, Doc, has my neighbor, the Reverend Stanley, called you lately?"

I knew by his laugh and the sound of his voice, he had been "up to no good!"

"Yes, he's been out here with his dog. He also said you told him our dog was the one that broke his dog's leg," I stated, knowing I was about to hear the whole story.

Bill threw back his head and roared with laughter. "Well, your dog did break his dog's leg, but he deserved it. I was looking out the window when it all happened. Your dog was trotting up the middle of the street minding his own business and that little mutt of his went out and started chasing him, yapping and nipping at your dog's heels. Pretty soon I saw your dog stop, grab his dog by the scruff of the neck, and toss him up in the air. When he came down, he broke his leg."

"What's so funny about that?" I inquired innocently.

"I told the reverend what happened, but then I added that you let your dog run loose just to drum up business for yourself. I didn't think he would believe it, but evidently he does," Bill acknowledged. "I'm sure sorry." He kept on laughing and every chance he got afterward, especially in my presence. He told the story over and over again.

As the old saying goes: "With friends like that, who needs enemies?"

BLUETONGUE

"We didn't have all these crazy diseases around here 'till we had graduate vets running around. That's the trouble. There's nothing wrong with our sheep other than that!"

Those were the words of a grizzled sheep rancher, with a few drinks in him, sitting on the floor in front of the dais where the state veterinarian had just finished speaking. The subject was the real possibility that sheep from our part of the state would be embargoed by other states because of bluetongue, a contagious and infectious disease caused by a virus. The meeting room was crowded to overflowing, with folks standing along the wall and sitting on the floor. It was hot in there, too—no such thing as air conditioning. And the weather had been unusually warm for fall. Like the grizzled rancher, a goodly number of others had been in town since mid-morning for the one o'clock meeting. The bars had obviously done a good business!

The outbreak had started sometime in July. That's about the time I began to get some rather oblique questions about lame sheep and sheep with "snotty noses." Questions like, "Doc, have you heard of anything going around among sheep? Jim, my neighbor, has got some that are acting kinda funny. Lay down a lot. When they get up they're lame. Their noses are dirty too." Or: "Doc, I hear tell there's quite a few sheep in the country with worms in their heads. Frank, my neighbor, took some sick ewes to a vet in Montana, and he diagnosed it as that. They're treating them now. Have you heard of it?"

I had been asked those or similar questions for almost a month. Each time I responded, "No. I haven't seen any sick sheep this summer. I have heard some talk, but no one has brought any in for me to look at."

A week or two would go by and the same roundabout queries would surface. Finally, late one afternoon, a young rancher brought a couple of bucks into the clinic for me to look at. One was obviously lame, though I could find no lesions to account for it. He lay down every chance he got. Though he was young, he was in poor flesh. When I offered him some good-looking alfalfa hay, he ate it with seeming relish, but from a recumbent position. The other buck was not lame but

183

had ulcers on his tongue and dental pad and quite a discharge from both nostrils. He was somewhat thin and didn't eat the alfalfa offered him.

Here were two animals from the same group of twenty bucks, each showing different signs of a disease. The rancher said a few more bucks were sick, too. He just brought these in for me to see if I could figure out what was wrong. Some in the ewe flock out on the range were acting like the bucks.

At last, I was having a look at some specimens, but the examination made no sense. "Just leave them here with me for a few days," I said to the sheepman. "I need to observe them awhile longer and maybe take some samples to send to the lab. By the way, have you lost any?"

"We've lost one or two ewes this summer that we counted, but that's not unusual. Whatever it is doesn't seem to kill them, but just knocks off their flesh as if they were starving. There's plenty of grass, so that can't be it. Some say the grass is tough, though, because of the dry weather we had earlier. But I don't believe that. Others figure they're eating a weed that's making them this way. I don't know what to think; that's why I brought these two in. Hopin' you could tell me what it is." He looked at me intently.

"I'll let you know in a day or two what I think, then we'll go from there," I offered, continuing to look at the two animals and dredging my mind for a clue. As soon as he left, and I got water and feed in front of them for the night, I headed into the office and the books.

I had only one book on sheep diseases, which I believe was the only one available at the time. In other texts, sheep diseases were treated as those concerning infectious, parasitic, poisonous plants, and so on. I was still studying them when Harriet called on the intercom and told me supper was ready.

"Who brought in those sheep?" Harriet asked while I was in the bathroom washing up. "I saw you out the window but couldn't recognize the pickup."

"That was Bob Bently. You know, Hap Bently's son. He brought in a couple of bucks for me to look at. You know, I've mentioned to you that there's something going on with the sheep in the country, but I didn't know what it was because I hadn't seen any. Well, now I've got a couple and still don't know what it is. I was studying the books when you called."

"What does it sound like, offhand?" she pursued.

"Well, if it's an infectious disease and I had to say something, I would think hard about a disease called bluetongue. Trouble is that neither buck has the same signs, and neither fit the book description of the condition. If I put together the signs I'm seeing in both animals, they would more or less fit the textbook, but I still have to try and rule out poisonous plants, too. I'll go back to the books after supper."

After supper, when the dishes had been put into the washer, the kids had been put to bed, and Harriet had gotten settled behind the desk to do some accounting, I went back to the clinic to study some more. I concentrated on the symptoms a sheep would show when exposed to various poisonous plants: St. John's wort, sneezeweed, rattlebox, corncockle, bluebonnet, jimsonweed. The bucks had symptoms produced by exposure to some of these plants, but I thought it was unlikely such poisonous plants would be as widespread as I was hearing this condition to be. It just had to be something else!

The book included nothing on parasites that even remotely fit the signs I saw. I went back to the books describing infectious diseases and read and reread the section on bluetongue. It was the closest thing to what I was seeing, but it really didn't fit either. Putting the books away, I went down to the house at close to ten o'clock. Harriet was just about through when I walked in.

"Have you figured it out yet?" she asked, looking up at me.

"Like I said at supper, I think it is bluetongue, but the only way to tell for sure is to do some animal inoculation work. Transfer blood from a sick animal to a well, non-exposed animal, and see what happens. I'll call the lab at Laramie in the morning and see if they will send someone to look over this thing with me and take some samples back. There's no way I can do the necessary testing here."

"That sounds like a good idea," Harriet replied, closing the journal and getting up from the desk. "Let's have a cup of tea. It'll make you sleep better. If I know you, you'll be tossing and turning all night, trying to figure this one out!"

By the time the state lab opened at eight the next morning, I had re-examined the bucks as well as taken care of the other animals in the clinic. John Wright, the laboratory director, answered after the first ring. "Good morning, Bob," he responded after I identified myself. "What can I help you with today?" John was always accommodating and willing to help every way he could.

"Well, Dr. Wright (I always called him Dr. Wright rather than using his first name, because some way it seemed more correct), I've got a problem up here with sheep." I then described the signs in the two bucks, plus what I had heard described by ranchers.

"I think it might be bluetongue," I concluded. "Have you heard of bluetongue being diagnosed in the state?"

John didn't respond immediately, and I thought for a second we might have been disconnected. "Hello! Hello!" I hollered into the mouthpiece.

"I'm still here," Dr. Wright said in a quiet voice. "I was just thinking if we ever had it reported before. I guess probably we haven't, at least in the past fifteen years since I've been here. In fact, I have even forgotten what the books say about it."

"Well, I'm wondering if you can send Harold Breen up here. Between the two of us, we should have a better idea what it might be."

"Yes, I can send him. He's just back from another trip, but I'm sure he won't mind coming. If you don't hear from me by afternoon, you'll know he is on his way. Should be in there by five or six tonight."

"Sounds good to me. He can stay here if he wants. There's plenty of motel space available if he doesn't want to."

"He'll no doubt stay at a motel, but we appreciate the offer."

I turned to Harriet and gave her the gist of the telephone call. "I hope someone else calls in before he gets here. I'd like to see a couple of flocks while he is here," I said, and, fortunately, that's just what happened.

"Doc, this is Dan Mackay." The voice coming over the telephone wires was familiar. Dan had a ranch up along the Little Powder River, and ran both sheep and cattle. "Got something wrong with the sheep. If you'll be there, I'll bring in three or four."

"I'll be here as far as I know, at least until noon," I responded. "What do you think is wrong with them?" I figured I'd get a fun response from Dan.

"Hell! I don't know what's wrong with them. That's why I'm bringing them in for you to look at!" came Dan's half-indignant reply. "If you want to know how they're actin', I can tell you that. Most lay around a lot and are lame in one or two feet when you get them up. Others have snotty noses. All of them are losing flesh. Does that tell you anything?"

"Yes, it does," I answered after suppressing a chuckle. "Tell you what. I've got another veterinarian coming up from the state diagnostic laboratory at Laramie. He'll be here this afternoon. We're going to be looking at some other sheep, and would just as soon see them under their normal range conditions if possible. We will come by your place, if you want, rather than have you bring them in. It will be tomorrow, though."

"That sound's good to me, Doc, as long as it doesn't cost too much. I'm busy putting up the last of the hay and hate to take out time to come in anyway. Do you have any idea what time you'll be here? I'll have to take you over to the pasture where they're at."

"I'll have Harriet call Blanch in the morning and tell her what time you can expect us. We have another place to go before we get to you."

"Okay, Doc, we'll see you tomorrow then."

Now, besides Bob Bentley's flock to look at, we would have Dan Mackay's. Both places were north of town so I expected to be able to make them in one day.

It was close to four-thirty when Dr. Breen drove into the yard of the clinic in a green pickup with the State of Wyoming decals on the doors and a stock rack on. "What have you got up here that you want me to look at?" Harold asked.

"I've got two bucks here in the clinic," I answered as I led the way through the garage door and on into the large animal section. "They came in yesterday. We can look at them now. Then, tomorrow, I've got the flock they came out of to go see, plus another one not too far away. Harriet will have supper ready about five-thirty. So if you don't feel like looking at the bucks until after that, we can wait until after we eat. I know what it's like after a long drive to have to go right to work."

"Let's examine them now," Harold responded. "Then we can relax and talk about it after supper."

After Dr. Breen retrieved his bag from the pickup and we got the animals restrained, he set to work going over every inch of each buck: listening to their lungs with his stethoscope; opening their mouths for a look at the mucosa and tongue; feeling the skin above the hooves for signs of tenderness; peering into each nostril with his ophthalmoscope. Finally, after he finished with the last one, he said, "Let him up, Bob. I'm ready to wash up and have some of Harriet's cooking."

"What do you make of it?" I asked, kind of pushing him a little for his diagnosis, or a confirmation of mine.

"I just don't know this minute. I'd rather wait to see what we find tomorrow."

I knew Dr. Breen well enough to know there was no use talking about it anymore for now. Veterinarians have a way of going silent when they are not sure what they are dealing with and want to sort things out. In administrative circles, this is called indecision, and is frowned upon. In scientific circles, it is called considering all aspects of a problem, and is lauded.

When we finished cleaning up and went to the house, Harriet and Harold greeted one another like long-lost friends, talking about the last vet meeting and, of course, the kids: our two and his four. As usual, Harriet had a great supper, and the kids enjoyed having company who would banter with them. Because it had been a long day for him, Dr. Breen left for his motel room soon after supper. We planned to leave at seven the next morning to visit the ranches in order to get as much done as possible before the heat of the day. It didn't work out that way, but we tried! We even arranged it so Harold would pick me up at six-thirty and we would eat downtown. That would save time, and would save Harriet the hassle of breakfast.

The next morning a nice breeze was blowing to take away some of the sun's
heat. Dr. Breen and I had breakfast at the Goings Hotel before heading out in his
pickup. The first stop at about eight o'clock was at Bob Bentley's, thirty miles to
the northeast after twenty-five miles of dirt road. Bob was glad to see us and had
four or five more bucks in a shed for us to look at. Some had developed the malady since he brought in the others. We examined them and they showed no more
nor less than the two at the clinic.

"Let's get a look at the ewes on the range," Dr. Breen directed, obviously as
confused as the night before.

"You follow me," Bob replied. "They're about two miles up the road from
here."

Because of the dust, we drove some distance behind him until finally arriving
at a wire gate, which he let down for us. A few ewes with their lambs were in
sight. After Bob closed the gate, he came to the window on my side of the
pickup. "Best we go over to where they water. There should be more around
there than anyplace else, even though it's still early for them to be very thirsty.
Just follow me."

Again we took off after him through the flying dust. Before we got to the
windmill, Bob slowed down and stuck his hand out the window, pointing at a
ewe and a lamb. They had been lying down but jumped up as we came close. The
ewe seemed to travel all right, but the lamb had a noticeable limp and wanted to
carry a front leg. Bob drove on to the watering area, which consisted of a tank
under the windmill into which water ran from a pipe coming out of the well.
There must have been twenty-five ewes with their lambs lying there or grazing
close by. We shut off the engines and watched them for a minute or two.

The half-dozen grazing ones appeared quite normal. No lameness. No apparent "snotty" noses. We got out of the pickups and wandered toward those lying
down. They stared at us for a minute, then jumped up and started to run away. A
good half of the lambs and some of the ewes were noticeably lame in one or two
feet. "Let's catch one or two!" Harold exclaimed. "As lame as they are, we
shouldn't have much trouble!"

With that he took off running in the direction of what looked like the one
most easy to grab. Bob and I each started after another one. Well, it turned out
we were able to get hold of only one, and then only by pooling our efforts. We
were winded, sweaty, and dirty by the time we caught that one! The others
seemed to "warm out" of their lameness or stiffness or whatever you wanted to

call it. Anyway, they were over the nearby hill and long gone, which ended the chase at the Bently ranch.

After regaining his composure, Harold conducted the same thorough examination of the lamb as he had given the bucks. And he didn't find anything more than was evident in the bucks. "Do you mind if I take this lamb back to Laramie with me?" he asked, looking at Bob. "We will need to do some laboratory work on this condition, and it's best to use fresh specimens rather than something that has post-mortem changes."

Bob thought a minute. "Sure, take him with you. If we can find out what it is, it will be worth it. Maybe we can find something to treat it with if we know what it is. I don't mind treating them if it will do any good, but when you have to handle six hundred head, you kind of like to think you're doing something to help them; otherwise, you might better leave them alone. In fact, I noticed a couple of old ewes that were off-feed and sore-footed a week ago, but now they seem to be doing all right."

"Well, I appreciate your giving us the lamb. Maybe I can get a ewe someplace else," Dr. Breen answered as he went around to the cab of the pickup. "By the way, I need to get a history of your flock." He pulled a clipboard off the seat and began to ask Bob about the flock: how many ewes, how many bucks, lambing percentage in the spring, worming history, past illnesses, and on and on. It took about a half-hour before Harold had all the information he wanted. "That'll do it," he stated when he got Bob's response to his last question. Then he turned to me and said, "Doc, where do we go from here?"

I glanced at my watch; it was 11:30. If we kept going, we could be at the Mackays' by 12:30 at the latest. "Well, we go back to the road and head north," I answered, not wanting to say in front of Bob exactly where. Breaking a confidence was the last thing a veterinarian or any other professional wanted to do. After we thanked Bob again for the lamb, I said, "I'll call you when I want you to come after the bucks at the clinic. I'd just as soon watch them for a few more days. By that time, the lab may have something for us, too."

When we got back to the road, I pointed to the direction we'd have to take to get to the Mackays'.

"Have you seen anything so far to make things gel?" I asked.

"Not particularly. There's definitely something up here all right, but it's like a shadow, so far," he explained. "Certainly, I've never seen anything like it before, and I've been looking at sick animals all over this state in the last eight years. Right now, your guess is as good as mine."

We were winging along about fifty miles an hour, and we soon came to a crossroads where I told him to go left again. We arrived at the Mackay ranch just as Dan came out of the house from dinner. "Hey!" he shouted from the porch after we got stopped. "Just in time for a bite to eat. Blanche is just cleaning off the table, but there's plenty left. Come on in!"

We protested in the name of time and bother, but he would have none of it. "Ya gotta eat somewhere. Might as well be here! Besides, I don't care for leftovers. If you don't eat, I'll have the same thing for supper I just had for lunch." Then he tipped back his head and laughed heartily at his own joke.

The time was not wasted anyway because as we were eating, Dr. Breen got the history of the flock; therefore, when we got ready to leave and he pulled out his clipboard to fill in the form, it didn't take long.

At the Mackay ranch we saw the same thing we had seen at the Bentleys'. This time, after much chasing, Harold tripped over a sagebrush and fell down, but he got hold of an old ewe. Dan told us we could have her to take to Laramie. When we finished and were heading down the road, I turned to Dr. Breen and said, "I'm glad we don't have any other place to go. I haven't run this much since I delivered milk as a kid."

He laughed. "You can say that again. The next time you call me to come up to help you, I'm going to make sure someone has a horse with which to chase animals. Most of the time all I need is to step out of the pickup with the post-mortem instruments and go to work!"

When we got back to the clinic, we unloaded the ewe and lamb and settled them in for the night. We checked the bucks, too. They both had eaten the hay and grain I had given them in the morning, and their water buckets were empty. Otherwise, the signs they showed the previous day were still there. Again, Harriet had a good supper for us. We retired to the clinic after we finished eating, to go over the histories in detail and to hit the books.

"You still don't think it could be bluetongue?" I asked Harold, again.

"No, I don't. Look at the book. It says they show the following signs: respiratory distress (panting). Hell, we didn't see any panting until we started to chase them, then we were panting too! Hyperemia (swelling) of the muzzle, lips and ears. There might be a little, but hardly noticeable. Elevation of body temperature. I haven't seen that either, but you said one of the bucks had a temperature of 106 when Bob brought him in. Depression. We haven't seen that either. Ulcers of the dental pad. The one buck you have here and the old ewe from the Mackays' show some ulceration; the others don't. I'm not sure but what you could find that percentage in any bunch of sheep at random. Swollen and cyanotic tongue. Again, the only things that had blue tongues were you and I after that last chase! Lameness. That we have seen, but you could hardly make a definitive diagnosis based on that. The only thing that's going to tell us what is going on is a series of tests at the lab. Thank goodness we will have live animals to get specimens from."

I couldn't refute Dr. Breen's logic, but something wouldn't let my mind get away from Bluetongue. I didn't pursue the subject further, however, because it was getting late and I had a telephone call to return before going to bed. "What time do you want to leave in the morning?" I asked Harold as I closed the books and put them away.

"The earlier the better. Probably by six at the latest. I'll eat at the hotel before I come up to get the ewe and the lamb. If you're not up, I'll just load them myself and take off. No need to get Harriet and the kids up that early."

"I'll be up, so don't worry. I won't meet you at the hotel, however. Got a little behind today, so have to catch up tomorrow."

A week later I got a call from Dr. Breen. "Nothing definite showing up so far in the tests. We took blood from both the ewe and the lamb and injected it into two normal healthy sheep. They don't show anything so far. We've got a call in to the federal laboratory at Fort Collins. They're studying bluetongue down there. On the chance it might be that, we thought it wouldn't hurt to talk with them. If there is any change after that discussion, we'll call you back. Otherwise, we'll just send you a report of our findings after we have completed all the tests. Sorry we can't be of more help, but that's the way it is sometimes."

I was a little downhearted, but from previous experiences I had learned that in the biological area many times there are no quick answers to the problems you encounter in the field. Sometimes, it's years before a disease entity is researched enough to determine a cause and give it a name.

When I told Harriet, she said, "I'll bet you're right. Surely the federal lab will be able to tell them something. Don't be too disappointed; you know how long it takes to get answers."

I left on a call south of town and when I returned three hours later Harriet told me to call Laramie. Harold had called about an hour earlier and had some more information for me, but didn't say what.

"Doc, I may have some good news for you. We talked with Fort Collins, and Dr. Hager, the chief in charge of the bluetongue project, told us we didn't go far enough in our testing. He said we needed to take blood from the normal sheep we injected with the blood from the sick ones I brought down. In ten days, inject their blood into two more normal sheep. If it is bluetongue, they would show signs of the disease. It seems the virus builds up enough to give the second-pass sheep the disease without the first-pass ones showing any signs. It's been just ten days since we started the process, so we are going on with it as soon as I hang up. We'll call you back in another week or whenever something shows up. Dr. Hager says it will take about that long. By the way, if it turns out to be bluetongue, he wants to go up and have a look. He said he would get clearance from the state veterinarian first, however."

Harriet happened to come up to the clinic about the time I hung up. She could tell from the look on my face that something had changed from Dr. Breen's previous call. After I told her what was happening, she exclaimed, "I bet they'll find out you were right. I can just feel it!"

"Well, if I am, I've got to start thinking about how to handle the thing, countywide. I know there is a vaccine for its prevention, but if that's what it is, there are a lot of sheep that have had it and are getting over it. To make matters worse, here we are coming up on the season to ship lambs to other states for feeding. Those states may not let them enter. I'll have to get in touch with the state veterinarian, too. It's a reportable disease and he'll have to inform other sates. What a mess!"

Within a week, Harold called me again. He was laughing.

"Bob, are you sure you didn't miss your calling? You must be psychic or something! The second two sheep are both showing lameness and both have ulcers on their dental pads. Their ears and muzzle are swelled, too. We just talked with Dr. Hager, and he says there is no doubt it's bluetongue. We also called the state veterinarian. You know we have to on a reportable disease. He's going to be contacting you."

I couldn't help but feel happy that I was correct about the diagnosis, but I had been thinking about the consequences. I was glad the state veterinarian had been informed and was going to call me. All of a sudden it ceased to be a private practitioner problem alone. It had become a regulatory one.

For a number of weeks, thereafter, I wore two hats: one, that of a deputy state veterinarian; the other, a private practitioner. Before it was over, I wished they had been hard hats!

The old story about the king's messenger was never more truly depicted than in what happened following the diagnosis of this outbreak. Suddenly, many people who wanted to know what was wrong with their sheep before the confirmed diagnosis, "didn't want to hear it" afterward. Some, liked the grizzled rancher at the meeting, were openly hostile.

What finally happened was this: the state veterinarian contacted the states surrounding Wyoming, as well as the states like Illinois and Iowa, where a goodly number of our lambs went to be fattened. All said they would not place an embargo on Wyoming sheep from our part of the state, provided they were vaccinated under the supervision of a veterinarian. The state veterinarian visited the area and held a public meeting with the ranchers informing them of that fact. Following that, we spent the next month getting in vaccine from all over the country and visiting ranches where the sheep were being processed—first, to make sure the vaccination was being done; and second, to answer questions and help overcome any problems that occurred. Fortunately, the hostility level was not as high when we visited the ranches as it had been at the meeting. Still, in many cases, you felt that the usual veterinarian-client relationship was strained.

This turned out to be an excellent training experience for me in my later role as a full-time regulator. First, even though you work diligently, using the latest scientific techniques and diagnostic abilities, you can't for one minute believe the truth will be gratefully accepted! Second, if you have bad news to convey, try to do it one on one. If at all possible, avoid making the news known in a public meeting where there are not enough seats on a hot day with no air conditioning. Try to hold such meetings in the morning, certainly not later than one hour after the bars open! Lastly, even though you completely wear out a five-year old vehicle (purchased second-hand three years previously) running up and down the road doing your duty, don't replace it with a new or another second-hand one for at least six months after an emotionally charged episode. Make it do or park it!

That was quite an outbreak, but when it was all over, we still had not seen one sheep with a blue tongue. But then, misnomers are not uncommon in medical literature!

THE DOG CATCHER

I learned the hard way about the changeability of public opinion. Of all things it happened over an incident with a dog catcher.

After we got our clinic built at Gillette, I was approached by one of the city council members about the possibility of using some of our dog facilities for housing strays picked up by the dog catcher. The pound then in use was little more than a set of old unheated buildings near the dump, and folks were beginning to complain about holding unwanted animals in such a place—even if it was just for a few days before unclaimed animals were shot.

Along with the request for housing, the council wanted me to put to sleep by lethal injection the animals not claimed in a certain number of days. They thought it was better than shooting, since folks were getting so they "didn't cotton" to that anymore. The city would pay me so much a day for board plus a fee for euthanizing the "unwanteds."

Harriet and I talked it over for several days. We didn't like the idea of associating a hospital with pound-like activities, but it was the middle of the winter and the city was not about to build a heated shelter for stray dogs and cats. Then, too, we had heard what happened from time to time during the shootings, so we felt we should take on the council's request, at least until they got public support to construct proper facilities.

All went well the first winter. The number of animals brought in by the various and sundry dog catchers was not great enough to overload the facilities, and no "wanted" animals were put to sleep. We even managed, through the help of the radio station, to place a number of animals into good homes. People concerned with animal welfare thought we were doing a real service for the community. However, spring came, and with it came problems.

First, the number of animals running loose in town grew exponentially. Although folks did a good job of confining and caring for their animals in winter, they didn't want to keep them cooped up when it got warm.

Second, the man who worked as dog catcher during the winter had quit and the city had hired a fellow who was afraid of animals. The city had a hard time keeping anyone in the job. It had issued two sizes of nets on the end of six-foot poles for the dog catcher to use in capture. If you've never tried to catch a frightened and fleeing dog or cat with a net on the end of a pole, try it! Now, someone who is scared of animals is not the best candidate for a job as dog catcher. Nonetheless, the council was desperate and acted against its best collective judgment. Before long the council knew "it wasn't going to work!"

After about a month on the job, the dog catcher requested that the council purchase a Cap-Shur Gun. This was a pistol-like air gun that shot a dart instead of a bullet. The dart contained a syringe, which in turn held an immobilizing drug. To use it correctly and safely, one first had to estimate the weight of the animal to be captured. (The margin between the safe dose and the lethal dose was quite narrow.) Next, the catcher had to estimate his distance from the animal since the size of the gas cartridge used to propel the dart was dependent on how far the dart had to travel. Last, but not least, the operator needed to have a better than average aim in order to hit the muscle of the shoulder or hip of a animal which was hightailing it. The equipment was really designed for use by game wardens or wildlife experts under field conditions.

I learned later, after much discussion at the council meeting, that the mayor was instructed to have me order the device. I did so without fully appreciating the implications such a weapon would have in the hands of a scared animal warden. It didn't take long to find out, however!

When the gun arrived, together with a supply of the active drug and the antidote, I read the instructions and had some misgivings about the course of action that the council and I had undertaken. And when I delivered it to the mayor at the city hall, I told him I didn't know if we were doing the right thing.

"Well, Doc, let's give it a try," he said. "The dogs are about to take over the town. People are calling all the time about them crapping in their yards, then scratching up their lawns when they get through. You know how they do sometimes—throw grass and dirt with all four feet! This guy we hired can't seem to catch anything with those nets, and he's too scared of them to try to call them and slip a noose over their heads like the other ones did. He said he tries to get close by offering them raw hamburger, but the only ones he gets that way are the old fat ones the owners have let out to do their chores."

"Okay!" I responded, handing the paraphernalia over to him. "Just keep an eye on the situation, though."

By the time the next council meeting rolled around, all hell had broken loose! The stories ranged from "gut shooting" a cat to implanting a dart into a car tire during hot pursuit of a mongrel that had just dumped over a garbage can. Fortunately, the cat made it and the tire did not go down. The revelation that made the council members twitch in their seats more than usual, however, was an incident relating to a puppy.

The warden had gotten several calls about the animal digging in neighbors' flower beds. In particular, it seemed to like bulbs, any kind of bulbs. Wherever he found ground soft enough to dig, he would keep at it until he found something to chew on. Anyone who knows how hard it is to grow flowers and other garden items in Wyoming would understand why people complained about anything that was wont to destroy them. At any rate, the warden tried on several occasions to catch the pup, but to no avail. Every time the animal saw the truck with the nets, he would scamper for home, get up on the porch, and just sit looking out at the man as if nothing had happened. He would not be enticed by hamburger, cookies, or anything, but would just sit there, looking dumb. Finally, after about the fourth or fifth complaint, the catcher decided to use the Cap-Shur Gun. Instead of shooting the animal when it was in the street, he waited until it was on the porch of its own home, sitting there looking out. Again, fortunately, the animal lived through it with the help of the antidote.

The council, nevertheless, decided they couldn't live through many more such incidents and voted to take the gun away from the warden. The mayor called me the day after the meeting and asked whether I could send the gun back to the company for a refund.

The whole setting caused Harriet and I to reconsider our arrangement with the city. We could see it would be just a matter of time before it would hinder our situation. Besides, the area was growing and really needed a specific place for lost, strayed, and unwanted animals. One was built during the summer, and our agreement terminated. We learned from experience that, sometimes, there is a fine line between sentiment and duty.

−−A bit of homely philosophy on Doctors by one of our best beloved Americans, the late *Will Rogers*

This is a day of specializing, especially with the doctors. Say, for instance, there is something the matter with your right eye. You go to a doctor, and he tells you, 'I am sorry, but I am a left-eye doctor; I make a specialty of left eyes.' Take the throat business, for instance. A doctor that doctors on the upper part of your throat, he doesn't even know where the lower part goes to. And the highest priced one of all of them is another bird that just tells you which doctor to go to. He can't cure even corns or open a boil himself. He is a Diagnostician, but he's nothing but a traffic cop, to direct ailing people.

The old-fashioned doctor didn't pick out a big toe or left ear to make a life's living on. He picked the whole human frame. No matter what end of you was wrong, he had to try to cure you single handed.

Personally, I have always felt that the best doctor in the world is the Veterinarian. He can't ask his patients what is the matter—he's got to just know.

Veterinarians loved to hang this Will Rogers saying in their office. It says we're the best doctors in the world because we can't ask our patients what's wrong—we've got to know.

That's me wearing on my head one of the "tools of the trade" for a veterinarian in Wyoming.

Practice was done using drugs and equipment stored in a custom-designed box that I carried in my pickup, which is fully loaded here in this 1952 photo.

My wife Harriet (middle), Edna Binney, our "girl Friday," and me at the
drugstore in Sundance.

You are cordially invited

to attend the opening of the

Veterinary Hospital

at 10th street and 4-J avenue

on Saturday, March 17, 1956

Gillette, Wyoming

HOURS: 10 a. m. to 12 Noon
2 to 4:30 p. m.
7 to 8 p. m.

The announcement of the opening of our Veterinary Hospital in Gillette.
I believe there were only three or four in all of Wyoming then.

My son Harry and daughter Jen are coaxing an antelope to eat. The antelope was actually a pet, but not ours!

Watering our garden patch in Sundance.

The clinic in Gillette.

Part of a private herd of buffalo south of Gillette. At time of slaughter, I inspected the carcasses for wholesomeness for human consumption.

An on-call trip to Arch Creek in 1953. Like the mailman, we were expected to show up and deliver in any weather.

SHEEP TRADERS AND THE DOG

An unwritten law of survival waxes strong in the Westerner, akin to the law of survival of the fittest, except that it "kicks in" under stress situations rather than over a long period of time. It is a bit more selfish, too, not unlike the PYA designation existing mostly in organizations. Probably the closest description of it, however, is the physiologists' concept of "fright and flight." This story is a second-hand account of how the "law" works.

A breeder of German shepherds in the Gillette area unfortunately selected for his breeding program a pair of dogs whose offspring turned out to be unusually vicious. It was just a bad mix; in fact, in the two litters they raised, all but one had to be "put to sleep" by the time they were two years old because neither the owners nor anyone else could handle them. Putting them to sleep usually took place after an unprovoked attack during which someone was bitten or nearly so. It was even more pathetic because when the puppies were small, they were lovable balls of fur, full of life and affection! Everyone in the household adored them. Yet as they got older, they became overly protective of family members, and then problems would arise, first with friends being intimidated and finally with strangers like the mailman or milkman being nearly chewed up. Protectiveness turned into uncontrollable behavior.

Jake, the dog that survived, did so by being sent to a sheep and cattle ranch east of town. The ranch house was located next to the main east-west highway running through that part of the country. The rancher, like Jake, was quite protective of the family, and the dog turned out to be just what he wanted to keep strangers from dropping in unexpectedly—especially unwanted strangers like drifters and bums. He was real tickled to get Jake when the previous owner didn't want to have him put to sleep and tried desperately to find him a home. Jake took to the new family in just a short time and you couldn't have taken him from them with a gun!

I met Jake the first time when he was a pup and I gave him immunizations against "doghood" diseases of distemper, hepatitis, and leptospirosis. I met him the second time when I drove into Lance Early's on a call to deliver a calf. I had driven through the yard and past the house to a gate leading into the corral. Lance was waiting for me and opened the gate for me to drive into the enclosure. Jake was with him, looking intently at the whole proceeding.

As I drove past the house, I had noticed a sign on the yard gate saying in big red letters: "Beware of The Dog." So when I got out of the pickup and greeted Lance, I looked down at Jake and said, "Is that the dog the sign on the gate is referring to?"

Lance laughed, with a kind of sinister chuckle, and patted Jake on the head. "Yep, old Jake here keeps everyone honest," he said.

By the time I got my gear out of the box on the pickup, Jake had left his "mark" on all four wheels and was giving my boots and pants a good sniff. Lance took the calf-puller and headed toward the shed with Jake and me following.

A preliminary examination showed the cow had a torsion of the uterus, a condition in which the uterus is twisted on its axis. This results in partial closure of the cervical opening so that when the animal strains to expel the calf, the closure becomes complete and normal delivery is impeded. More often than not, the calf inside the uterus is lying on its side rather than presenting itself with its head between its front legs, in a "diving" position. It would take more than an hour of heavy physical work to get the calf on the ground—plenty of time for Lance to "spin a few yarns," as he was wont to do, and it didn't take long for him to start.

"Ya know, Doc, since we got that dog over a year ago, we haven't had any trouble with people dropping in off the road, mooching us for a handout or something. That had got so bad one time, I was afraid to leave Elsie alone in the house. Seemed like every other day, there was somebody come by. Some were pretty rough-looking characters too. Old Jake here has taken care of all of that," he said fondly, looking over at the dog who was lying in the straw, watching my every movement like a hawk.

"The only trouble is, he doesn't know the good guys from the bad. Last fall, George Kantrell and Sid Amsley came down to see about buying my lambs. They didn't tell me they were coming; they just showed up one day, right after dinner. I was having a snooze and Elsie was doing some sewing in the other room. Everything was quiet, except for cars going by. All of a sudden, I heard the damnedest hollering and racket out in the yard I'd ever heard. Someone was screaming, 'Open the door! Open the G—D—door!'

"When I jumped up and looked out, there was old George up on the hood of the car with Jake jumping at him from the ground, trying to get a hold of his britches. Sid was sitting behind the wheel of the car with the doors locked and the windows rolled up. George was just hollering like a mad man and beating on the top of the car with his fists."

By now, Lance was red-faced and laughing like crazy. His description of the scene and his laughter settled on me, despite my labor; I got to laughing, too. Pretty soon I had to withdraw my arm from the cow and wipe my eyes. Because of the story, it took me longer than it should have. Later, I would hear George's side of the tale!

George, about six-foot-four inches tall and weighing close to 200 pounds, was normally "rough and tough." Not much phased him. Sid, on the other hand, was short: about five-feet-six or seven inches with a Casper Milquetoast sort of personality. For sure they were opposites, but they had a loose partnership in a livestock-buying operation. That is, there were no formal papers drawn up between them; they just pooled their ideas, orders, and resources. I don't believe either of them really needed the income; they just enjoyed the chase.

One day, shortly after Lance told me about Jake's encounter with George and Sid, I was sitting in their car at the railroad yard, waiting for some yearling heifers they bought a few days earlier and were sending by rail to Illinois. I was waiting to give them the health inspection required by law, and Bill Able, the brand inspector, was sitting in the car with us. I thought about the story Lance told and decided to see what George and Sid had to say about it.

"I hear tell Lance Amsly's got a real good 'watchdog' at his place," I said off-handedly, when the conversation was getting dull.

George looked over at Sid, who jerked himself into an erect position from his normal slump and looked straight ahead through the windshield without saying a word. I knew I had hit a soft spot.

"Watchdog, h—!" George exclaimed, looking back at me and then at Sid. "Why the S—of a B—would eat a man alive! Sid and I went down to see Lance last fall about buying his lambs. We noticed a sign on the yard gate saying 'Beware of the dog,' so after we stopped, we waited and looked for the dog. We didn't see any sign of one and decided he must be in the house or somewhere. I shook the gate and waited again before I went through it. Sid was right behind me. Neither of us saw the dog, until we were halfway up the walk to the front door.

"All at once that big man-eater came around the corner of the house and headed right for us. His lips were laid back and his teeth just a clickin'. By the time I got turned around to run back to the car, Sid was already through the gate and was jumping into the car. When I reached there and tried to get in, Sid had locked the doors and was winding up the open window on his side!"

I could tell by Sid's body movement, he wasn't enjoying this one bit. "There was nothing for me to do to get away from the B—except to get on top of the hood. He already had taken hold of my pant leg and I had a h—of a time getting him loose long enough to get that far. Even then he kept jumping up trying to get another hold. About that time, Lance came out and called him off. It was a terrible experience, I can tell you that!" George paused, half wild-eyed from reliving the experience.

What happened after that?" I prodded, figuring there might be a little more to it.

Again, George looked over at Sid, who by this time had gone back into a slouch. I don't think he wanted to hear what was coming next. "Well, we didn't get Lance's sheep. It's hard to 'work a deal' when you've been put at a disadvantage from the outset. When we were on the way home, I asked Sid why the H—he locked the doors and wound up the only window I might have dove into. You know what he said?

'You don't think I wanted that animal in here with me, do you?'"

OLD FAT LADY AND OTHER STORIES

When they are around, the children of veterinarians have a way of interjecting humor—and embarrassment—to a scene. Ours did on more than one occasion since they were born and raised during the Spock era: No inhibitions! No thwarts! Let it all hang out!

It wasn't quite that permissive in our house, though. We expected the kids to behave to a certain extent, especially to do what they were told, after awhile, or when I could reach their hind ends with the toe of my Blucher's. Where we fell short on discipline, however, was in the area of verbal expression. Basically, the kids were allowed to say what they thought, when they thought it. No inhibitions! No thwarts! Let it all hang out! Now all of us who have youngsters know the child between three and six years old is somewhat of a "free spirit." That is, they are not yet "halter broke." They do cute things innocently. They change every day or at least every week. They are both curious and observant.

Those who agree with this description can easily imagine, then, the things around a veterinary clinic and practice for a young, agile mind to be curious and observant about—and to comment upon. No inhibitions! No thwarts! Let it all hang out!

The first time it happened to me was on a cold winter day, when son Harry was about four. (I'm told by colleagues I am lucky it didn't start sooner!) Kate Goodly called about her Chihuahua.

"Doctor, this is Kate. Can I bring Nancy right out after dinner? She hasn't been eating too well at all. She started throwing up two days ago so I went to the drugstore and got some Pepto-Bismol. I had a time getting it down her and it didn't do any good. I had some paregoric in the medicine chest from when our daughter was little, about ten years ago, so I gave her some of that. She threw it up right away. I think it was from the excitement. Now she is running off at the bowels. I do hope you will see her."

A typical Kate call: non-stop talking, trying everything at the drugstore and at home before letting me see her. Half the time, I felt the animal was a surrogate for Kate's imagined disorders, because invariably when I examined Nancy, Kate would be telling me of her own maladies. Somehow, they always seemed related. If the complaint wasn't "throwing up," it was constipation. Constipation was sure to bring poor Nancy a dose of soapy water with an old bulb syringe.

This time the scene wasn't any different. The only variables were son Harry and Kate, who had on a fur coat—a very shabby and moth-eaten raccoon, as I remember.

Kate was a little on the plump side, and with the fur coat on, she looked more stout than usual. However, I didn't notice it particularly when she walked in, holding Nancy under her coat to shield her from the cold and ever-present wind. Placing the furtive-eyed dog on the table, she started her incessant line of babble. I saw Harry, hands in his Levi pockets, saunter into the room. Standing by the refrigerator, he observed the scene without saying a word. Kate's back—hence her widest part—was facing him. Obviously, Kate had not noticed him, at first.

I was conducting the examination on Nancy, and Kate had paused in her description of how she gave an enema, when all of a sudden, I heard Harry muttering over and over, "old fat lady, old fat lady." I couldn't believe what I was hearing, but he started again, "old fat lady, old fat lady." There was no mistake. I shifted the ear pieces of the stethoscope in my ears.

Unconsciously, I guess I was trying to keep out the chant. Anyway, I became more intent on the examination and hoped Kate didn't hear what he said. When he started up again, however, she pulled herself up to her full four-foot-nine-inch height, drew her coat around her body and asked, accusingly, "Do you hear what he is saying?"

I looked up from Nancy, with what I hoped was a questioning look and said falsely, "No, what is he saying?"

"He's saying 'old fat lady'," she stated as if she had been insulted. Then she began to laugh. "I probably do look big in this coat."

I looked over at Harry, but didn't say a word. He pushed his hands deeper into his pockets and sauntered out as quietly as he had sauntered in. When Kate left, I was going to say something to him about talking in front of clients, but it was the Spock era. No inhibitions! No thwarts! Let it all hang out! Besides, I knew I couldn't have kept a straight face if I tried.

The next time it happened, Harriet was the one to get caught, and she told me about it later. It was late spring, and the flies had already started to move about on the southern exposure of the clinic. Harriet had brought Harry along to the clinic since Jen was having a nap, and Harriet didn't want to leave him alone while she took care of some client's needs. I was busy in the large animal section, delivering a calf.

In the spring, folks you seldom saw during the rest of the year showed up at the clinic, usually to get some advice, or medicine, or both for a sick calf, heifer, ewe, lamb, or what have you. When I was busy, Harriet would take over and help them with their needs, consulting me as needed, through the intercom or by coming out to where I was working.

This particular day, one of the clients happened to be Silas, a familiar acquaintance from the Sundance area. He lived close to the Devil's Tower on a little place "just big enough to starve to death on," as the locals said.

Most winters, after the first snowfall, the only way in and out of the place was by team and sled, or tractor. It would be well into April before a pickup could get through. I'd been there several times and always felt I was hastening his impending bankruptcy by charging him anything. The house he and his wife lived in was little more than a tar-paper shack. However, it was always immaculately clean, and fresh cake and coffee were always ready when we got through with whatever I was there for. Silas's wife who was short, with a tendency toward being fleshy, looked as clean and neat as her house.

Silas, on the other hand, was always either unshaven or half-shaven, and his Levis were usually so caked with dirt, they looked as if they could stand by themselves. That particular day he had a piece of baling twine around his waist holding them up instead of the usual belt, and he surely hadn't shaved in a couple of months. Indeed, the only way Harriet recognized him for sure was by his old pickup.

With Harry in tow, she was just leaving the clinic for the house when she saw the pickup coming in the drive. She waited to see if she could handle whatever the need might be. After the pickup stopped and Silas rolled out, he said, "Hi Harriet, remember me? Silas McGovern from over near the Tower. I used to come into the drugstore in Sundance."

Harriet did a double-take, for she remembered him as being fairly clean-shaven and a little cleaner looking the last time she saw him, which was all of three years ago.

"Oh! Yes, I remember you now," she said. "How is your wife?" Womenfolk out there had a tendency to inquire about wives and kids, when there were any. Harry, who was four years old, had been running ahead of her but turned around and came back when Silas started to talk. Silas had walked closer to them before he answered. "Oh, she wintered good," came the reply through his heavy beard.

"We've had a lot of snow out there this winter. This is the first time she's been out since last fall. She's downtown doing some shopping."

Harriet looked down at Harry about that time and could just tell by the way he was studying Silas that something untoward was going to come out of his mouth if she didn't get him moving soon.

"Bob is busy working on a cow. Can I get something for you?" she asked, trying to hurry things along a little.

"Well, maybe you can. You used to be better at giving me the right medicine than he did, anyway," he laughed. Then he proceeded to tell her about a calf he had that was sick. It took him about five minutes. Harry was still staring at the fiery red beard.

"Let's go into the office. I think I know what to give you," she responded, getting a little panicky by this time. All three went into the reception area where the drugs were kept on shelves. As she reached for the bottle of pills, she knew it was too late to avoid an embarrassing situation, for behind her she heard a little voice ask, "Do your whiskers itch?"

She turned quickly to see Harry's innocent face turned upward, the eyes still fixed on Silas's beard. She looked quickly at Silas to see if he might be offended. Suddenly, his nose twitched and his eyes sparkled and he let out a great guffaw. He reached up with his right hand, stroked the hairy red mass as he looked down at the little face. "Yep, they itch once in awhile, but when they do I just scratch 'em," he said.

Harriet was glad when that scene was over and did her best to get Silas on the road before another client arrived. She needed to get the boy to the house before he "broke loose" on anyone else!

Daughter Jen was something else. She was born in Gillette so it was three or four years before we really had to be on our guard with her. The tip-off that she was old enough to create embarrassing situations came one day when Dr. Gale, the State Veterinarian, visited. He was in the area inspecting the sanitary conditions of the saleyard that I was responsible for—sort of a quality control mission. Since he had been a deputy under Harriet's dad at one time and had seen her grow up, he always made it a point to come to the house and visit a little with her. Jen was close to three at the time and, like Harry, "didn't know a stranger."

Harriet always had a chocolate cake or some other sweets on hand so that when someone stopped by, which was quite often, she had something to offer them to eat. This particular day, Dr. Gale and I had just finished a bit of cake and had pushed away from the table to talk a little, when sister showed up. (We called Jen "Sister" from time to time.) Going directly to Dr. Gale, she stood by his knee and, of course, he was taken with her at once. "What is your name?" he asked, looking down on her upturned face.

"My name is Jen," she responded forthrightly. "What is your name?"

With a chuckle he said, "I'm Dr. Gale, and I live in Cheyenne." He obviously was enjoying this bit of repartee. Pretty soon she had climbed up into his lap and they were visiting back and forth, oblivious to Harriet or to me. After a few minutes I heard her ask him, "Do you want to hear a poem my daddy taught me?"

I looked at Harriet and she looked at me. I had gotten the kids to memorize a couple of ditties as well as a bedtime prayer, and of course, grace at meals. I wondered which she was going to recite to Dr. Gale.

Dr. Gale looked questioningly from Harriet to me and chuckled again. "Sure, I would like to hear your poem," he answered.

That was all the cue she needed. Still sitting on his lap, she looked directly into his eyes and in a sing-song voice said, "Ladies and gentlemen, take my advice, pull down your britches and slide on the ice." Well, as you might have guessed, this was one I never had taught her to memorize and certainly I have no clue as to where she may have learned it!

It was a second or two before Dr. Gale got the full impact of what she had just recited. Again, he looked back and forth from Harriet to me. This time he looked as if he couldn't believe what he had just heard. When it finally struck him, he convulsed in laughter, almost dropping Jen off his lap in the process. She acted a little curious about the extent of the frivolity but joined into his fun after a bit, slapping her little leg and oh so satisfied with herself! When I looked over at Harriet, she was not smiling or laughing, just staring at me in anger and humiliation.

Well, to make a long story short, Dr. Gale never forgot the visit, for every time I saw him afterward, he always asked after Jen, with a chuckle, of course. Neither did I forget his visit, for each time I tried, Harriet would tend to remind me! I doubt that Jen remembers the incident, for, after all, what is memorable to a parent is not earthshaking to a child. Besides, I thought it was a nice little ditty!

Those of you who are old enough will remember that the Hippie movement was coming into its own in the early '60s. Up to that time, males wore their hair fairly short and Butch haircuts were not uncommon, especially among World War II veterans. Beards were unheard of except on very old men.

The movement was slow in coming to Wyoming, however, and I believe we saw pictures of hippies on television a good two years before we actually saw a live one. When we did, it wasn't quite believable that a human would elect to look so unkempt, with very long hair, bushy beard, and ill-fitting clothes, all showing various amounts of dirt—from dust to crust.

The first one I saw came one morning with its mother's dog. A week or two earlier, I had heard that a couple of them showed up at a rodeo near Broadus, Montana. The cowboys didn't take much liking to them and before the hippies could escape, the boys shaved them a little with a pair of clippers they used to trim their horses' manes and tails.

Boys with long hair started showing up behind the counters of fast-food chains. Since, at that time, women food handlers could be required to wear hair nets, the regulation was also extended to long-haired male food handlers. It didn't do anything to slow down the movement, however. It just kept coming, and eventually, even those in the hard-hat industries wore their hair long and had beards.

It happened that when the first hippie came to the clinic, Sister was there. A dog was placed on the examination table by this long hairdo, unkempt creature, which I couldn't distinguish as a boy or a girl. I surmised it was a beardless boy but wasn't quite sure until it spoke.

"My mother wants you to give her dog a rabies shot," he said.

As I was getting the vaccine from the refrigerator, and otherwise preparing to carry out the task, Sister came wandering in to watch. She looked at the dog and reached up to the table to pet it. Apparently, she then first noticed the hippie, for she pulled her hand back and began to stare up into his face.

Now, everyone knows how disconcerting it is to have someone stare at you. And a little kid's stare can be devastating. I guess the hippie was beginning to feel the heat of her stare for he glanced down at her and sort of shuffled his feet. Suddenly, I sensed she was prime to say something, because I could read curiosity all over her face. Without batting an eye and in all innocence she asked, "Are you a boy or a girl?"

I heard the hippie mutter something unintelligible as he shuffled a bit more. About that time, I asked her to get me something from the waiting room. Anything to get her out of there and "break the spell." She complied without another word and I finished what I had to do to get the scene over and the hippie gone.

Unfortunately, this wasn't the last time Harriet or I had to cope with her curiosity and exuberant nature. The most memorable occasion involved the Episcopal Bishop of Wyoming, his wife, and a visiting Episcopal Vicar and his wife.

At the time, I was the Senior Warden of Holy Trinity Church, the little mission church in Gillette. We were currently without a clergyman so I was "next in command." Therefore, when the Bishop came to town, he contacted me. This visit was for the purpose of introducing us to the new Vicar of the church at

Newcastle. He and his wife were natives of Virginia and had never been "out West." They were fascinated with both the country and the people.

It happened to be spring, my busiest season, with calving and all that went with it. At that time, too, it was common to have a goodly number of stallions to geld—mostly quarterhorses, but also ponies. Folks wanted it done before they turned them onto pasture for the summer. Stallions had a way of fighting and getting hurt. Geldings, on the other hand, were more interested in eating and were more docile.

On this particular day, when the clerics and their wives showed up, two very small pony stallions were admitted to the clinic for surgery.

Harriet always liked to have a bite to eat for the Bishop, and this time she had prepared a nice lunch for the visitors as well as sandwiches for me and the kids, in case I couldn't make it to the table. Oftentimes, I'd be so busy I'd just grab some food between patients. As the morning went on, it was obvious I would eat on the run. When the kids came home from school, they could eat with me. Harriet and the visitors could lunch in leisure, around the kitchen table. That became the plan but somehow along the line, the leisure part never materialized.

When the folks arrived, the Bishop and the new Vicar came up to the clinic to say a few words. There was a pregnant cow in the chute, and I had just finished examining her when the Bishop came through the door with the cleric in tow. I had on my black OB suit, and my right hand and arm were covered with blood and mucous. Obviously, we omitted the normal hand shaking formalities. I noted, too, the Bishop kept his eyes on the floor as he talked. He was not at all his usual ebullient self but was in obvious discomfort. In about five minutes he turned and hurriedly exited the environment. The client, who had been silent all during the conversation, expressed himself after they left.

"God, Doc, I didn't know what to think when I saw those two preachers with their 'backwards collars' coming though the door. I didn't think the heifer was in that much trouble that she needed to be given the Last Rights!" he laughed.

I smiled a little and went back to work. It was a fairly simple delivery. One of the front legs of the calf happened to be laid back along its side instead of presenting in a forward position along with the other foot and head. As soon as I got it straightened out, I slipped chains over the two front feet and we pulled it the rest of the way by hand. The calf was lying on the floor catching its breath when Jen came through the door. She had on her school clothes so I wouldn't let her come in very far because of the debris and blood on the floor. Ordinarily, she would have gotten a pan of cold water and poured it on the calf's head, a technique I used to get a newborn animal to take deep breaths. It's something akin to the slap on the rump that MDs use when they deliver a child.

"Mommy wants Harry and me to eat our sandwiches with you," Jen said. "Are you about ready?"

"Yes. You get them and go to the office. I'll be in as soon as I clean up," I responded. "Maybe Harry will be home by then."

It took us about half an hour to eat and when we finished the kids went out to the corral to the back of the clinic to look at the animals. Despite being around animals all the time, they never seemed to tire of seeing more. It didn't take Sister long to discover the ponies. When she saw them, she called out to me, "Daddy, what are you going to do to those ponies?"

"They're in here to be castrated," I remarked matter-of-factly, both children having been raised to understand correct medical terminology. By that time she was in the pen with the little animals, and they were nuzzling her for something to eat. It was love at first sight!"

All at once, she started to scream and cry. "No, Daddy, you can't casterate my ponies! I won't let you." By now she was hugging one and then the other around the neck as if to protect them. She hadn't acted this way before, so it kind of took me aback.

"You go to the house and get your clothes changed," I said, hoping that she would be gone long enough for me to get things underway a little. Maybe it will settle her down, I thought to myself.

She ran out of the clinic and to the house crying loudly. Harriet and the folks were seated around the table, and were right in the middle of lunch. Harriet said the Bishop, as usual, was recounting some experiences he had in the missionary district, when Jen came running into the house crying and shouting, "Daddy is going to casterate my ponies! Daddy is going to casterate my ponies!" She ran over and put her head in Harriet's lap and kept on sobbing and screaming.

You can believe the outburst brought the Bishop's story to a halt, and there were many red faces around the table. Harriet said it was the first time she had ever seen the Bishop speechless. He was the first to speak, however, a few minutes after the initial shock had passed.

"Oh, I think this is just great!" he insisted. "Sex education in the home and everything. There should be more of it!" All the time, the bishop's wife, the Vicar, and his wife were trying to keep straight faces, while Harriet patted Jen's head and tried to quiet her down.

It seems things were just settling down when Harry came bursting onto the scene. "Daddy wants the Polaroid camera," he announced. "He wants me to take a picture of him castrating the ponies."

I had decided to take some pictures in case I wanted to write up the cases. When Harry had come up to the clinic after Jen left, I sent him down to get the camera, not thinking what commotion it would cause at the dinner table.

According to Harriet, this outburst from Harry stopped the Bishop completely. He had to join in the unrestrained laughter that had now taken over. The folks just sat helplessly by while Harriet got the camera and sent both Jen and Harry to the clinic. All was quiet then and normal conversation resumed for about ten minutes—things like the church needing more prayer books or hymnals or something of the sort.

Then came the final attack on their sensitivities. Harry came rushing in again, this time waving the picture he had taken. It was as clear a picture of the mid-stages of the procedure as you would ever want to see. Harriet said he took it directly to the Bishop. He wanted him to see it first! By that time, Jen came in breathlessly with another picture, one showing a little later stage in the operation. Harriet tried to grab the prints but in vain. She just resigned herself to the fact that lunch was a complete disaster.

Soon the party broke up as the guests wanted to be away and it seemed as good a time as any to make a break and leave. Harriet commented later that the Vicar was still laughing as he shook hands to leave. He said, "I don't want to go back East. In the first place, I love this country, and in the second place I know no one will believe me when I tell them about this trip!"

THE MONKEY

The Western sense of humor could often be counted on to liven up even the most common experience. For example, if someone got bucked off a horse unexpectedly, the onlookers responded with great glee, provided, of course, that only the feelings of the dislodged rider were hurt. Or people would laugh when an old cow came charging out of a herd and knocked a person down or made him jump up on a fence. As long as the individual was not skinned up too much and had no broken bones, the merriment that followed was something to behold! So when Bill Wrangler told a bunch of us who were having dinner at his place the story about his monkey and its encounter with an oil patch worker, we nearly choked to death on our food!

Bill had a good-sized outfit about twenty-five miles south of Gillette, and in those days, theirs was the last telephone on the line for almost another thirty miles. Then, the calls had to go through either Douglas or Kaycee. At any rate, a lot of country down that way was not covered by telephone.

When oil exploration started down there, a lot of seismograph crews and other oil-related personnel were running around, and it was not uncommon for them to ask Bill to use his telephone. Some had two-way radios but not very many.

Even though Bill was very conservative and pragmatic, most of the time he also liked the unusual. Although he ran a good-sized spread of mostly registered cattle and had never called me for anything except something related to them, this one time he called with something else on his mind.

"Doc, this is Bill Wrangler. Do you know anything about monkeys?" he began.

At first I thought he might be engaging in a little Western humor down at the bar. In spite of that, I answered his question as if he were serious. "Well, I haven't had anything to do with one since I was in school. That was a chimpanzee. I remember when the Prof put a thermometer in his rectum to take his temperature and turned away to write something on the chart, the thing reached back with his hand, pulled it out and threw it against the wall!"

I could hear Bill chuckle a little. "Well, I got this monkey out of the Montgomery Ward catalog about two weeks ago, and he's running off at the bowels. If I bring him in, do you think you can help him?"

I knew then Bill was plumb serious. "Sure, bring him up. We'll see what we can do for him. I can always call back to school and get advice if I can't figure it out." I was down at the house having a piece of cake when the call came in, so after I hung up, I said to Harriet, "Bill Wrangler is bringing in a monkey for me to look at."

"You're pulling my leg! What would Bill be doing with a monkey way down there in the ranch?" Harriet responded, looking at me intently for any sign of my kidding with her.

"I'm serious. He got the thing from Montgomery Ward."

"Well, don't let the kids see it or they'll go crazy. You know how they act sometimes!" she admonished, after accepting the fact that Bill was actually bringing a monkey in.

When I saw Bill's pickup driving in, I quickly sent the kids to the house. It wouldn't help to have a monkey with diarrhea being upset further by children's voices and impetuous movements. Bill came into the clinic holding the monkey inside his Levi jacket, next to his big belly. It made quite a sight, especially when the only part of the animal you could see was his little head with big, anxious eyes peering out. Pretty soon he bared his teeth and began to chatter, at the same time turning and reaching up with his long arms to hug Bill around the neck. I thought by that time I'd seen everything. Here was a six-foot tall grizzled, big-bellied rancher with a little, wild-eyed spider monkey hanging onto him for dear life!

I stifled a laugh. "Let's see if we can get a temperature on him," I said as I reached for a thermometer. "Best if you just hold him like you are rather than try to get him on the examination table. The only thing I've got to restrain him is a canvas bag I use for cats, and he wouldn't like that."

Bill just sort of grunted. "I'll hold him unless he starts to dig in," he advised. "Then we'll have to do something else."

The temperaturing procedure went okay, but then, remembering the experience with the chimpanzee, I held tight to the thermometer and didn't take my eyes off his arms, either. He had about a degree of fever.

"What have you been feeding him?" I queried Bill.

"He's been getting bananas and other things they recommended in the papers that came with him." He reached into his pocket and pulled out a sheaf of papers, which he handed to me. "Evelyn's been getting the stuff at the grocery store. He's been kinda loose ever since we got him. Thought he'd get over it, but he's been getting a little worse if anything." Then he laughed a little and confessed, "We wouldn't want anything to happen to him. It might sound crazy, but Evelyn and I have really become attached to him. Don't that beat hell?"

It truly was incongruous when I thought about it. And still is even after all these years.

"Well, you wouldn't be the first one to get hooked on an exotic animal," I finally said. "There's people all over the country that have strange house pets. Even, right here we have people that keep bobcats in their houses, not to mention skunks and coons!"

I had collected enough fecal material on the thermometer to do a quick microscopic examination for evidence of parasites. None were present in that sample nor the one I had Bill send me the next day. I read the directions about caring for the monkey that Bill had handed me. In quizzing him about the diet again, I thought that one thing that could be causing the problem (other than getting acclimated to new surroundings) was the amount of bananas he was eating. Far too much, according to my reckoning. I told Bill to cut back on them and also dispensed some anti-diarrhea medicine, similar to Pepto-Bismol. In a week's time, Bill called to say the monkey was okay, but getting into more mischief all the time. "We give him the run of the house, and he's gotten so he likes to hide and jump out at you when you least expect it," Bill sniggered before he hung up.

Before he got through telling us the story about the oil patch worker and the monkey, I knew what was going to happen. The story went like this:

About nine o'clock one morning in the fall, Bill had come to the house for a cup of coffee with Evelyn, after finishing the chores around the barn, and before riding out to "bunch" the heifers he wanted vaccinated against Bang's disease. Just as they sat down, an engineer for one of the oil outfits knocked at the door, wanting to use the telephone. Bill and Evelyn never turned anyone down, but they admitted it was getting tiresome, especially since, before that, they had been used to their own seclusion.

"Sure, come right in. It's hanging on the wall right there in the dining room," Bill said, pointing through the kitchen to the other room.

The man doffed his hat and went on in, saying a few words of greeting to Evelyn as he passed through the kitchen. He had cranked up the phone and was talking with a loud voice to his party on the other end. The conversation had been going on for about three minutes when Bill and Evelyn heard a commotion and what Bill called, "this God-awful shriek, coming from the engineer." He went on, "I jumped up and ran into the living room, thinking lightning or something else might have hit the line, giving the man a shock. What I saw made me stop in my tracks and double over with laughter. The monkey was on his shoulders, pulling at his hair, chattering wildly. The worker had a 'death grip' on the mouthpiece of the phone and it looked like he would pull the thing clean off the wall! The cast of the man's eyes was one of absolute terror! Lucky for him, Evelyn came in about that time and grabbed the thing off his back, 'cause I was paralyzed by then. Shouldn't have laughed about it, I guess, but I just couldn't help myself. After the 'dust settled' the fellow laughed over it, too."

Bill told me the oil worker's account of what happened: "There I was talking to the office in Gillette, when that monkey came out of nowhere and landed on my shoulders and started to holler and pull my hair! I couldn't for the life of me figure out what was going on! It was an awful sensation, I can tell you that!" As Bill explained it, the oil worker told this story while watching the monkey jabbering in Evelyn's arms. When he got hold of himself well enough to carry on a phone conversation, he called the office again and finished his business.

Yes, Westerners have a "funny" sense of humor—some funnier than others. Some even have monkeys where you least expect them!

ADVENTURES IN FLYING

As at Sundance, but not as frequently, I elected to fly on some missions from Gillette. Two occasions are memorable. The one time I thought the best way to find a heifer that had gotten loose from the clinic was to spot it from the air, and the other time, I wanted to save time.

It was close to eleven o'clock one spring night when the heifer got loose. I had just finished doing a cesarean on her and had opened the chute gate to let her out and drive her to the pen where her calf had been placed. Several ranchers and ranch hands were also there, waiting to unload their heifers, which were having difficulty calving. They had been standing around watching me or sitting on the corral fence kibitzing. When I let her loose, a couple of them started to follow her along the alley to the open door of the pen. She was very docile, so the men just sort of ambled along behind her. I had turned my attention to cleaning up the chute area to get ready for the next animal when suddenly someone hollered, "Look out, Doc!" When I looked around, she was bearing down on me like a freight train. The two cowboys who had been following her were on the fence.

The large-animal operating area had three doors: one was an overhead door leading to the pen area; another led from the receiving pen into the chute; and the other one led from the operating area to the garage where the pickup was kept during the winter. In the spring and summer, the garage was mostly unoccupied, and mostly, too, like this night, the overhead door leading to the outside was open. Much of the time the door leading into the garage was open, too, except of course, when we had a fractious animal that might try to bolt through it. I didn't close it when I turned this heifer loose, because there was no indication that she was the "bolting kind." One thing you continue to learn throughout your practice days is the unpredictability of animal behavior. (That holds for the human as well!)

In this case, although I knew the door to the garage was open, I felt it wiser to jump on the chute gate than to try to "head her off." As a result, she ran by the chute, through the open door to the garage, through the open overhead garage door, and out into the night. At first, we looked at one another in disbelief, then began running in all directions to see if we could head her off, and back into the "catch pen." After about fifteen minutes, during which time several of us tripped over things in the dark and had fallen down, or had become winded, or both, we still had no sign of her, so we decided to get on with the rest of the night's work. It was nearly two-thirty in the morning when I finally turned out the lights in the clinic and headed down the walk to the house and bed.

In addition to being "bone tired," I had done five cesareans since seven o'clock in the evening, and I was worried about the heifer. Once in awhile, a heifer will go into shock after surgery and need emergency treatment. There was the remote possibility the stitches in the uterus could tear loose, resulting in hemorrhage. Then, if she ran off some place where water was not available, she could get dehydrated. Finally, if we didn't get her back by the next day, she probably wouldn't accept the calf as her own and let it nurse. This situation would be critical for the calf since it should have the first milk at least from its mother, and it would be a terrible bother for the owner. If she didn't "take her calf," if would mean trying to "graft" the calf to another cow, which is not easily done, unless you happen to have an old cow around that would "mother" anything. (At times, some have been known to mother lambs or even colts.)

Harriet looked at the clock as I rolled into bed. "What a night you've had!" she exclaimed sleepily. "How many heifers have you worked on since you went up last night? I saw five trucks lined up one time."

"I did five cesareans and pulled one," I answered. "That's only the half of it, though. One got loose and is still out there someplace. We couldn't find her in the dark."

Harriet became completely awake. "You're kidding! How could one get loose?"

I told her how we'd all been "faked out," and what I planned to do to find her after daybreak. "If I can't spot her down the road, I'm going to call Jim at the airport and have him fly me around. She should be pretty easy to see from the air, if she's not with a bunch of cattle."

I was up by six. The day had broken with a good forty-mile-an-hour wind blowing, and with gusts to fifty or sixty—the kind of day where you had to pull your hat so tight on your head you got a headache, and every corral you walked into had a "horse shit" blizzard raging. Before the telephone started ringing, and after I checked all the animals in the clinic, I drove down the 4J Road about ten miles. I figured the heifer couldn't have gone any further than that, but there was no sign of her. There was a bunch of cattle near the road at Les Catlick's, just below our place, but I couldn't see her among them. When I got back to the clinic, I decided to call Jim, in spite of the wind. "What are the chances of getting you to take me heifer hunting this morning. Is it too rough?"

"If you don't get airsick easily, it's not too rough for me or the airplane," he replied. "At least we won't have to worry about the lift."

"I'll be out in an hour if I don't get caught here before that," I stated. "If I do, I'll have Harriet give you a ring."

Fortunately, that morning there was a lull in the clinic activities. When this happened, as it did every so often, you wondered what "turned the spigot" off and on.

The wind had died down a little by the time I got to the airport just north of town but it was still blowing hard enough that Jim and I climbed into the little Cessna while it was still parked in the hanger. He started it up inside and taxied out toward the runway. Before we made it that far, Jim turned the nose into the wind and applied full throttle, and we were airborne. That was the quickest take-off I ever saw or felt. Even though I was strapped in, I had to hold onto parts of the frame to steady myself while the plane bounced around like a cork in rough water. Jim had to keep it at full throttle as we flew into the wind.

Sometimes I thought we might even be going backward. Finally, we got over the clinic and headed south. I looked down while Jim kept the plane as steady as he could. Even then, sometimes we would drop precipitously, but just as quickly would be thrown up in the air, like a kite on a windy day. We flew around for perhaps a half-hour, long enough that I was satisfied the heifer must have gotten in with another bunch of cattle, for there was not an isolated animal in sight. I felt a little better, believing at least she wasn't dead or would have water.

When we got back to the airport, Jim was reluctant to set the plane down on the runway, afraid the wind would flip us over as we touched down or surely as we were taxiing toward the hanger. If he said what he was going to do, I didn't hear it above the roar of the engine and the rush of the wind. Suddenly, however, as we neared the buildings, the plane dropped, and it looked as if were flying straight into the open door of the hanger. Jim still had it at full throttle as we hit the ground (the entrance was coming up fast) and he didn't pull it back until the nose had entered the building. When he did, he hit the brakes hard, and we stopped as the propeller was within five feet of the back wall!

Cutting off the engine, he turned to me and grinned. "Sorry it wasn't better flying weather," he said.

I managed a half-hearted smile, relieved to get out of that alive.

The heifer? We found her that afternoon mixed in with Les Catlick's cattle. We got her back, so all was not lost. However, like I feared, she wouldn't take her calf even after we tied her up. It wasn't the most profitable day for either the rancher or me, but I'll never forget that airplane ride or the landing.

Jim and I made another trip that I kind of laugh about. One Saturday afternoon late in the spring at the "tail end" of calving season, when there were no calls and no animals on their way in to be treated, I began to think I could repair some of the equipment that was appearing worse for the wear.

The phone rang. "Doc, this is Junior Rohm. I'm up here at Bob Walker's telephone. I got a cow out here that's 'cast her withers.' She's wilder than ape manure, so I hate to think of hauling her in. Can you come out and fix her up?" The term "casting her withers" refers to the condition where a cow's vagina, usually with the bladder inside, is hanging to the outside and has to be repaired surgically. This occurs as a result of infection or trauma, but also seems to be an heritable weakness in some lines of breeding.

The road leading into Junior Rohm's ranch from the highway was a good thirty five-five miles south of Gillette, and the house was at least five miles from there. I judged it would take most of the afternoon to go down and back. Not comfortable with leaving the clinic unattended that long, I thought about having Jim take me.

"Is the cow at the house or somewhere else?" I asked Junior.

"She's at a branding corral about three miles west of the house. You know, where you vaccinated the heifers last winter."

I knew immediately where he was talking about, and I knew, too, it would take that much longer to get there and back. Still, I was undecided whether to fly or drive. I didn't say anything to Junior except, "I'll try to make it down by three o'clock. If you don't see me by then, you'd better figure on getting her loaded and brought here because I will have gotten caught here with an emergency."

Okay, Doc. I'll be working along the road so I won't miss you. Sure hope you can make it, though."

It was one-thirty. If I could get Jim to fly me, I could get out there and back by three-thirty or four at the latest. If I drove, it would be close to five-thirty or six. I called Jim, and luckily, he was free.

"Warm her up. I'll be out in ten minutes." I said, ending the conversation. There was no way to get back in touch with Junior because he had no phone, so I called Harriet on the intercom and told her what I was going to do.

"You take care now," she admonished like she always did when I was to fly on a call. "I'll handle things here, so don't worry."

I got to the airport within my allotted time, and we were airborne within five minutes. To get to Junior's place from the airport, we had to fly over the west side of town, and when we passed over the clinic, about a hundred feet up, I looked down and saw Harriet and the kids in the yard waving. Jim waggled the wings in acknowledgment. Kids always like that!

"Do you know from the air where this place is?" Jim turned to me and hollered over the roar of the engine.

"I'll be able to tell you as soon as we get close. Just fly in the direction of Douglas for now!" I shouted back.

It was a beautiful afternoon, warm, and clear for miles. After we passed Reno Junction, I looked to the southwest in earnest and spotted Junior's place. I tapped on Jim's shoulder and pointed. "The corral is about three miles west of that set of buildings!" I spoke loudly in his ear. He changed the plane's direction slightly. In five more minutes we were close enough and low enough that when we passed over the corral, we could see a single cow in it. Sure enough, she had an everted vagina. "That's her!" I shouted at Jim.

"Hang on then!" Jim hollered back as he swung the little plane around and lowered the flaps. The landing was bumpy because of the sagebrush. He taxied right up to the corral fence and shut off the motor. "Okay, Doc. Now it's your turn to work," he laughed as he opened the door and we got out.

It turned out to be a short job. She was a "snake" all right, as Westerners sometimes call a highly excitable animal, but Jim helped and we got her into the squeeze chute in good fashion. The anesthesia I used (a local nerve block) worked just fine, and once I got the mass pushed back in and sewed up with umbilical tape and gauze, we turned her into a pen that had a water supply. We were back in the plane ready for takeoff within a half-hour. Junior must not have seen us, because he didn't show up.

"Shouldn't we fly over toward the ranch house, so he will know you were here?" Jim offered.

"No, he'll know soon enough when he comes over and finds she's been fixed up. That should be this afternoon sometime. If not, the cow has water, so she will be all right, anyway," I answered. "I don't want to be gone any longer than I have to."

Jim started the engine and taxied away from the corral. Soon we were heading north.

We landed at the airport at three-ten. After paying Jim, I was back at the clinic by three-thirty. Right on target, I thought to myself as I drove into the yard.

As luck would have it, no calls or animals were waiting. I just sort of relaxed for the rest of the afternoon. Harriet and I laughed as we thought about the expression Junior must have had when he went to the corral to get the cow and found her "back together."

It was at least two weeks later that Junior called about another matter. When we had finished the conversation, I asked, "Say, how did the old cow with the withers get along?"

"She's just fine, but I still can't figure out how you slipped past me to get over to where she was. I left the road to come to the house for only about ten minutes. How did you do it?" he quizzed.

"I had Jim fly me down. We didn't stop because I was in a hurry. I knew you'd see her that afternoon or in the morning and then turn her out, so I wasn't worried. When are you going to get a phone?"

Junior laughed and said, "I told Anna you'd pulled a fast one on us. She'll be tickled to hear how you did it. As for the phone, I never want to get one. Hell, the kids or Anna would be hangin' on it all the time. Wouldn't get anything done down here!"

I had other airplane trips in small planes. Most often the pilots had commercial or instructor licenses. Sometimes, however, a rancher had his own plane with a private license. I always thought twice about offers to ride with them—but most times I went anyway!

A CLOSE CALL

Working with animals, particularly when they are sick or injured, sometimes can be perilous. That's always a "given," so to speak. What you don't expect, however, is to be "pinned down" by two hunters blazing away at a deer, from the back of a speeding pickup, while you're treating a "downer" cow in a pasture!

Now, I don't believe all hunters are crazy. I even support the need for reducing to a manageable level the numbers of wild animals that would overpopulate the countryside, until they died of starvation or an epizootic disease. I just want to tell this one story about hunting, not because it was typical but rather because it was atypical. Besides, what turned out to be amusing could well have had tragic consequences for a cow, a rancher, a young and struggling veterinarian, or all three!

That particular fall, we were having a real pretty Indian summer, though a little dry. One night I received a phone call from Pat McCarthy, a rancher east of Gillette, down Rozet way.

"Doc, I got this cow out here whose slobbering at the mouth and her nose is all dry—looks like the skin is peeling off. She doesn't want to move either. Sort of acts stove-up. Anyway, can you come out in the morning and look at her?" he asked me.

As I remember, this call came in on a Friday night, and I didn't have anything lined up in the morning except to care for the animals in the clinic. "Yes, Pat, I can get out there by nine if that's okay. Will you have her there at the house or over at your other place?"

"Well, actually, she's still out in the pasture about a mile from here. I didn't want to move her, so I took some hay and water out to her. She's not going to be hard to get a rope on so you just come here to the house and we'll go on from there."

"Okay, I'll see you about nine then." As I hung up the telephone, I thought about the cow and the signs of illness Pat had described. I bet she has ulcers on her tongue and dental pad, too, I thought to myself.

A ruminant, such as a cow or a sheep, doesn't have upper teeth in front. Rather, they have an area of hard tissue known as a dental pad. The disease condition Pat described was something new at that time. At least, we thought it was new because it was not described in textbooks. Going by the signs we saw, we called it ulcerative stomatitis. Some years later, after much research, it was determined to be the disease entity bluetongue, which we saw in an earlier account, though in sheep.

I checked the pickup to make sure I had the drugs I needed, plus a can of water. If I had to treat her in the pasture, I knew I would be without water and that after giving her the medication intravenously, it would be nice to be able to wash up a little.

The next morning broke as pretty as the day before. I put the dog patients out in the runs and fed them, after giving them their medications. Then I cleaned out the stalls and medicated the large animals. I was ready for the road by eight-thirty, plenty of time to get to Pat's without hurrying. As I was driving down main street in town, on the way to Rozet, I noticed quite a few cars with out-of-state license plates, parked diagonal to the curb. "Hunters," I said to myself. "The merchants must be doing a pretty good business this year." I didn't think anymore about them until I got to Pat's.

"By golly, Doc, you're right on time," Pat said at the gate when I arrived.

"Well, everything went right this morning," I responded. Then, to make a little more conversation I said, "Noticed quite a few out-of-state cars in town when I came through. Must be a goodly number of hunters around."

Pat was standing beside the pickup. "Well, we don't allow any hunting, except a few close friends, so I wouldn't know about that," he replied. Then he pointed off to the south at a trail. "Just follow me down that road. It's about a mile and couple of gates to where I left her yesterday, before I called you. I'll take my old pickup just in case we have to 'cowboy' her. Just leave the gates open. We'll be coming back this way and will close them then."

When we got to the place where Pat had left the hay and water, there wasn't a cow in sight. He hollered out of the pickup, "The old rip's gone off, but she's not far, I can tell you that! Not in the shape she's in. Just drive over that little hill, yonder." When we crested the rise, we saw a cow lying down about fifty yards away, sort of on the level. An old road heading into a wooded area was just beyond.

"That's her! Doc, I knew she couldn't have moved far," Pat sang out gleefully. "Wouldn't cha know, she'd move away from feed and water when it was right there for her?"

When we drove up closer to her, she got to her feet and made an attempt to run. She didn't go far, however, before she stopped and just stood there watching the pickups.

"Gimme your rope, Doc," Pat ordered, after we had jumped out of the trucks and I was getting the equipment and medicine out of the box on the back. "You just stay where you are 'til I get it on her. I'll holler if I need help."

With rope in hand, he headed around to the front. I kept quiet and watched. Though she tried once again to run, he caught her on the first loop. She took off, again, this time dragging Pat with her. I didn't wait for him to holler; I ran over and got on the end of the rope with him. Together, we stopped her. "She's stronger than I thought," Pat offered, when the dust had settled.

"Let's see if I can get a closer look at her," I said as I began to "walk up the rope" toward her. Pat held firmly on the rope behind me. As I got close to her head, she suddenly fell over on her side. In her weakened condition and with the rope tight around her neck, we had cut off her wind a little too much. Pat dropped the end of the rope and ran around me as I reached down to open the loop. He was on top of her in a second and, grabbing the upper front foot, he bent the leg back at the knee. She didn't try but she couldn't have gotten away even if she had wanted to. Not with the hold he had. "That's just the way we wanted her, isn't it, Doc?" he laughed between breaths. "Now you can examine her or treat her or anything else you want to do. I'll guarantee she won't get up 'till we're ready."

"She's just right, Pat," I affirmed as I reached for the thermometer to take her temperature. As I knelt down behind her, I noticed swelling of the skin above the hoofs of all four feet. She was panting pretty heavily, too, for no more than we had to wrestle her around. Her temperature was 106. Normal is 101.5 Allowing a degree or two for the wrestling and the excitement, it was definitely above normal. I went to her head and opened her mouth. Sure enough, there were ulcers on the dental pad and tongue. "What do you make of it, Doc?" Pat inquired, looking at me but still gripping the leg and hoof.

"We call it ulcerative stomatitis," I answered. "Nobody knows what causes it. Some think it comes from eating hard dry grass and weeds. Others think it is a virus. Whatever, we do see it most often this time of year. Most get over it with treatment and a little care."

Pat didn't say anything for a second, then he laughed. "Guess I shouldn't have asked you, Doc. I don't know any more what it is now than before, just another big name."

I laughed a little, too. "Medically, all it means is that she has ulcers of the mouth and its parts. It describes the signs of the disease rather than its cause."

"I had some ulcers in my mouth awhile back I had to doctor for," Pat said. "You don't suppose I got them from these old cows do you?" He was dead serious as he looked at me.

Suddenly, a ludicrous picture crossed my mind, so I smiled a little when I answered, "Not unless you've been out here kissing these old heifers!"

Pat got to laughing and almost lost his hold on the front leg. When he quit he exclaimed," If you could draw cartoons, you'd make a better living than you are now!"

I had already started back to the truck for the gear and drugs I needed. When I returned, I prepared the drugs I would give intravenously. When I got ready to insert the needle in the jugular vein, I said to Pat, "Hold her real still. It won't take long to run this stuff into her."

With that, he took a little extra hold on the leg and leaned back. The cow thrashed around a little when the needle hit her, but not too bad. I got the apparatus hooked up and was holding the bottle in the air watching the fluid bubble nicely, which indicated it was running into the vein with no blockage. Everything was real peaceful. The only noise, other than that emanating from the bottle and the cow's labored breathing, was what sounded like a pickup coming through the wooded area below us, to my back. Pat looked intently past me, in the direction of the wood. "I wonder who's coming through there?" he said. The words were no sooner out of his mouth than he exclaimed. "By golly, there's a buck coming out of those woods and heading right towards us!"

About that time, "all hell broke loose," as they used to say out there. First, I heard an engine roar and what sounded like a pickup bouncing over the low brush in the pasture. Next, I heard the sound of gunfire not too far away. For a minute, it took me back to the war zone on Saipan.

"Duck! Doc, for God's sake get down!" Pat hollered, as he huddled down closer behind the cow, but still hanging onto to her leg. "There's a couple of people in the back of a pickup firing at the deer. The deer is swinging wide around us now, so we're right in the line of fire!"

I dropped my arm and the bottle, scrunching down behind the cow, on the opposite side from Pat. We could hear the bullets ricocheting off the rocks as well as hitting the ground with a thud, not fifty feet away. After a few more shots, the firing stopped. The pickup was not 200 feet from us. Instead of stopping, however, it started up and tore off in another direction. Pat was the first to speak.

"Hurry up, Doc! I need to go after them. There's not supposed to be anyone in here. I want to see who it is and have a little talk with them."

I had already gathered up the bottle, still attached to the intravenous outfit, and a good three-quarters empty. After I cleared the air from the tubing, it didn't take long to run in the rest.

"Okay, Pat, let her go!" I said, pulling the needle from her vein and raising up with the bottle and other equipment in my hand.

Pat was on his feet in one second flat. "I'll be back in a few minutes. You just wait for me!" he called out as he ran for his pickup. With a roar and a cloud of dust, his truck was fairly flying over the brush, in the direction the other truck had gone. Pretty soon the sound of the engines stopped. I could see the two pickups together over a little hill, maybe 200 yards away.

Just as I finished cleaning up, Pat returned. His face was a little flushed, to say the least, and I didn't attribute it to holding down the cow.

"I guess you know I told those fellows a thing or two. It wasn't really the hunters' fault; it was the damn guide. Those town boys don't know half the time where they're at. They shouldn't give them permits to guide if they don't know when they're on posted land or not."

By that time, I had regained my composure and decided that we were just plain lucky. No one in the pickup had seen us, and the shots had been wild, but high instead of low. I was glad to be back talking about the cow, which by that time had regained her feet and was ambling off toward the woods.

"If you can, you should try to work her toward home so she has hay and water in front of her all the time. It would help to give her two or three pounds of 'cake' or other grain, too. Those ulcers make the mouth awful sore to be pulling on this tough grass. She should be all right in about two weeks if she has good care and the medicine I am leaving with you. Give it once a day in the muscle of the hind leg," I instructed.

"Okay, Doc. Sorry we had all the trouble, but it could have been worse." Pat had regained his breath and his sense of humor. "You can tell this one to your kids when they get older. They won't believe it, but tell them anyway. Call it, Comrades Without Arms!"

We both shook with laughter. This used to happen on Saipan, too, after coming off unscathed following a strafing by the Japs.

"How about naming it The Close Call?" I retorted.

"That's even better, Doc! I do believe you missed your calling!"

THE PUBLIC HEALTH
PHYSICIAN

Early in August, about the fifth year Harriet and I were in Gillette, we experienced a mild outbreak of equine encephalomyelitis (sleeping sickness) among horses. The first one to contract the malady was too ill when we were called, and of course, it died.

Word spread throughout the county about the outbreak so I was busier than the proverbial "cranberry merchant," vaccinating horses, ponies, mules, and asses, wild and gentle, of every color and stripe. Nothing strikes more terror into the heart of a rancher than the prospects of losing his best horse or string of horses!

The vaccination program called for two intradermal injections of the vaccine to be given, seven to ten days apart. That meant, of course, traveling over the same roads and visiting the same ranches within that time period. It also meant each animal had to be handled twice. I can tell you not all the animals forgot the hassle and pain in seven to ten days! The "second time around" is not always better. In fact, during that time between, I swear some of those equine were just waiting … waiting for the needle prick to make them come "unglued!" Then it was anyone's guess what would happen. And what happened ranged anywhere from jumping forward, trying to run over whoever was holding the rope, or holding the needle, to whirling quickly and attempting to kick both the "holdee" and the "injectee." Ponies were the worst for aberrant attitude and behavior!

Anyway, if ever there was a time to have "horse sense," it was while working with them under those circumstances. You had to watch both eyes, the position of each concha or external ear, the attitude and changing attitude of all four feet, all at once. From all of these working in unison, a person with experience in handling horses can get some idea what the animal might do: jump forward, whirl and kick, strike out with one or both front feet, try to bite you, rear up on its hind legs, or just run straight over the top of you! The predictability rate as to the outcome was, at best, forty to forty-five percent, then only if you'd been around broncs all your life, with bowed legs to show for it. These are the things the vet had to keep in mind about the horse, mule, ass, or pony. Another concern, was the "human factor."

If I was vaccinating a pony, of course, the kids would be around. Ponies have a way of "faking out" kids, and they extend that thought process to adults as often as they can. I am sure they consider vets in the same vein as they do the kids. Anyway, between the "spoiled" pony, and the sympathetic or scared kid holding it by the bridle reins or halter rope, and me knowing the struggle it would be, two or three attempts were often needed to get the needle in, the vaccine injected, and the needle withdrawn. That in turn meant at least two or three attempts at biting whoever was closest to the mouth and for sure, it meant both of my feet being trampled on.

With wild equidae that had never had a rope on them until the day of the vaccination, the human factor was different. Usually you had some "top hands" handling the situation so when one hollered "Ready, Doc!" you could just about bet you could conduct the procedure without fear of bodily harm. In such instances, the animal was subdued by being pushed against a corral fence by half a dozen cowboys, or he'd be "eared down," or both. In the earing-down process, a cowboy gets hold of both ears and either twists them or chews on one with his teeth—not enough to draw blood, just enough to take its mind off the needle! Although there was a lot of dust flying in this environment, in some ways it was a lot safer for the vet than vaccinating the ponies and so-called gentle horses.

The absolutely worst situation was the combination of a half-broke horse and a half-scared owner. Some way or another, about the time I was to stick the needle into the skin of the animal's neck, these owners always managed to get around behind me, while holding the halter rope of their wild-eyed steed. Thus, if the animal sprang toward us instead of pulling away, I was first in "the line of fire." In such situations I was lucky not to get the vaccine in my finger or arm before we got untangled and off the ground. One thing for sure, next to humans, the equine has to be the animal species with the most unpredictable behavior. Put them together under stress, and, as the statisticians say, "the possibilities and probabilities are staggering," for someone to get hurt.

Despite the odds, all that fall only one person got a broken leg from a kick, and there were no other injuries except a few mashed toes, bite marks here and there, and a few wrecked feelings. I thought for sure the odds would change, however, when the Public Health Service Physician called from the Center for Disease Control in Atlanta and wanted to ride with me to look at the cases of sleeping sickness I was treating. Then too, he wanted to learn how to take blood samples from a horse in case he got to an area where there were only a few vets. In those days, you could tell whether an animal (or human, for that matter) had been exposed to the equine encephalomyelitis virus by comparing antibody titer of blood samples taken a week or two apart.

The Public Health Service physician called because, coincidentally, an epidemic of encephalitis in humans was raging in the county and he was conducting an epidemiological study. Humans can contract a virus that causes equine sleeping sickness the same as horses—that is, mainly from mosquito bites. Mosquitoes get the virus from feeding on wild birds that harbor it. Thus, horses and humans are both "dead-end hosts" for the virus; they don't transmit the disease to one another or to other animals.

When one of the local physicians who owned horses was in discussion with the doctor from CDC, he told him of the outbreak of encephalitis occurring in horses. It was only natural, therefore, that he would want to check it out. So early one evening this PHS doctor telephoned me.

"Doctor Baldwin, this is Dr. Brown. I'm from CDC in Atlanta, and I'm here investigating the outbreak of encephalitis in people you may have heard about. (Indeed I had heard about it as I was on the county hospital board at the time.) Doctor Pete Mason told me he heard you have some horses under treatment for equine encephalomyelitis. Since there is an outside chance there might be a link I would like to see some of the cases you are treating, if you don't mind."

"I'd be happy to have you," I responded. "In fact, the day after tomorrow, I have to re-treat the two cases I have. Then I have other horses to vaccinate. It will likely take most of the day. Do you want to be gone that long?"

"That's fine with me. What time do you want me to meet you?"

"Let's make it around eight o'clock at my clinic. Dr. Mason can tell you how to get to it. The one case is right across the road from the clinic so it will be handy for both of us to leave from here."

"Suits me fine. I'll call Dr. Mason and tell him where I will be in case the Center tries to contact me. By the way, have you sent any blood samples in for confirmatory diagnosis? I can bring some blood vials with me to take samples if you want. CDC won't charge for the analysis."

The offer was like "manna from heaven." I had not sent samples into the laboratory, first of all because I was sure enough of the diagnosis through clinical signs. Second, any lab I sent specimens that had the capability to do viral work would charge for it. I felt there was no need to add an already expensive treatment regimen. However, I seldom turned down a "free lunch," so I quickly accepted his offer.

"That would be great!" I responded." I haven't sent in any samples but would be real happy to see if I am right. Might give you a good comparison with the samples from the humans, too."

"Right," Dr. Brown agreed. "Will see you at eight, then."

By the time he arrived, I had everything ready to go: Vaccine in a cooler with ice packs. Plenty of intradermal needles. The medicine for the two sick horses. A thermos of cold water. Before we left, I showed him through the clinic since he had never seen a large animal hospital. (They were not common at the time).

We got to the first stop in just a few minutes. The owner greeted us and led the way around the corner of the shed to the sick horse, which was down on its side, almost comatose. It could neither eat nor drink, so I gave it food and water by stomach tube each day. It was not responding to treatment, and was the one that died later.

Dr. Brown asked the owner what he'd noticed different about the animal when it first became ill.

"One morning when I went to feed him, he acted kind of droopy. He stood with his head down. When I got his grain, he nickered a little like he usually does, but when he went to eat, the grain just stuck to his lips. He couldn't seem to chew. When I offered him a bucket of water, he just slobbered around in it. He seemed to be swallowing but none went down. That's when I called Doc here. It's been about a week, hasn't it, Doc?" he asked looking at me.

"Just about a week," I acknowledged. "He went down day before yesterday. By rights we should put him to sleep. I've never seen one get up once he gets down."

I could tell Dr. Brown was not comfortable in this situation. "How about getting a blood sample?" he asked as if trying to hasten our departure. "Two samples taken ten days apart would be better, but at least one sample is better than nothing."

The owner and I talked about euthanizing the poor beast but decided to wait one more day, just in case things turned for the better. In twenty minutes Dr. Brown and I were on our way up the Little Powder to the next call. We got into conversation about the various known causes of encephalitis in humans and animals. Finally he said he didn't think the human cases he saw at the hospital were the equine form, even though the initial diagnosis looked very much like it. He said, "A few years ago, this would have been called polio. I don't know what to call it now except an encephalitis. The blood samples will tell us for sure if I'm right or wrong."

By then we were close to Eric Hawkins' place. One of his mares was the second case I had been called to treat, and also he had about twenty other horses to vaccinate for the second time. Among them were three fractious yearlings!

"Hi, Doc!" he called out from his front porch as he came toward the gate of the picket fence surrounding the house. "Just got through talking to Harriet to see when you'd get here. Molly is going to fix us some lunch when we get through." By that time Dr. Brown and I were out of the pickup. I introduced him to Eric, who kind of kidded, "You doctors aren't ganging up on us poor folks, are you?"

I could tell right away he and Dr. Brown would hit it off because the doctor responded, "I'm not going to charge you anything for my services, so you don't need to worry about that. I'm just along to have you and Dr. Baldwin teach me about horses."

Eric laughed heartily. "Well, I'll be able to show you a thing or two, but you can't expect to learn much about horses from a vet!"

I decided to break up the banter before it went any further. Turning to Eric I asked, "How is the mare getting along?"

Still wanting to have a little fun, he winked at Dr. Brown and said, "Hell, Doc, you must have prescribed the wrong medicine again. She's getting along just fine!"

I smiled a little at the now timeless joke. "Let's have a look at her. Dr. Brown here would like to get some blood samples from her, too. He wants to do some comparison studies with the humans he's been looking at."

Eric just would not let up on his idea of fun. "Hell, no one in his right mind would compare a good horse with a human!" he shot back with a grin.

We all laughed again as Eric led us through the gate of the corral toward a long shed in the far corner. I noted a bunch of horses in another corner sort of staring at us as we walked through the corral. Pointing them out to Dr. Brown, I said, "We'll be vaccinating them right after we get through with the mare."

As Eric said, the horse was looking good and doing fine. She never had been as sick as the horse we'd looked at in town. I took her temperature and checked her over.

"She acts well enough to go back to work," I said to Eric. "Best give her a few more days rest, though, then only an hour or two at a time, to see how she takes it. Be especially watchful for any signs of staggering or stumbling. Sometimes this stuff leaves some brain damage."

Eric was all serious now. "Is there anything a man can do if she is affected? Nobody wants on top of a stumbling horse, you know."

"Nothing except time will help," I responded. "If there's not too much damage, they usually grow out of it. If they're not back to normal in six months, the chances are slim they ever will be much better."

Dr. Brown spoke up. "That's about the way it is in humans, too. We usually use some corticosteroids but there are no controlled studies to support its use, just clinical impressions and pharmacological rationale."

I took the blood vial and needle from Dr. Brown and while Eric held the mare by the halter, I drew a sample from her jugular vein. She didn't move or flinch. "That looks like something an MD could do," Dr. Brown joked as he intently watched my every move. "People often make more fuss than that."

The day was not over, however. The day was not over!

About that time, one of Eric's hired men came into the shed. After Eric introduced him to Dr. Brown, the cowboy said, "They're ready when you are," referring to the band of horses to be vaccinated.

"You can start catching them," I responded. "I've got everything ready." We all left the shed and walked into the middle of the corral. Two more hands were there with ropes and Eric grabbed his rope, too, as he went by his saddle. Soon they were whirling ropes over the horses' heads and settling them around their necks. Like most animals, they had not forgotten the first shot, so they tended to act up a little. The last one or two were always the worst and when we got down to them, it took Eric and all three hands to hold them. I was knocked backward against the fence once, and almost got a front foot in my belly a second time.

Dr. Brown looked on intently, from a distance. He didn't say a word until we were leaving the corral. "They're a little wilder than the mare," he observed.

"Hell, they're gentle compared to the ones we have on the range," Eric chuckled. "Some of them will walk up and put a front foot right in your shirt pocket! I had a stallion one time that would pull you right off your horse with his front teeth when he was with his band of mares and you rode anywhere near them. Like I said, this bunch was plumb gentle."

Dr. Brown did not laugh with Eric this time. He just remained silent and followed along to the pickup where I put away my syringe and needles and returned the unused bottle of vaccine to the ice chest. Since it was close to lunch time and Molly had it ready, we couldn't refuse. Dr. Brown perked up a little as we were finishing the last of the fried chicken. "This is a real treat for me," he offered. "I don't get a chance to visit ranches or eat in homes very often. Mostly, I am at hospital cafeterias or something like that." Then turning to me, he asked, "Do you get to eat food like this very often?"

Before I could answer, Eric spoke up, "Hell! Look at his belly, you can tell he doesn't push himself away from the table all that fast. Either that or he is in the 'buck pasture,' and Harriet wasn't pregnant looking the last time I saw her!" Then he slapped his leg and hollered laughing.

Molly's face got red. "Eric, you shouldn't talk that way in front of company," she admonished. "What will Dr. Brown think?"

"Hell, he knows about the birds and the bees!" He went on with his tomfoolery, looking over to catch his reaction.

Dr. Brown knew something was supposed to be funny about the "buck pasture" reference, but he didn't know what it was. "I've never heard that expression before. It must be a colloquialism peculiar to the west. What does it mean?" he asked seriously.

"You tell him, Doc." Eric looked at me with a grin on his face while Molly grabbed up some dishes from the table and headed for the kitchen.

"It's a saying some of these more robust souls use to describe the extra weight a man puts on when his wife becomes pregnant. They think it comes from forced abstinence, like what happens to buck sheep when you take them away from the ewes after mating season," I explained as lightly and quickly as possible. Not to be outdone by Eric, I added, "Harriet's not going to have another baby, though. We found out after the last one what caused it!"

The laughter and wild talk quieted down when Molly came in with dessert. She was anxious to hear what Dr. Brown did and the places he traveled to. He seemed reluctant to leave so I had to push a little more than usual to get away.

The next call was twenty miles away, over on the D Road. The sick horse there was a gelding, and he belonged to one of the hired hands. Besides treating him, we would have fifteen head to vaccinate. At this place, everyone was all business—no joking like at Eric's. The horses were "snakes"—that is, they seemed to know every mean trick in the books. One almost got me with a hind foot, in spite of being "eared down" by one cowboy and being pushed against the corral fence by another. It happened so quickly, I still don't know how it happened. All I know is when I slipped the needle between the layers of the skin, the hand holding him against the fence went flying, and the left hind foot went whisking past my head as I jumped back. I should have stayed in close to him, but as the fella says, "my feet would just not hold still!"

Dr. Brown, watching from outside the corral, had grown serious indeed. After we were back in the truck heading home, he didn't say anything for a few minutes, then he opened up. "After seeing that last display, I'm going to look up one of you guys if I ever need blood samples from horses. It goes to show, there's a knack for doing anything. I thought it would be so easy to hit a vein as large as the jugular on a horse, and I believe it would be. But the trouble is getting close enough to do it without getting killed or maimed!"

As he was leaving, he said he would send me a copy of the laboratory test results on both the humans and the animals. In mid-winter the folder from CDC arrived after I thought perhaps he had forgotten. The papers showed that the samples from the three horses were positive for sleeping sickness while those of the humans were negative. A note penned at the bottom said, "Looks like you were right about your horses and we were wrong about our humans. Sincerely, Ed Brown."

MEMORABLE TRAIN TRIPS

Traveling by train in the 1960s was akin to traveling by air now. It was certainly the easiest and best way to go long distances, because before that time motels and hotels were few and far between, especially throughout the West. When you did find one, it was not the most elegant. During the late '50s and early '60s, however, Harriet and I noticed a change in the way folks traveled.

First, we noted more motels being built in the little towns. They would be advertised on the billboards as being "modern," which meant there was inside plumbing. Next, we saw an increase in the automobile tourist trade each year we operated our drugstore. Finally, after we were in Gillette only a couple of years, we noticed the passenger train running through there carried fewer and fewer cars. It wasn't long before the dining car was removed, also. Harriet and I felt that an important bit of history was passing and wanted our kids to sample a little of it. Little did we know what was in store for us!

Our first trip was relatively short, just up the track about 80 or 100 miles to Sheridan. We were invited to stay at a friend's place for a weekend and decided to go by train so the children could get a new experience. Harry, about six, was in the process of losing his deciduous or baby teeth, with at least two incisors missing. Jen was close to three.

The train we boarded about four in the afternoon was only three cars long, the diner having been removed at least a year earlier. Our car had a few passengers toward the front, and Harriet, the kids, and I arranged ourselves on the right side toward the back, after I flipped one of the seat backs over so the youngsters faced us as they rode backward. Before long they became restless and tired of looking out the windows, so they began wandering up the aisle.

Harriet and I watched them inch their way toward the people at the front. Soon, we saw Harry talking with them; he never knew a stranger. Suddenly, peals of laughter came from the couple he was visiting, and they turned and looked back at us when they were able to control themselves. Harriet and I knew he had "let the cat out of the bag" about something, for he, too, turned to look at us but was not laughing. He just had a puzzled look on his face. Jen was laughing because the adults were laughing.

I decided it was time to get them back to their seats so they wouldn't bother the people anymore. When I reached them and told them to return to our place, the man smiled and said, "I understand you are a veterinarian."

"Yes, I am," I replied, a little perplexed about what that had to do with the jocularity Harriet and I just witnessed.

Still snickering a little, the gentleman went on, "I just asked your son how he lost his two front teeth. He told us his Daddy had pulled them. I then asked him if his Daddy was a dentist, and he said, 'No! he's a veterinarian!'"

Suddenly, I could see why the remark was so amusing, and I laughed, too. As I shooed the children down the aisle, I turned to the couple and said, "Best I get them back in their seats before they tell you anymore."

When we got off at Sheridan and walked past the car to the station house, the strangers were still smiling as they looked down at us and waved. Doubtless, the trip was memorable for them too.

The second trip took place about a year later. Harriet's brother and family lived in the Chicago area, and we hadn't seen them for several years. After a particularly tough spring calving season, and being up at all hours for over two months, we were "beat" and needed all the rest we could get for a week or so before bull-testing and other early summer activities began. We decided to take the train from Cheyenne to Chicago, and since it would be an overnight trip, we elected to get a sleeping compartment.

We drove the 300 miles to Cheyenne the morning of our scheduled departure, which was to be about four in the afternoon. We arrived there in time to do enough shopping for me to get a pair of pants and a sports jacket before boarding the Sante Fe, "City of San Francisco." The kids were well-behaved and enjoyed all the new sights. When we got on the train the black Pullman porter in his white coat and black hat escorted us to our compartment.

The children looked at him very intently, with what I called the "Wyoming Stare." I knew right then Harriet and I were about to experience something, for as we moved up the aisle I said to her, "Do you see how the kids are looking at the porter?"

She half laughed. "Yes, I do. Why don't you try to divert their attention before they say anything embarrassing. You know they never saw a black person before. Take them to the observation car while I follow the porter to the compartment and unpack."

Thus, when the porter opened the door to our compartment and carried the bags in, I took the kids' hands and hurried them on by. We quickly climbed the stairs to the upper deck of the Astradome and took seats as the train started to move out of the station. They were so busy staring at the passing sights from that height, that whatever they might have said about the porter's color passed. Before the trip was over, they talked and visited with him like they were old friends. They saw a lot more black folks, too, before we got home. Harriet said later, "Well, we got by that one okay!"

Toilet facilities in the compartment consisted of a commode with a heavy cover that could substitute for a seat. It was so well camouflaged, at first we had a time finding it. When we did, however, the kids thought it was the greatest thing they had ever seen and couldn't wait to "try it," midst much giggling and poking one another. It "worked" all right on the first go-round. They took turns, then they headed back to the observation car, laughing and having fun. Harriet and I were glad just to sit back and relax a little as we talked. It was getting on toward supper time, and we had planned to go to the dining car. The two of us had to be prepared for any eventuality that might occur there, for it would be another new experience for the children.

As it turned out, the meal was delicious: grilled lamb chops for Harriet and me; hamburgers (by choice, besides being less expensive) for the youngsters. They were on their best behavior, with no hint of embarrassments until the end of the meal when the waiter set silver bowls half full of water down in front of them. They both looked at us quizzically. Harry was the first to speak, "Daddy, what is this for?" he asked, pointing at the vessel. Quickly, I looked at the waiter and saw his lips break into a big wide grin.

As he bent over the boy, he said, "Here, young man, let me show you what to do with that." Quickly and deftly, he dipped his fingers in the water, withdrew them and wiped them on the napkin he had placed beside the bowl. "There, you see. It's to clean your fingers off after you eat. Now let's see if you can do it."

With grins as big as the waiter's, first Harry and then Jen did as he directed, then looked at us to see what we thought. Both Harriet and I laughed and thanked the waiter for his interest. We suspected he knew "country" when he saw it!

When we got back to the compartment, the bunks had been made up for the night. It was dark outside, and we had had a long day, so we decided to turn in even though it was only about eight o'clock. Harry and I stayed out of the compartment, looking out the window while the "girls" got into their nightgowns. When Harriet called out, we went in. Jen in the bunk she would share with Harry was already fast asleep. Harriet lay in our bunk reading while Harry and I got ready. I didn't realize it until we started to undress, but the train seemed to have picked up speed since we were in the dining car. It was going so fast, and the car was lurching from side to side so badly, I had a hard time standing on one leg then the other, trying to get my trousers off. I finally made it with Harry standing there waiting for me to get out of the way so he could use the toilet.

The minute he lifted the cover and stood up to the bowl, I could see it wasn't going to work; his body was swaying in one direction and the car in the other. He "let go" anyway. The result was that the only water that got into the toilet was that expelled during the middle one-half of the pendulum. The rest was deposited, alternately, on first one side, then the other side of the seat and floor.

"Harry, watch what you're doing!" I admonished, visualizing what would happen when the next person got up in the night and got their feet wet.

"I can't help it, Daddy!" he half-cried back. I could see he was trying desperately to at least diminish the range of the arc. About that time, Harriet looked over to see what was going on. She burst out laughing and said to me, "You'll just have to get something and wipe it up. You're the one who wanted a boy, you know!"

Neither Harriet nor I got much sleep that night, but the children slept like logs. We had chosen the bunk perpendicular to the train for ourselves and had given the parallel bunk to the kids. So while either our feet or heads were being crushed against the ends of the bunk, the youngsters were being rocked, as if in a cradle, albeit a high flyer. In the name of a "new experience," we decided to change that arrangement on the way home. Then, too, we opined the shorter bodies would have a lot more "clearance."

Well, the trip was great. We got a lot of visiting done and I got to eat quite a few of those special hot dogs, the kind with all sorts of different toppings, famous in the Chicago area at the time. We went into town on the bus to the museums and got lost coming home. By the time we headed back West, we were ready to "look it in the eye" for another year.

As I look back on all of this, I'm convinced Harriet and I deluded ourselves when we thought we were giving the kids "new experiences," for *we* were never the same!

UNUSUAL PETS

It appears that some folks have to be different in their choice of a pet, like Bill Wrangler and his monkey. Others have unusual pets simply because of circumstances, like someone who is hunting wildcats and happens to kill a female with kittens or about to have some. Sometimes, the one who can kill an adult cannot bring himself to kill a kitten, so when that happens, somebody gets an unusual pet to raise. And, more often that not, sometime the services of a veterinarian will be requested.

"Doctor, this is Mrs. Tebo. I just got home from the hospital and need to have you de-claw Nettie," the caller explained.

Now I knew Nettie to be her thirty-pound, eight-year-old bobcat that I had given a rabies shot about a year earlier. She didn't like men, much less someone who smelled of medicine, like vets!

"What seems to be the problem?" I asked, hoping to solve whatever was wrong without tangling with Nettie.

"Well, about a week ago, Nettie was lying on top of the piano where she usually does, and when I went by and reached out to pet her, she hit my hand with a front paw. Just playin', I figure, but anyway, she drew blood. Then she became excited and made a lunge for the hand, acting as if she wanted to chew it. I don't know how I got away from her, but when I did, my wrist was tore up enough so I had to go to the hospital. They kept me there for three days and gave my a shot for lockjaw and a lot of antibiotics. They said I may have to have reconstructive surgery, too. It scared my husband to death. Otis thinks we should put Nettie to sleep, but I don't want to do that. I've had her so long, and this is the first time she's done anything like this. Before you got here, I had her spayed, so it couldn't have been anything to do with her cycle that caused it."

I was not then and still am not an advocate of people owning or having essentially wild animals in their homes. Too many accidents can happen. And more than that, the animals will have little chance to express themselves normally or to develop normal behavior. When the time comes to dispose of the animal, as it most often does, there is really only one choice: put them to sleep. Here it was again!

"Well, if you've decided not to have her put down, I guess it might be best to remove her claws, her front ones at least. I hate to do it, but she's too old now to think of turning loose in the wild," I responded, dreading the difficulty of getting her under anesthesia and doing the surgery on this age cat. Like so many procedures in veterinary medicine, the procedure itself was relatively straightforward; getting an animal restrained or anesthetized was the greatest problem.

"You or Otis will have to come to the clinic for some tranquilizers to give her before you bring her in. We'll never be able to give her the anesthesia unless she's already knocked out a little."

"I don't think we'll be able to do that," Mrs. Tebo exclaimed. "You know how a cat is!"

"Well, you'll just have to get it down her, maybe in some food. There's no way we can handle her without it." I had made up my mind after a previous near-miss with getting clawed by a bobcat, and I would not attempt to handle one in strange surroundings, without taking at least that precaution. Mrs. Tebo must have sensed I meant business.

"I'll send Otis in after it, then. When do you want to do the surgery?" she asked.

I glanced at my calendar. "Make it the day after tomorrow. You can give her the medicine in the morning, say about eight o'clock, then have her in here by eleven, if she's good and sleepy. Otherwise, let me know when she is sleepy and we'll work her in later in the day. The main thing, she has to be woozy enough that we can get an ether can over her nose and mouth without her fighting us too much. Otherwise, I'll have to use a bucket with ether-soaked cotton on the bottom."

There was a moment of silence at the other end of the line. I doubted it was one of prayer, but thought rather it was the realization of why it was necessary to get the pills into the cat. "Mercy, is it going to take a bucketful of ether to get her under?" Mrs. Tebo asked incredulously.

"Not a bucketful," I laughed. "The ether dispenser I normally use for cats is too small to go over Nettie's nose and mouth, so I'll have to make one that is large enough, or put some cotton in the bottom of a bucket and soak it with ether. A few whiffs of that and she'll be under in a minute."

Otis came in for the tranquilizer pills that afternoon. "I just couldn't talk her into putting that cat to sleep," he fretted. "She hasn't liked me from the beginning. Every time I walk past that piano where she rests, she lays back her ears, opens her mouth, and hisses at me. I have to go by there to get to the bathroom, too."

I couldn't help smiling to myself. I could just envision poor old Otis having to make a weighty decision every time he had to go to the toilet! And, "running a gauntlet," so to speak, if he decided he had to. I handed him a bottle containing enough pills that if he had to put them in her food, it would still do a good job of tranquilizing her. "Don't you or Mrs. Tebo get hurt giving Nettie these pills," I warned. "If she'll take two dissolved in her milk, okay; if not, give her three in some meat she likes. That'll require a little longer to take effect, but you'll be able to tell."

At ten o'clock on the day we were to do the surgery, Mrs. Tebo called. "Doctor, Otis is on his way in with Nettie. She's good and sleepy. I couldn't stand to come in so you will have to help get her out of the car. She was something to get loaded, as heavy as she is."

In less than ten minutes Otis arrived. I went out to help him in with the somewhat limp Nettie wrapped in an old sheepskin coat. When we started to get hold of her, she raised her head, looked around glassy-eyed, laid back her ears, opened her mouth baring her very sharp prominent fangs, and hissed! Halfheartedly, but it was there.

"She's not out of it, that's for sure," I grunted to Otis as I reached for the coat and wrapped it tighter around her.

"Here, Doc. Let me cover her head some more with the collar of the coat. Maybe that will quiet her," Otis offered. "I'll get hold of her front if you'll carry the back end." With that arrangement, we got her out of the seat of his old pickup and onto the table in the operating room. So far, so good.

Now, there are three stages of anesthesia an animal has to go through: induction, maintenance, and recovery. The induction stage is further subdivided into three periods: excitement, rigidity, and relaxation. When an inhalation anesthesia such as ether is used, the excitement stage can be quite pronounced. In cats, that means the minute they inhale that first breath after the ether can is placed over their nose and mouth, the fight is on until relaxation occurs. Normally, domestic cats are placed in a canvas bag or some other device, with only the head left protruding, so they won't injure themselves or the anesthetist while the claws on all four paws scratch wildly during the excitement stage. In addition, the animal tries to get its nose away from the ether can. Before the days of giving a tranquilizer for pre-anesthetic sedation. the scene was worse. Even so, I knew getting Nettie relaxed would be a challenge. Usually, Harriet helped with the anesthesia. This day, however, I decided the situation was too dangerous; Otis and I would do it or it wouldn't be done!

Covering Nettie's head had been a good idea, for normal respirations were the only movements coming from the sheepskin coat while I added ether to the gallon can containing the cotton. When I finished, I turned toward the table and looked at Otis. "Okay, we're ready. You just wrap that coat a little tighter around her body and lay on top of her a little," I instructed. "I'll expose her head just far enough to get this can over her nose and mouth. When she starts to struggle, hang on tight and don't let those legs get loose! I'll handle the head."

"Okay, Doc, I'm ready. Just don't let her sink her fangs into you." Otis's eyes were as big as the proverbial saucers. The room was wreaking with ether, too. I had poured a whole quarter-pound can full of it into the gallon can to be sure she would get plenty in the first few breaths. I'd take a chance on an overdose because it would be an underdose that would give us the trouble.

It worked like a charm! There were only a few scratching movements inside the coat and one brief yowl, then the steady breaths. I pulled the can away for a second, then placed it under her nose and mouth a little further away. That provided more air-to-ether ratio to be inhaled.

"Take the coat off her, Otis, and hold the can where I put it. You watch her breathing, too. If it changes from what it is now, let me know." With that, I began to clip the hair on her front paws and make other preparations for the surgery. After removing the first claw, I glanced over at Otis to be sure he was all right. I had seen owners of animals faint or nearly so any number of times when I was examining or doing a brief surgical procedure on their pet. I even had it happen to a young lady in the loading chute when she came for her horse after some surgery on him. In this case, Otis was sweating but otherwise doing fine, in spite of the surgery and the heavy odor of ether in the room.

It took only fifteen minutes to complete the procedure, including the bandaging. I thought controlling hemorrhage would be a problem, as big as the claws and arteries were, but the blood-clotting mechanism in a wildcat is very well developed. No blood was showing through the bandages when Nettie left.

When I was about through bandaging, I said to Otis, "Take the ether away from her. We're about through. We'll want to wrap her back up in that coat. Got to keep her warm on the way home and after you get there. She's breathing all right so it's just a matter of putting her in a good quiet place until she gets back on her feet. She should be up and around within an hour—two hours at most. You can call me if you are concerned about anything."

"What about the bandages, Doc? How are we going to get them off?" Otis asked somewhat apprehensively.

"You won't have to worry about that," I responded. "You can bet those will be the center of her attention the minute she recovers in good shape. She'll take them off and start licking her paws. That's the way it is with cats. You couldn't keep them from it if you wanted."

With that, I helped Otis wrap her up to carry her back to the pickup. The outside air was particularly refreshing, not only to get away from all that ether but also because a very unpleasant and potentially dangerous procedure was over without a mishap. There was always something exhilarating about the successful completion of a difficult task. Like "acing" the final exam.

"What happened with Nettie?" Harriet asked a couple of days later.

"Mrs. Tebo called this morning to ask how much she should feed her. She said the cat seemed ravenous ever since the surgery. Nettie removed the bandages just like I said she would. No blood or anything. Otis was amazed. He had a bad headache after he got home. Thought maybe it was from the ether."

Then, to give Harriet an additional bit of information passed on by Mrs. Tebo, I laughed and said, "Nettie has started to hiss at Otis again every time he walks by the piano to go to the toilet, so everything must be fine!"

BACK-HANDED
COMPLIMENTS

Veterinarians have an unusual way of eliciting unusual compliments from clients. At least, I took some of these whimsical comments to be compliments, of sorts. The body language and tone of voice used by the clients, or their offspring, made me believe they were compliments!

The first time I remember being "complimented" was at a ranch where I had been called to remove a large tumor from a cow. The growth, located on the animal's side just behind the right elbow, was bigger than a man's head and hung down like a second udder. I had seen the animal a few days before when I was at the ranch vaccinating heifers against brucellosis. (It happened then as it happened more times than I liked, after I had completed the original task I was called to do, the rancher would begin, "Say, Doc, while you're here, I got an ol' cow, or an ol' bull, or a young calf, I want you to look at. Do you have time?" Well, what can a fellow say under those circumstances? Particularly, when you're more likely than not a good twenty or thirty miles away from the office.)

On this particular occasion, he had the cow handy and it took me only a few minutes to examine her and determine that the mass was probably a fatty tumor.

"There are three things you can do to her," I said to Ray. (The rancher's name was Ray Kaskov). "Sell her, let her go the way she is, or remove it."

"Heck, Doc, she wouldn't bring anything with that thing hanging off her. You know those buyers knock off all they can for any little thing wrong. It's growing all the time, so it's not going to go away. That leaves taking if off as the only thing to do ... unless it's going to cost too much. Then I might have to shoot her. I don't want the old thing to suffer. How much would you charge to take it off?"

This was early in my career, so I had not thought of the fourth option. Besides, one doesn't think of that as a viable choice when he dreams of becoming a veterinarian and then strives mightily to get into veterinary school and stay in.

I thought for a moment how far it was from town (twenty-five miles), how much time it would take (probably a couple of hours until we got her down, I did the surgery, and I got cleaned up), and how many drugs she would need afterward (a 10 cc bottle of penicillin, given over a three-day period).

"Well, it will be twenty-five dollars plus the cost of a bottle of penicillin, which is seven-fifty," I responded, looking directly at Ray to see how he would react. Cows were only worth about $100 at the time. They had come down from $300 the year before.

He shuffled a little and shoved his hands deeper into his pockets. Finally he said, "Well, if you think you can cure her, let me know when you can come out and we'll have her in. I guess she's worth that much if she lives."

That kind of response to a disease problem was always such a confidence builder. "Let's figure on doing it day after tomorrow," I said, "about ten in the morning."

"That will be fine," Ray replied. "The kids will be home from school and can help if we need them."

When I arrived at the ranch about nine forty-five on the morning designated, Ray had the Hereford in the corral, and his son (twelve) and daughter (fourteen) were with him. With no chute in which to hold her, that normally meant throwing an animal to the ground and tying the legs so it couldn't get up. In those days, there were no tranquilizers, and the standard general anesthetics were not considered very reliable for use in cattle. Thus, we used manual restraint, plus local anesthetics, to control the surgical patient and to relieve pain.

It just so happened that a few weeks before this event took place, a new drug had come on the market that was touted as a safe anesthetic for cattle. I had obtained a bottle and was anxious to try it, even though it would take at least $10 worth to see how it worked. (Harriet was always scolding me for "subsidizing" my services!). I told Ray about the product and told him I'd like to try it.

"As long as it doesn't kill her, and you won't charge me any more than what you said, go ahead and experiment on her," he retorted.

After I got the instruments ready, I told Ray to get a halter on her and tie her to a post in the center of the corral. I estimated her weight and started to withdraw the correct amount of anesthetic from the bottle into the syringe. Only then did I notice that the product was a rather thick suspension as opposed to a solution, which was the normal medium for an intravenous product. It must be all right, I thought to myself, else the company would not have marketed it. Deftly, I hit the jugular vein on the first thrust, and slowly pushed the plunger of the syringe. I had given her about three-fourths of the dose when she started to wobble, so I gave her the rest before she moved enough to get the needle out of the vein. Then she collapsed without a struggle, landing in the best position possible.

"Boy, that stuff sure worked fast!" Ray exclaimed.

"It sure did," I answered, very relieved and pleased, for I really didn't know what to expect from a new compound.

Quickly, I washed and disinfected the mass and held it up out of the dirt while Ray's daughter slipped an old bed sheet under it. Then, I went over to the table holding the instruments, washed my hands with disinfectant soap, and pulled on a pair of sterile rubber gloves. As I turned to face the animal, I overheard the girl say to her brother, "See, just like a real doctor."

Ray chuckled and said to her, "What do you mean a real doctor?"

I could see her face redden. "Daddy, you know what I mean," she replied, embarrassed.

I smiled a little, too, as I set about the task in front of me. Come to think about it, that was my normal response when I received such compliments.

The cow? She got along just fine. The anesthesia was wearing off just as I placed the last suture. She had what we call in medicine an "uneventful recovery."

The anesthetic agent? I used it on at least five other animals, one of which was a $3,000 bull. Later in the month I went to a veterinary meeting and discovered that several veterinarians had lost valuable animals with the stuff. I didn't encounter a single "untoward effect," but I never used it again. It wasn't on the market long anyway!

A compliment I got on more than one occasion was from clients who became disgruntled with the treatment they received from one of the three MDs in town or at the county hospital. One, in particular, I remember vividly.

L.A. Brown, a rancher from down toward Moorcroft, came to the clinic to get medicine for a sick steer. He had just come from a doctor's office where, evidently, he felt he had a rather rough physical examination to determine if he had stones in his bladder. His face was ashen, though normally it was red and ruddy. His hands were shaking and the minute he got inside the door, he had to sit down on the couch in the waiting room.

I was somewhat alarmed when I saw him. "Are you feeling all right, L.A.?" I asked, thinking perhaps he was having a coronary.

He didn't answer until he got seated and gained his composure. "By gosh, Doc," he let loose, "I've just had about the roughest exam since I was in the army during the war. I went to ol' Doctor … 'cause I got a lot of pain in my bladder region last night, and I think I passed a stone. Leastwise, it burned enough down there when I passed water I had to holler to Mabel because I thought I was going to faint. Anyways, when I got the doctor this morning and told him my problem, he made me take off my pants and underwear and get on that damned old metal table he uses for examinations. Then he proceeded to stick a catheter up my you-know-what, without any dope on it. Christ, it hurt! When he got through with that, he made me bend over and he prodded around with his finger 'til I thought I would die. Finally he said, 'You can put your clothes on.... There's nothing wrong with you now. If you had a stone, you've passed it, so there's nothing to worry about unless it happens again.' Then he proceeded to leave the room to see another patient, without as much as a by-your-leave."

"What happened then?" I asked. It was hard to believe Dr.... would act like this with a patient, unless he was under stress from some other source.

"Well, I just spoke up and said, 'Gosh, Doc, aren't you going to give me any-thing for pain, in case it happens again? It was awful, what I went through last night'!"

So he pulled out his pad and scribbled something on it. "Here, take this to the drugstore," he told me. "If you feel something like this coming on again, take two of the pills and get in here as soon as you can. If it's after office hours, go to the emergency room at the hospital. They can get a hold of me from there." Then he turned and left while I cleaned myself up as best I could.

"That doesn't sound much like Dr..... to me," I proffered.

"I know it doesn't," L.A. acknowledged. However, he was still pretty upset about the episode. "When I got back in the car, I told Mabel that if ever anything like last night happened again, she was to bring me right up here to you. Heck, Doc, you treat sick animals better'n I was treated down there. I'm sure you know more about treating someone with stones better than those MDs. After all, you handle waterbelly steers all the time, and most of them get well!"

I smiled a little and said I might get sued for malpractice, or practicing with-out a license, if I took him up on his wish. I thanked him for the compliment anyway.

Despite these back-handed compliments, it was truly a compliment when, over the years, Harriet and I witnessed a procession of clients' sons or daughters become part of the veterinary profession. Somehow, we felt we were part of the reason for their making that choice.

THE PONY AND THE
ELEPHANT

Fair time usually turned out to be a crazy time for me. It occurred in the fall when I was busy inspecting animals for shipment to other states. It was also the time when there were larger than ordinary sales at the livestock exchange where I was expected to be on hand most of the time to provide health certificates for purchasers and to test or "doctor" animals that required it. I also had to tend sick animals that were brought to the clinic.

On top of all this, fair time brought show animals to the fairgrounds just outside of town. This included cattle, sheep, horses, ponies, rabbits, chickens, gerbils, and of course lots and lots of young, middle-aged, and old people. Everyone wanted to see the fair!

One year, in addition to all this, a circus was in town at the same time. A circus has animals, too, and this one had an elephant and a pony that "gave me a go," for a few minutes. As we looked back on it years later, Harriet and I laughed about the experience. At the time, it was a little "hair-raising."

That September day broke unusually hot. By noon, the temperature was close to ninety degrees and the sun was really beating down. I had been to the fairgrounds already once that morning, checking on a bloated bull. Every animal that could pant was doing so. People were fanning themselves with their hats or programs. It was "bloody hot!" as the English would say. When I returned to the clinic from the fairgrounds, Harriet called on the intercom.

"Bob, you've got to go downtown and look at a sick pony that belongs to the circus. They called just a minute ago. The pony will be standing on the street beside the trailer that holds the elephant. And the fellow said somebody will be around there to tell you how it's been acting."

"Did he say what he thought was wrong?"

"Just that it is lame, doesn't want to move."

"Okay, I'll go right down!" I hollered into the box, at the same time running through my mind what the malady could be: arthritis, founder, torsion, whatever. I could always run back after making the diagnosis if I didn't have the medicine I needed on the truck. It wasn't easy to find a parking space in the vicinity of the trailer. The town was full even at that time of day and people were milling around the circus display on the streets, but finally I got parked and walked over to the trailer. There was a pony tied to a parking meter nearby, its head hanging lower than usual. There wasn't a bit of shade and the pavement was sizzling hot.

"What a place to tie an animal!" I muttered to myself. When I got close to it, a man came around the back of the trailer.

"Are you the vet?" he asked as he came over to me and the pony.

"Yes, I am. Is this the pony someone called me about?"

"Yep. We were in Sheridan yesterday and he didn't act right then, sort of gimpy on his feet, so we pulled him out of the ring, thinking he just needed a little rest. When we unloaded him from the truck this morning, he couldn't hardly walk. That's when we called you. What do you think it is?"

"I'll tell you better after I examine him," I answered as I reached down to pick up a hoof. (It always beat me how some people expected me to know immediately what was wrong with their animal, even before the examination!)

After examining each hoof, I untied the animal and tried to lead him around. He was reluctant to move and did so only after much urging. "You said you just noticed this yesterday?" I asked.

"Yep. During the opening ceremonies. We pulled him out the minute we noticed he wasn't right."

"Where were you the day before yesterday?" I had already pretty much decided he had the condition called founder. The event that precipitated it must have occurred at least a couple of days earlier. It would take that long to show up at least.

"We were in Hardin, Montana, putting on a show for the Indians," he answered. "It's been awful hot this total trip. Would that have anything to do with it?"

"Well, it could have. The pony has been foundered. That's where the blood vessels in the feet expand and press against the nerves running along them. Since the hoof wall cannot expand, it causes intense pain. There are a number of causes, from drinking cold water after being exercised, to being worked out unusually long on hard surfaces. Overloading on grain can cause it. Ponies have been known to get it just eating green grass in the spring of the year. Whatever the cause, it usually leaves them permanently lame."

"Does that mean he won't be able to work in the ring again?"

"It depends on how he gets along with the treatment I'll give him. If we can reduce the inflammation in those hoofs soon enough, he'll probably be okay for light work. If he doesn't respond well within twenty-four hours, I'd say he'll need extensive foot surgery plus constant medication to keep him going."

The man looked at the pony a few minutes then said, "Well, the boss said to have you do what you could for him as long as it didn't cost too much. We will be leaving here right after the show tonight for Rapid City, South Dakota. We'll see how he gets along on the medicine you give him. You can give us enough for a few days and we'll reassess the situation then. It's for sure we can't afford to have a lame animal in the ring with all those people looking at him."

"Well, the first thing we've got to do is get him into some shade and off the street," I said, looking around for some space that would do.

"How about the front of the trailer where the elephant is?" The man pointed toward the covered overhang of the trailer, where hay and other feed for the elephant was kept.

"Looks good to me. I'll treat him now, and you can get some men to help you get him in there after I've gone. I've got a busy schedule but will come back about four o'clock and give him some more medication. Then I'll leave you enough for three or four days. By rights, his feet should be placed in ice water for several hours at a time, but that isn't possible unless you would be willing to leave him behind."

"Can't do that. We won't be back this way until next year at least. Maybe never," the man responded. "You just come back at four and holler if you need any help, then come out to the office trailer for your money."

It sounded all straightforward enough. However, I didn't reckon with the elephant in the trailer!

It was closer to four-thirty when I got back to see the pony the second time. I had been called to the fairgrounds twice during the day to treat injured animals. One steer had gotten loose and cut his leg on a fence before he was finally caught. One horse kicked another and tore a gash in its rump. In between times, I had to inspect several carloads of calves going to Illinois. When I got ready to go back to the pony, I asked Harriet if she wanted to go. (I've forgotten where the kids were, but they were not with us.) When we parked and walked over to the trailer, we first went to the back where a group of people were feeding peanuts to the elephant, which was inside the trailer, facing the back, extending her trunk through the bars that separated her from the onlookers. She had a big chain around one front foot, with the other end bolted to the floor. I judged there was about three feet of slack in it so she could move around a little.

As I looked past her toward the front of the trailer, and saw a partition with a door in it, I turned to Harriet and pointed. "The pony must be behind that door. You just wait here and I'll go in and treat him. I shouldn't be a minute," I said.

Black bag in hand, I went to the front of the trailer, climbed the temporary steps that led from the street to the inside, walked behind the elephant, which was still busy munching peanuts, and went through the door of the feed room where the pony was standing eating hay. Closing the door behind me, I hooked it and examined the animal again. His temperature was still high, but less than in the morning. He drank a little water from the bucket I offered to him. He seemed more alert, but I couldn't tell if it was from the effects of the medicine or just getting away from the intense heat of the sun.

As I was giving him a second injection, I felt the trailer sway perceptibly. I figured the elephant was just moving around a little trying to reach some more peanuts. After a bit, though, I heard the door behind me rattling, and then a noise like an animal sniffing heavily. The trailer began to rock even more. I looked toward the door and suddenly saw the end of her trunk coming over it, reaching, as if to unhook the latch. The sniffing noise got louder. The trunk was extended farther in toward me. Pushing the pony between me and the trunk, I got as far against the front of the trailer as I could get. Just when I thought her trunk would reach me, it stopped coming, but she got hold of the top of the door and started to shake it. I knew that door wouldn't last long against all the power and strength of that elephant.

Hoping Harriet was still where I left her, I called out, "Harriet, can you hear me?" The trunk disappeared for a minute.

"Yes, I can hear you. What do you want?"

"Try to get the elephant to turn around so I can get out of here!" I shouted back. "If you can't, find one of the circus people!"

The rattling of the door and the sniffing started again, then the trunk came over the door ... searching ... searching. I stood very quietly as the end of the trunk touched the pony .. and went on, finally returning to the top of the door. I thought for sure that time it would give way.

I could hear Harriet calling and calling, trying to get the animal to turn around. At last the trunk disappeared, and the trailer swayed violently again. "She's turning around!" Harriet hollered. "You can get out now, if you hurry!"

I didn't wait, but dropped the syringe into the bag, stepped around the pony, opened the door wide enough to see that although she was indeed facing the back of the trailer, she was beginning to rotate her body on the chained front leg. I grabbed the bag, flung open the door, and got to the outside door just as she made the complete turn. I jumped out of the trailer to the ground just as her trunk touched my back! Harriet ran around to greet me.

"Are you all right?" she exclaimed.

"Yes, I'm okay. But she sure gave me a fright! You know I forgot what an elephant caretaker in St. Louis told me several years ago. He said that elephants, for all their size, are very dependent upon their caretaker for peace of mind, that they are easily frightened by little things when the caretaker is not around. I was dumb not to find some of the circus people before I went in there."

By the time we gathered our composure and were ready to leave, the old girl had returned to her original position, begging peanuts through the bars at the back of the trailer.

Harriet and I talked about that experience many times afterward, sometimes even making up mock newspaper headlines that might have appeared if I'd been injured or worse: "Vet Injured By Elephant In Wyoming!" "Frightened Pachyderm Clobbers Vet In Cattle Country!" "Elephant Thought Vet Was a Mouse. Gives Her a Start!"

THE DOG HATERS

Some time, it happens in every practice—usually late at night. Not one call, but anywhere from half a dozen to ten or twelve within an hour. The calls end as abruptly as they begin, and the stories are all the same, conveyed in the same manner, at the top of the caller's voice. "Doctor! this is—; our dog is having fits! I think he's dying! Can I bring him right out?"

For the first couple of calls I would ask, "How long has he been having fits?" I was thinking initially the animal had canine distemper or some other disease that could result in convulsions. Maybe it was something that had been going on for some time and the owner was just getting concerned.

However, the answers came back: "We let him out to run before going to bed and about fifteen minutes after he came back in, he started breathing hard and then fell down in fits. The fits are worse when we try to get hold of him, or if there is a loud noise around." When I heard that answer I knew it was time not to ask questions but have the animal brought out immediately to the clinic. It was a pretty close bet that a dog poisoner was on the loose, so time was of the essence!

The first time it happened, it was about ten o'clock at night. Harriet and I had just listened to the news on the radio (we did not have a television) and were getting ready for bed. When the telephone rang, I knew instinctively it had to be trouble, for early fall is not normally a time for emergencies. (After a few years in practice, too, you get so you can just "feel" big trouble.)

When I picked up the phone at the head of the bed, Mrs. Benjamin's voice came screaming through the receiver: "Doctor, I think Sandy is dying! Can I bring her right out?" I knew the voice as well as the dog. The Benjamins were clients and Sandy was their blonde cocker spaniel, close to three years old, and had had all of her immunizations.

"How is she acting, Pat?" I asked, wanting as much information as I could get before she arrived.

"We let her out to run before we went to bed. When she came back in, she acted all right, but in about ten minutes she started to run around the house like a crazy dog, yelping and barking. Pretty soon she just fell down and is now having fits!" Pat was breathless. I could hear her husband and the kids shouting something in the background.

I knew the Benjamins well enough to know the story was correct. If Sandy had been ill before now, they would not have waited until ten o'clock at night to bring her out. I suspected poisoning. Nothing else had an onset as rapid as what she described. Animals with rabies might have some of the same signs, but normally they show other signs of being ill for a period of time first.

"Wrap her in a blanket or old rug and bring her right out!" I responded. "Keep your hands away from her mouth in case she tries to bite you, too. I'll be waiting for you at the clinic."

When I hung up, Harriet, who was already in bed, looked at me questioningly. "What in the world was that all about?" she asked.

"It was Pat Benjamin. Sandy is in convulsions, and they're bringing her right out," I answered as I got ready to go up to the clinic. "I'll be back as soon as I can."

"Do you want me to get dressed and help?"

"No, I should be all right after I get it figured out. I should be back in half an hour if everything goes okay."

By the time I had the lights turned on at the clinic, a car came speeding in the drive. I held the front door open as Dan, carrying Sandy in a blanket, came straight in and placed the animal on the examination table, with Pat puffing and blowing right behind him. "By golly, Doc, we don't know what happened," Dan sputtered. "Sandy was perfectly all right when we let her out tonight. Now look at her!"

I was looking at her: breathing rapidly, foam around her mouth, the pupils of her eyes widely dilated. When I touched her, she went into a convulsion. There was only one thing it could be: strychnine poisoning! Turning quickly, I grabbed a syringe and needle and a bottle of apomorphine, a drug which will make a dog throw up. In a few seconds I had given Sandy a shot and carried her outside with the Benjamins right behind me. As I was carrying her out, I heard the telephone ring but knew Harriet would answer it.

Almost immediately Sandy started to wretch, finally emptying the contents of her stomach. While this was going on, I turned to Pat and Dan and explained, "I suspect poisoning, probably strychnine. That's why I gave her a medicine to get it out of her stomach, at least. The poison circulating in her system will have to wear off or be dispelled through her liver and kidneys. That will take some time, maybe five to eight hours. In the meantime to stop the convulsions, I'll have to put her under anesthesia, and she can just sleep it off. Otherwise, she would keep convulsing until the effects wore off or she died from paralysis of the respiratory system. Either way, she is completely conscious even though she doesn't look like it, and every contraction of the muscles is very painful—like a giant charley horse! The anesthesia will give relief from the pain even if we cannot save her."

Pat and Dan looked at me as if they couldn't believe what they were hearing. Then Pat began to cry softly as she looked down at Sandy. Finally, Dan exclaimed, "Where would she get hold of strychnine? We don't keep anything like that around the house. Do you suppose somebody put some out deliberately? Someone who doesn't like dogs?"

Seeing that Sandy was through expelling her stomach contents, I picked her up to return to the examination table and started the anesthesia into her vein. I hadn't responded to Dan's question, but I didn't have to, for about that time Harriet called on the intercom, "Bob, you've got another dog coming in. It's in convulsions. I'm getting dressed and will be right up to help!"

When Pat heard what Harriet had to say, she stopped crying and became angry. "There has to be someone around that either hates dogs or hates people that own them. Anyone that would poison a dog is sick, sick, sick. I wish I could get hold of him!" she bellowed.

After I had given Sandy enough pentobarbital to quiet her, I asked Dan to get a paper cup from the sink area and gather up the emesis from the lawn. "I need to send a sample to the lab to confirm my suspicion, and I don't want another dog getting into it, either," I explained.

By the time I had Sandy far enough under to stop the convulsions and had placed her in a cage, under a blanket, the other dog had arrived. The big black Labrador retriever, weighing close to seventy pounds, was breathing hard and foaming at the mouth, with only an occasional convulsion. It required the owner, Dan, and me to carry the big guy from the back seat of the car to the front lawn. They held him while I went into the clinic to get the apomorphine. Like Sandy, soon after the injection, he retched and heaved, expelling his stomach contents. Like Sandy, a chunk of meat was evident amidst the rest of the emesis. It took all three of us again to get him into the clinic and onto the table. Meanwhile, Harriet had come up and was talking with Pat and the wife of the other client as they watched over Sandy.

"Isn't it something?" Pat was saying. "Imagine anyone poisoning a dog!"

Harriet didn't have time to respond before the telephone rang again. This time someone from the same neighborhood was calling about a little Boston Bull that was "acting funny ... sort of having fits, I think," is the way the owner put it.

I heard Harriet say, "Bring her right out. Wrap her in a blanket to keep her warm and to keep her from accidentally biting you!" After she hung up, she came into the surgery where Dan and the other client were watching me slowly inject the Lab with anesthesia. She looked at me and said, "You probably heard, but you've got another dog on its way in. Sounds like the same thing."

"'It never rains but what it pours,' Grandmother used to say," I answered, trying to bring a little levity onto the scene.

As usual, no one understood my sense of humor. Dan, now getting into the routine of things, got a paper cup and left to gather up the mess from the Lab before the Boston arrived. As often happened under stressful situations, at least one person would become an angel and just "move in," taking over the manual chores while I, or in this case Harriet and I, carried out the medical tasks. Our good friend and neighbor, Dr. Frank Hadley, was especially good at this. After the Boston arrived, Pat left to get back to the children. Dan stayed on through the tenth and last one for the night, and it was close to one o'clock when he left in our old Jeep station wagon. We had dogs asleep all over the place, including some on the straw in the stalls of the large animal section. I kept a vigil until three o'clock, but then I lay down on the couch in the reception room and slept for about two hours.

When I awoke, it was time to give Sandy some more anesthesia since she was beginning to show signs of convulsions again. It took a lot of pentobarbital to get her "under" again. The idea was to give just enough drug to eliminate the convulsions, then hope by the time the animal "woke up," the strychnine would be metabolized out of the system. It worked well in most cases, especially if the stomach was emptied before too much poison could enter the bloodstream. Little dogs seemed more vulnerable to the lethal effects if the strychnine than large breeds did.

By daybreak, eight of the ten patients were in various stages of "the wobbles." That is, they were coming out of the anesthesia nicely and were wobbling around trying to regain their feet. No further signs of convulsions ... just bleary-eyed and unsteady. At that point, I could identify with them!

Dan and Pat brought the Jeep back about six-thirty, just as I came out of the house. They looked at me apprehensively, as if they were afraid to ask. "How's Sandy?" Pat spoke up.

"I had to give her some more pentobarbital around five this morning, but I think perhaps this round will be enough. She must have taken on quite a load of whatever it was," I answered, as we all entered the clinic. We went directly to the cage where Sandy was just trying to arouse herself. Pat and Dan couldn't wait to open the door and talk "sweet talk" to her.

Finally Dan said, "Isn't it a fright how you get attached to an animal? Too bad some kids don't get the same attention. Our kids are all just waiting for us to get home and tell them how she is." They both laughed, little embarrassed laughs.

How many times would I encounter the same scene with the same rhetorical question during those clinical practice years? I never tried to answer the question, for I always thought that whoever asked it just sort of went on in his own mind and answered it for himself. Better to leave it that way. To me a more puzzling question was what kind of mind sought to kill someone's pet in order to solve a problem? I don't know if that has any coherent answer either. Maybe they just don't like dogs. Maybe they just don't like *some* dogs. Maybe they don't like dog owners that allow their animals to run loose when they are supposed to be confined. Maybe ... Maybe ... Maybe.

With that much activity—in the middle of the night—in a small town, it didn't surprise me that both the manager of the radio station and the editor of the newspaper called the next day to get a story. There hadn't been that much excitement since the New Year's Eve dance at the Legion Hall!

There wasn't another such incident for several years. Then it involved only a couple of animals, likely from someone trying to poison magpies or some other pest. Anyway, you can bet the dog catcher didn't have much business for a few months after the word got out. The city's leash law was never so well obeyed.

Yes, I must add, we lost the Boston. I hated it all the more because I grew up with one. It didn't seem right that I couldn't "save" one of the breed that was a real pal during my early years. Her name was Buddy. But you see, all Bostons were Buddy to me!

THE INSPECTOR

One role for which a veterinary college prepares its graduates is the pursuit of public health. This can take on many aspects, from full-time employment inspecting meat, poultry, and other food products, to managing broad programs for controlling diseases of animals transmissible to man. Rabies and brucellosis are examples of this.

At the local, private practitioner level in Wyoming during the 1950s and '60s, a small but significant part of my work was public health related. Inspecting restaurants, grocery stores, bakeries and establishments such as the local meat locker plant was one of the tasks I carried out under agreement with the Wyoming Department of Agriculture. Since it was difficult to hire qualified inspectors to cover the vast territory encompassed by Wyoming, they liked to use the local veterinarian whenever possible because their formal training gave them the requisites for this job. Before I went to veterinary college, I also trained as a sanitarian at a health department in Michigan. So kitchens and coolers of restaurants were nothing new to me. Neither were meat locker plants, or dairies. I filled out inspection forms correctly, too!

In relation to the meat locker plant at Gillette, I not only had to inspect animals brought in for slaughter, I also had to see that the premises and equipment were in a sanitary condition—that is, during the greater part of the year. During hunting season, things were different, even though they really weren't supposed to be that much different. The difference was due to the crush in the numbers of game animals that had to be processed during that season. In fact, during the hunting season, few if any domestic animals were brought in for slaughter because the plant had too many other things to do. There was always the potential for an exception, however, and that was the situation when I got a call during my second year in practice at Gillette.

"Doc, this is Bill Ashby. Will you come down to the locker plant? I've got a Hereford-lope that needs to be inspected." I could hear some very excited voices in the background. It was seven o'clock on a Saturday night, the last day of hunting in Campbell County. Bill Ashby was the state brand inspector. Being at the locker plant to inspect antelope was not part of his job since only cattle, sheep, horses, and mules came under the purview of the state brand inspection system. Certainly wild animals were not covered. I never knew Bill to take a drink either, so I figured he was not calling from a bar to "fun" me a little, like some of my friends.

"What's going on, Bill?" I responded dubiously.

"You better come down here and have a look for yourself. You wouldn't believe me if I told you," he laughed.

When I hung up the receiver, Harriet looked over at me curiously. "What was that all about? Surely you don't have to got out on a call. This is Saturday night!"

"It was Bill Ashby. There must be something screwy going on down at the locker plant. That's where he called from. Says I need to go down, something about a Hereford-lope."

"Well, don't be too long ... remember, we were going to the movies at eight. Sally is coming over to sit with the kids."

I grabbed my Stetson and jacket and ran up to the pickup. With luck and a little hustle, we could still make the movie. In five minutes I pulled up in front of the plant. Bill's car was there, sure enough, along with about six others. Most had out-of-state license plates. I saw Bill standing in the front entry talking to a couple of fellows, obviously hunters. When he saw me, he hollered, "In here, Doc. Come in the back."

The back of the plant was where, depending on the season of the year, game or livestock were skinned out (they called it scun out) and otherwise prepared for final cutting and packaging. Right now, it was a mess! The hunters had really unloaded on the plant. Dead deer and antelope lay everywhere there was spare space. Game was also hanging from the rail leading into the cooler. Suddenly, I caught sight of something that was incongruous. It was more than incongruous, really—it was incredible. I saw a Hereford heifer laying amidst a pile of antelope! She had been "field dressed" like any wild game. It took me aback, somewhat, but then I remembered the experience I had with Straitor's milk cow.

"What do you make of it, Doc?" It was the voice of Lee Barrows. He had come up behind me as I was looking at the heifer. Lee was a rancher south of town, and I surmised the heifer was one of his. I was correct.

"Well, it's quite a site, I'll give you that," I responded. "This your heifer?"

"It was, but by gollies, these hunters are going to own it before this thing is over! One of my best animals, too. I just called the sheriff; he'll get this straightened out!" He said all this loud enough so Bill and the strangers with him could hear it. It couldn't hurt any, come settlement time.

"What do you want me to do, Bill?" I asked, turning toward him.

"Well, these fellas here figured on payin' Lee for the heifer, but they wanted it cut, wrapped, and shipped back East to them. Since you normally inspect any cattle that are slaughtered, we figured you better look at it before they processed it."

By that time, word of the debacle had gotten around to the other hunters who were milling about, waiting to check their game in. Must have been at least a dozen of them. Thus, in addition to Lee, Bill, and the two sportsmen beside him, who by now I assumed to be the culprits, these others were all looking at me for my pronouncement.

I stepped out from among the carcasses, looked at Bill, and said, "As far as the rules and regulations governing the slaughter of domestic livestock is concerned, this Hereford-lope, as you called her, has to be considered as a game animal. There is no way I can inspect and pass her for wholesomeness and put the state stamp on the meat. If anyone wants to eat her, they'll just have to do it like they would deer or antelope. If I put the stamp of approval on the carcass, the meat could be sold anywhere in the state. For all I know, that critter could have died by itself."

The cacophony that had accompanied the whole scene ceased, for a minute at least. About that time, the sheriff's car, with all lights flashing, wheeled up and stopped in front of the open overhead door. The sheriff himself got out. He was a kindly man, most of the time, and had been a cowboy in these parts for many years. He knew everybody, and everybody knew him. He was honest and fair. That's what they wanted in a lawman. He ambled over to where Bill and I were standing.

"Hi Bill, Doc. Lee called and said some hunters shot and killed one of his heifers. Wants them arrested. Is the animal in there?" he asked, pointing to the open door.

Bill responded, "She's in there all right. So is Lee. He's madder'n a hornet, too. For your information, these fellas here that killed the animal by mistake said they are plumb willin' to pay for her. I think we can settle this thing without anybody bein' arrested and going to jail, if we can get Lee settled down." That's when Lee came "hot footing it" out the door and started telling Ned about the whole thing, with gestures! The two antelope-stalkers just stood there intently watching the sheriff's face. As was typical for Ned, his expression didn't change. When Lee finished, Ned looked him right in the eyes and asked, "Do you want me to arrest them and put them in jail or just let them pay you and get out of town?" Ned had a way of getting right to the heart of the matter, no fooling around.

Lee glanced over at the hunters, then down to the ground. He jammed his hands into the pockets of his Levis, looked at Ned, and grunted almost inaudibly, "If they pay me a hundred and fifty dollars for her, let 'em go. I feel sorry for anybody that don't know the difference between an antelope and a cow. No use spendin' tax money lockin' 'em up."

The sheriff turned his eyes upon the hunters. "You fellas willing to pay this man a hundred and fifty dollars for his animal? If not, I'll have to put you in jail until Monday. The judge doesn't work Saturday night or Sunday."

Now, I can tell you, those men did not even have to look at one another to get agreement. "Sure, sheriff, we'll give him cash money right now. We want to get this thing settled!" It was the biggest of the two who spoke, the first time either had spoken to anyone except Bill.

Ned turned to Lee. "Guess that settles it. Wish all the cases I have to handle were this easy." With that, he turned on his heel and headed back to his car.

I glimpsed at my watch. It was quarter to eight. Still had time to get back to the house, pick up Harriet, and get to the movies. As I jumped into the pickup to head home, I noticed Lee and the hunters talking together. One of them was even offering him his hand. I thought to myself: there is forgiveness and reconciliation under the strangest circumstances.

What became of the heifer? Well, the hunters paid the processing fee, but left her with the locker plant operator. He fed out mink for their pelts. We always figured that's what he did with the meat. That's only an assumption, of course.

"WATER, WATER, EVERYWHERE..."

The worst kind of call a veterinarian can go on is one where there is no hope of saving the dying—and the "innocent dead" are lying in bunches here and there, or maybe strung out along a fence they couldn't get through. Even though you determine the cause of the catastrophe and time passes, the eyelid of "the mind's eye" never quite closes over the scene. Neither does the picture of agony, manifested by seasoned stockmen. One of the worst situations I was ever involved in had to do with water—a lack of it! It reminded me of a couple of lines from Samuel Taylor Coleridge's, "The Rhyme of the Ancient Mariner."

"Water, water, everywhere
Nor not a drop to drink."

"How could we have been so stupid?" Oscar asked me after he and I had ridden around the fence line and counted at least twenty dead heifers. Five others, still alive, were in their death throes. All the rest looked normal and healthy.

I had been at Oscar's place just a week earlier and vaccinated these same heifers against brucellosis. His 150 cattle were as pretty a bunch as I'd seen all winter. They were in good flesh, their hair coats were shiny, and their eyes were bright. You can tell a lot about an animal by "how it looks out of the eye," as they used to say out West. You can tell if it feels good or not so good; if it's gentle or not so gentle; if it's frightened or at ease with it's surroundings—a lot of things that make sense to someone working with livestock.

Oscar had called me a couple of hours earlier. "Doc! can you come right down?" His voice was high pitched, and he was obviously mighty upset over something.

"Yes, I can leave in just a few minutes," I responded. "What seems to be the matter?"

"You know those heifers you vaccinated for us last week? Well, when we finished with them, we took them over to the Banks' place. You know it's about five miles from here. We trailed them over and turned 'em loose in the big pasture. We didn't look at 'em until this morning after Jim Parson called and said we had some dead cattle along the fence joining him. We just got back from there and sure enough, there's some dead ones and a couple alive, but down and can't get up. We haven't been over the whole pasture yet. There's about ten sections in it. I rushed right back to call you. The boys were to keep riding to see how many more there are."

(A section of land contains 640 acres. Out West, it is not uncommon to have ten sections inside one fence. In that part of the county, it took twenty-five to thirty-five acres to support one animal unit; i.e., a cow and calf.)

Mentally, I quickly ran down the maladies that might be involved. I always thought first in terms of the etiological classifications of disease: infectious, chemical, physical, nutritional. I dismissed nutrition as a potential cause. Nothing dies that fast from a nutritional ailment.

"Did you see any up and walking around?" I probed.

"Yes, I saw a few. They looked good to me. Didn't notice any sickness in 'em if that's what you're askin'."

Probably not an infectious disease, I thought to myself, but I would have to check that in more detail. That left chemical or physical as likely causes.

"Are there any old buildings or dumps in that pasture?" I went on.

"Nope! That pasture is as clean as a hound's tooth. The only thing in it is a well with a windmill on it. Of course, there's a water tank, and we put some salt blocks around it."

I mentally checked off a chemical toxicity. That left something physical as the most obvious answer to whatever was going on.

"You said there was a well in the pasture? Is there a reservoir too?" I was thinking that was a pretty big pasture to have only one water source.

"No reservoir, just the well. It's located smack-dab in the middle of the place," Oscar replied. "You'll see when you get down here. We'll take you over to it."

"Okay. I should be there in about a half hour." His place was a little over thirty miles away, and ten miles were dirt.

When I pulled up to the gate, Oscar and a couple of his hands were waiting. The men were on their horses, and Oscar had his pickup. He opened the gate and as I drove through, he hollered, "Best take my pickup for now! It's pretty rough in spots. If you need anything, we'll come back and get it. There's a couple of dead ones right close here. You may want to look at them first. A little way over the hill, yonder, there's a live one that's down."

I did drive over to the dead ones because I wanted to conduct a post-mortem examination on at least a few.

When I got out, I looked at Oscar and then the men. "How many dead ones have you found?" I queried.

Oscar answered, "Twenty dead ones and five down that can't get up. God, Doc, do you suppose something in those shots you gave them coulda' done this?"

"Not likely. We'll "post" some and find out, however."

The only thing the autopsy showed was edema of the lungs, probably from thrashing around in the dust before dying, and very little liquid in the paunch or rumen (one of the four compartments of the stomach of a cow). In this size animal, there should be at least twenty-five gallons of fluid and grass. The contents were mainly grass, and darn little at that. I had to hunt hard to find the sites of the vaccine injection. I opened the skin over them and found that they were not unduly inflamed. Oscar and the boys were looking on intently.

"Nothing showing up on these two that would indicate the shots had anything to do with it. The only thing I see is no water in the paunch. Tell me again what happened after we vaccinated them."

"Well, sir, you know it was about two o'clock when we finished vaccinating 'em. As soon as you left, we turned 'em out on the road and trailed 'em right over here. It's about five miles. I followed the boys with a horse trailer 'cause we knew it would be close onto dark by the time we got 'em there and got back. We just threw 'em through the gate and come home. Didn't think anything more about 'em 'til Jim called this morning."

"You said the well is in the middle of the pasture?"

"Yep, already been over to it and the windmill's working all right. Most of the dead ones are along the fence over by Jim's. We'll drive over to 'em if you hop in."

I took my post-mortem equipment and climbed into the front seat of the pickup with Oscar. The cowboys hopped in the back. When we went by the well on the way to the other fence line, I saw a few heifers standing around the tank. They looked hale and hearty. Like Oscar said, the windmill was pumping okay, too.

Arriving at the line fence, we noticed Jim Parson riding up to the other side of it, and we also saw about ten head of dead heifers strung out for a short way.

"Hi, Jim!" I called over to him. Oscar and the boys said their howdies, too.

"Nothing to be worried about so far," I remarked, not wanting to say what I thought it was, for fear of embarrassing Oscar.

"Well, I've got a reservoir just down over the hill there," he said pointing toward the west. "If they got somethin' catchin', it would run off of 'em right down toward it."

I prepared to conduct some more post-mortems, even though I knew I wouldn't see anything different than I saw in the first two. Each one had taken a number of hours to die. You could tell that by the way the dirt was all dug up around them. The sides of their heads next to the ground were all swollen and the hair worn off, no doubt from beating them, trying to get up. I glanced up the fence line. The ground was churned to powder. It looked like a racetrack. It was obvious the cattle became thirsty, didn't find the well in the middle of the pasture, and kept walking and walking along the fence. The reason so many were at this place was probably because they could smell the water in Jim's reservoir. After wandering up and down so long, they just went down from exhaustion and dehydration.

Suddenly, it dawned on Oscar what most likely had happened. He looked over at me. "You don't suppose they couldn't find the water at the well, do you?"

I didn't answer immediately, since I was about ready to open up another animal. When I finally got to the paunch and it showed the same as the others—little or no water—I didn't have to say anything. Oscar, Jim, and the boys just looked from one to the other. Finally, Oscar took off his hat and wiped the sweat off his brow with the forearm of his shirt. That's when he exclaimed, "How could we have been so stupid!"

We went back and tried to rehydrate the ones still alive, but they were so far gone, they didn't make it either. All died within another few days.

"Water, water, everywhere,
Nor not a drop to drink."

THE OPEN HEIFER EPIC

An "open heifer" is a young bovine female, usually between one and two years old, that is not pregnant. At one time (and to some extent even now) they brought a premium price for fattening in feedlots, as opposed to heifers of unknown pregnancy status. There were several reasons for this. First, a feedlot operator usually loses money on a heifer that has a calf under those conditions, since he has been feeding her to be slaughtered and her having a calf delays the time she can be finished out. Second, expenses are usually greater because such heifers are likely to have problems delivering, and that means the cost of professional help. In most every way, they are "losers." Finally, for the heifer to have a calf upsets the whole operation!

Now there are abortifacients, drugs that cause pregnant animals to abort with little or no loss, providing they are not too far along. But at that time, the drugs were not very predictable; hence, the premium price paid for "guaranteed open heifers."

Raleigh Hansen, a rancher not far north of town, bought open heifers during the winter and spring, turned them onto pasture during the summer, and then sold them to a feedlot operator in the fall. He gained his profit from their growth and gains, plus the "guaranteed open" designation. This guarantee was always given in writing, so if something went wrong, such as a neighbor's bull jumping the fence or breaking it to cavort with them, he was stuck!

One day in mid-September, during one of the prettiest Indian summers we had had in years, Raleigh called before breakfast.

"I hate to disturb you this early in the morning but I got troubles," he began. "You know that seven hundred head of heifers you inspected for me last week before they went to Colorado? Well, I got a call from down there last night. They said they checked some of those heifers and at least twenty-five percent have calves in them. I just can't believe it! We rode on them all summer. Only once did we find a bull in with them, and couldn't have been for more than a day because we saw him in his own pasture just the day before. There is no way he could have bred 175 heifers in one day! There was a penalty clause in our contract that anything over one percent pregnancy rate would cost twenty-five dollars a head. That's damned near the profit on the whole bunch. I need some help. Is there anything you think you can do?" For Raleigh, his voice sounded desperate.

I quickly calculated in my head 25 times 700 was $17,500. Quite a bundle in those days!

"I tell you what, let me think this over and maybe make a few calls. You come in about ten o'clock, and we'll talk about it. I'll be around all morning," I answered finally.

"Okay, Doc, thanks a lot. May and I didn't sleep a wink all night. We may grab a little rest before we come in. Do all you can and charge us for any calls you need to make."

The "ball was in my court," as the saying goes. But "the monkey is on your back," was perhaps a better euphemism to describe how I felt after hanging up the telephone.

"Who was that at this hour?" Harriet grumbled. "It must have been pretty important." She had just made French toast and bacon and had the kids around the table ready to eat. She was trying to get breakfast over early because she had to help me with small animal surgery most of the morning.

I told her about the call while we were eating. After we finished and the kids had left the table, she asked, "What can you do about that mess? The cattle are in Colorado. You don't have a license to practice down there."

"Well, the first thing I have to find out is who did the pregnancy check, whether they had a veterinarian do it or a layman. In either case, I've got to get someone else to confirm the results. I could do it, but as you say, I don't have a license to practice there. Besides, it would be my word against whoever they had do it in the first place. I'm going to call Ed Katz at Colorado State and see if he would be willing to do a confirmatory check for us. There would be no question on anyone's part if he conducted the exam. He's an expert in this field and is into these old cows every day! 'I could feel the monkey getting ready to jump.' I'll call him after we finish spaying the first dog. He should be in the office by then."

So I called Ed, who said, "Hope you have something for me up there. It's always good to get to Wyoming. Especially when I can get a free meal!"

Same old Ed, I thought to myself. Always ready to help but have a little fun doing it.

When I finished telling him of Raleigh's plight, I said, "Is it possible for you to meet us at the feedlot and check the heifers they say are pregnant; then, if they are, be around to run all seven hundred through?"

For a minute there was no answer, and I could hear him talking to someone else. "I can meet you at the airport any morning this week. You'll probably want to fly down, won't you?" He had anticipated my thought exactly.

"That's great!" I responded. "Raleigh is coming in at ten o'clock and we'll decide then. He might want you to go over and check them without us, but I doubt it. I'll be back in touch with you the minute we figure out what we want to do." Then, realizing the potential conflict that could arise between a local practitioner and the interests from someone from out of state, I added, "Sure appreciate your offer to help us out. I know this could put you in a bind."

"Thanks, Bob, but don't worry about that. We get caught in the middle all the time. It isn't pleasant, but we just call things as we see them. It's the only thing to do. I'll be waiting for your call, either way."

Raleigh and May were waiting in the reception area when Harriet and I emerged from the operating room. (The last animal had taken a little longer than I expected. Fat old bitches always took more time to spay! I often thought of what human surgeons had to go through when doing abdominal surgery on "stout" people.) After the usual greetings, Raleigh asked, "Well, Doc, what have you figured out?" His whole expression, as well as May's, was hopeful.

I told him that I thought the best approach was to have Ed Katz recheck the heifers and then do them all if he found they were pregnant. It would cost some money, but that couldn't be helped. I told him it was up to us whether we wanted to be there or not.

Without hesitation, Raleigh said, "Hell, I want to be there. Want you to go, too, if you can get away. This thing is too big to not be around to see everything is going right. I'll get Jim at the airport to fly us down and back tomorrow if you can get things lined up. The sooner we get this over with, one way or the other, the better. It's about to worry May and me to death!"

I felt the same as Raleigh. Even though the problem was just a few hours old, I knew it wouldn't "heal" itself. No use putting it off.

"Why don't you call Jim and see if he can take us down in the morning. If he can, ask him what time we can expect to land at the Greeley Airport. I suppose that's the closest to the feedlot. After that, I'll call Dr. Katz."

As it turned out, the earliest we could get there was close to ten o'clock, if we left at daybreak, about six o'clock. Jim would use the four-seat Cessna. I conveyed all this to Ed, who said he'd be there to pick us up.

"By the way," he said before hanging up, "did you find out who checked those heifers down here?"

"We don't know his name, but it was the vet in charge of the feedlot."

"See you in the morning then, Bob."

Raleigh and May left after everything was planned for Ed to pick us up, and I joined Harriet in the surgery where she had about completed the cleanup. I explained the arrangements for the next day, and she said, "I wish you and Raleigh would drive down. It wouldn't take much longer and it's a lot safer."

I didn't respond. I knew she didn't like me up in small planes, so there was no use talking about it.

I met Raleigh and Jim at the airport at quarter to six the next morning. It was a great day for flying, with not a cloud in the sky, and we were airborne on schedule. I looked down at the house and clinic from perhaps 400 feet up as we flew over it, heading due south. Harriet was hanging out clothes and waved when Jim waggled the wings. We stopped to take on fuel at Cheyenne, less than an hour from Greeley. Raleigh had talked most of the way down, but when we took off from Cheyenne, he went silent. We landed at Greeley about ten minutes after ten, and Ed was waiting when we taxied over to the little building they called the terminal.

"Well, it looks like you made it all right," Ed laughed as we shook hands and I introduced him to Raleigh and Jim. It was five miles to the feedlot from the airport, and only Raleigh and I went. Jim decided to stay and check out some minor problem with the plane and to get some rest. Having flown in from Denver just the night before, he was more than a bit tired.

On our way to the feedlot, Raleigh told Ed about the arrangements he'd made with the feedlot operator. They had run a hundred head through the chute and found twenty-five pregnant. The twenty-five would be ready for us to check. Their vet would be there also, but as far as they were concerned, anyone who wished could check them. Everything was completely "above board," not a situation where somebody decided they had paid too much and were trying to either get out of a deal or knock the price down a little.

Checking a heifer for pregnancy entails entering the rectum of the animal manually and then picking up the uterus or ovaries, or all of them, and feeling for changes that indicate the pregnancy status. Experienced veterinarians can tell that an animal is pregnant as early as twenty-five to twenty-eight days after conception. By sixty days most can tell fairly easily. These heifers were supposedly ninety days along, according to the initial examination.

When we arrived at the feedlot, it was decided that Ed would examine each animal and determine its status. This done, either the feedlot veterinarian or I could verify it. The feedlot operator and Raleigh would stand by and keep the records, writing down the ear tag number on each heifer and marking whether open or pregnant. Tension was high when the first animal was run into the chute and Ed slipped on a long-sleeved, plastic glove and entered her rectum. As he moved his arm around, all eyes were glued on his eyes and face for any clue to his findings. In what seemed like an hour, but was actually less than a minute, he withdrew his arm quickly and said "Open!" He then turned to me and said, "Dr. Baldwin, do you want to check her?"

"Nope, I've felt them before," I answered, trying to sound jocund in a situation that was deadly serious.

Ed looked at the feedlot veterinarian. "Do you wish to examine her?" He declined until Ed had declared the first six to be "open." Then he decided to have a "learning experience" as Ed helped him correct some major misconceptions about what he was palpating.

As it turned out, none of the animals were pregnant, much to the embarrassment of the veterinarian and much to the chagrin of the feedlot operator. When Raleigh and I entered the office, the operator was most apologetic, stating that he understood the veterinarian had just gotten out of the service and was new to this procedure. But Raleigh and I did our best to convince him that everyone has to get experience. When we left, Raleigh was "flying high." Like most people after a fateful emotional experience, he "talked like a magpie," but only until we got in the air heading home. Then he fell asleep and didn't awaken until we were circling the Gillette airport.

"Gosh, are we home already?" he asked, as he shook his head and looked down. "I haven't slept two hours a night since this happened. Guess it finally caught up with me."

This epic is but one example of the responsibility for competency that veterinarians carry with them each day. Since mistakes can be costly, both monetarily and in terms of human anguish, there is a need for vigorous training and demanding standards. As one of my professors said one day when the class complained about his pop quizzes, "With few exceptions, every case you will encounter in practice will be a 'pop quiz.' You will either know the answer or you'll fail."

I've often thought about just how right he was!

THE MAIL-ORDER BRIDE

From time to time, the veterinary practitioner has a way of getting intimately involved with his clients. Not in the sense of the iceman and the housewife, nor the traveling salesman and the farmer's daughter; but rather, while caring for an animal, the veterinarian discovers the owner's behavior patterns that are odd or different from normal. The marital machinations of Edgar and Mary Leadbetter are a case in point.

Edgar and Mary lived east of town on a kind of poor man's ranch. By that I mean the whole place was not over 500 acres in size, and a lot of that scrub-oak and jack-pine, with a lot of rock outcroppings, too. As they used to say out there, the place was just big enough to starve to death on.

It didn't help either that Mary was not from that part of the country. Edgar got tired of living alone trying to grub out a living, and in a weak moment, so the story goes, he sent off for one of those "mail-order brides." No one knows for sure how he heard about the service, because they said he could just about read well enough to pass the test for his driver's license. But as is often the case, "where there's a will, there's a way," and before many folks knew what was happening, old Edgar had himself a housemate. What's more, it turned out, the little lady was a schoolteacher from somewhere "back East."

Please understand, Harriet and I can't vouch for any of this since it was mostly hearsay, and had happened long before we moved to Gillette. One thing for sure, however, we witnessed a couple of mighty peculiar things that made us believe the story, at least halfway, because there didn't seem to be too much compatibility between them at times. To us, their behavior reflected many a cultural difference emerging from simple old marital disagreements.

One time when I was scheduled to vaccinate some calves at their place, I heard hollering and screaming inside the chicken house as I walked past it toward the house to get Edgar. Lo and behold, Edgar and Mary had had an argument the night before, and he had locked her in with the chickens. The temperature that night had not been very warm, either.

The second time was when they brought in her Boxer dog. I had just finished working on a heifer about nine o'clock one spring night and was about to go down to the house for the night … I hoped. As I stepped out of the door of the clinic, I saw old Edgar's pickup coming up the drive. I knew it was Edgar's because there wasn't another one as beat up in the whole county. I waited while he pulled up to one side of the clinic and stopped. I could see Edgar and "the Misses" were both in there and as soon as he shut off the engine; I could hear her wailing. When he got out of the pickup, he sauntered over to me. "Hi, Doc," he said. "We got the old lady's dog in there with a hurt leg. The thing's been gone two days and come home like that. I'd have shot the damn thing, 'cause it ain't good for nothin', but I wouldn't have been able to stand all the cryin' and car-ryin' on. So we brought it in."

Going over to the passenger side of the pickup, I saw poor old Mary with tears running down her cheeks, holding the dog's head in her lap. "Do you think you can do anything for him, Doctor?" she managed to blurt out.

"Well, let's get him inside and we'll have a look," I responded. "Which leg is injured?"

"The right hind one," she replied, sniffling.

"Okay, Edgar. I'll take the front of him and you carry the back. Hold him real easy in case he's got a broken leg."

"If he's got a broken leg, I'm sure enough going to shoot him. We don't have the money to pay for all it'll take to fix that."

He'd no sooner got the words out of his mouth than Mary began to scream and wail some more.

"If you'd helped me look for him when he first disappeared two days ago, this wouldn't have happened! I can't drive and you wouldn't take me over to Benson's where the female is in season. We knew that's where he likely would be." Mary was now hollering at the top of her voice. Despite that, we got the dog on the examination table, and I began to palpate his leg while Edgar held his head and forequarters. It didn't take long for me to feel the distinct crepitations signaling a broken femur. Both Edgar and Mary were watching me intently, and they knew by the dog's attempt to withdraw its leg from my grasp, and my stepping back quickly, that the animal had a broken leg. Neither said anything until I announced, "It's broken all right." Then Mary began to scream at old Edgar again. She was a fighter; I'd give her that!

About that time, Edgar turned his face toward me and said, "Doc, can you hold this here dog for me while I knock some sense into that woman? Golly, the way she's carryin' on, we'll all be deaf or crazy." With that, he let go of the dog and started around the table after Mary. The screaming and crying reached a cre-scendo.

About the time he was ready to hit her, I said in no uncertain terms, "You'll have to settle this argument someplace else. It's getting late and there's going to be a lot of work to get that leg set!" Edgar dropped his clenched fist and muttered something I couldn't hear. I went on, "Mary, why don't you go in the waiting room and lie on the couch to settle down? Edgar, I need you here to help with the dog!" With that, Mary stopped crying and wailing, but she left the room sniffling, holding a handkerchief to her mouth and nose.

I decided to use an intramedullary pin, as well as a light external splint to affect the repair of the break. While I was sterilizing the pin and getting the dog under anesthesia, Edgar stood on one foot and then the other, talking. "I don't know what's worse, the dog or the old woman. It's first one thing and then the other. About how much is it going to cost, Doc? We don't have any cash to pay you with. You'll have to take it out in eggs. Won't have much of any cash 'til we sell some calves this fall. I could bring you a couple of dozen eggs a week if that's all right with you."

At that time, Harriet and I ate eggs for breakfast regularly, and used about two dozen a week. "It'll cost close to thirty-five dollars, if there are no major complications," I responded. He didn't say anything for a minute; I figured he was deciding how many dozen it would take.

"I get seventy-five cents a dozen, so it will take most of a year to pay you off, the way I calculate. Is that about right, Doc?"

"That's real close, lacking a few weeks."

It took me most of an hour and a half to set the leg and get the snoring animal in the cage. Mary came into the kennel room when I was putting him in. Patting his head, she said to the unconscious beast, "You have a good sleep, and Mummy will be after you in the morning!"

Edgar dug his hands deeper inside his pockets and moaned, "We can't come after him in the morning; I promised Bill Marks I'd help him brand." Mary looked like she would have another outbreak of emotion, but she held back.

Edgar went on, "Will it be all right if we pick him up tomorrow afternoon sometime?"

"Fine with me," I answered. "Might be best anyway. It will give me a little longer to observe him and to see that the splint is staying on."

After they both turned to leave, Mary turned back to me and said embarrassed, "I'm sorry I acted up so, Doctor, and thank you for taking care of Dan tonight."

"Don't worry about your crying," I said. "It happens all the time. Folks get kind of excited when a pet is injured. Sometimes, if it's bad enough, they even faint dead away on the floor," I went on, trying to relieve the tension between them.

As they went out the front door, I could see Edgar shaking his head in disbelief.

It took another few minutes to clean up the surgery so it would be ready for the next day. While I was doing that, I heard the telephone ring, and pretty soon Harriet called over the intercom, "Bob, you better come down and get a piece of chocolate cake and a glass of milk. Sam Ormby's on the way in with a heifer. Says it will likely need a C-section." By then it was ten-thirty, five hours since supper.

I groaned inwardly at the message. I had hoped to get a good night's sleep for a change, but it was not to be. "Okay, I'll be right down!" I called back. It was as some would say to me from time to time, "You wanted business when you moved here, didn't you Doc?"

As for Edgar and Mary, I understood from our good friend, the optometrist, that his family was supplied with eggs for service nearly the year round, for no sooner had the payment for repair of Mary's glasses been completed than they were broken again—usually accompanied by a black eye. That went on for all the years we lived there. Some folks thought it was comical at the time. Now we call it the "battered wife syndrome," and there are houses, other than chicken houses, for the Marys of the country.

INNOVATIONS IN
PRACTICE

One of the great things about a veterinarian practice was having so many opportunities to be innovative. Hardly a day and certainly not a week passed that a situation didn't arise calling for altering a usual surgical procedure or the use of an instrument in an unusual way. There seemed always a different and better way in some situations to accomplish an objective.

For instance, I used a towel forceps, a sharp pincer-like instrument designed to hold a surgical drape in place during surgery, to break up urinary calculi (stones) lodged in the urethra of steers suffering from a condition the locals called "water belly." The standard operating procedure was to incise the urethra directly over the stone and remove it intact. Suturing of the wound ordinarily would provide for first intention healing and, of course, make the urethra normal again. Right? Wrong! Fifty percent of the time urine would enter the wound and prevent first intention healing. The result was chronic urine seepage through the wound and into the underlying tissue. Correcting this condition required a second operation. This time the penis was amputated above the wound and the stub sutured to the skin in such a manner that the animal urinated thorough the original incision—"out the back," in other words. Needless to say, no one was happy with this situation, I least of all. It meant handling an animal twice and that halved its economic value in the market place. It took considerable thought and some experimentation before I perfected the towel forceps technique, but after I employed the procedure routinely there were less than twenty percent of the steers returned for further surgery. Not a perfect score, but a lot better than a return of fifty percent!

Broken leg bones in horses and cattle posed another interesting challenge. The old axiom that it was necessary to shoot a horse or cow with a broken limb was, to me, unacceptable. Therefore, after we built our hospital at Gillette, I took on several animals with broken bones. As a result I devised various splints and/or slings in an attempt to manage these cases for a successful outcome. Soon enough I learned, however, that in spite of all the innovative handling and using various and sundry methods of external fixation the prognosis in these cases was always very poor. Patients were lost, not because their bones would not heal like any other creature but because it was impossible to maintain the animal in a tranquil enough state to allow healing to take place. In order for broken bones to "knit," the segments must remain together and immobile for three to six weeks, depending upon the age of the animal. My experiences taught me that in spite of innovation, some things just didn't work, although I did learn that if the broken bone occurred in the distal extremities it could be immobilized properly and healing would occur. Otherwise, the axiom was correct.

Late one morning as I was about to go to the house for lunch I heard a truck back up to the unloading chute at the back of the clinic. When I looked out the door I saw that the truck contained a horse, a big horse, a Belgian to be exact. A closer look revealed this Belgian mare had a placenta hanging from her birth canal … a very unusual event since mares shed their placentas very shortly after giving birth. Another reason the placenta would still be attached was, of course, that the mare had not foaled. In such a case, it was very probable the foal would be dead because once the placenta begins to detach from the uterus, the blood supply to the foal is interrupted and death ensures very rapidly.

When I saw Ed Markley get out of his truck I walked up to him and asked, "What have you got there, Ed?" We then walked around to the back of his truck and raised the truck tail gate in order to unload the mare.

"Well sir, Doc, Old Nell here's got a colt stuck inside her. That's what's going on," came his reply. "I saw her trying to have it earlier this morning and I thought it was funny nothing was showing up, what with the way she was straining and all. I watched her for about an hour and just knew something had to be wrong. That's when I got the truck out and brought her in. I don't mean to be tellin' you your business, Doc, but you know when a mare doesn't have something on the ground a little bit after she really gets down to straining, there's something mighty wrong. My daddy told me that long years ago and it's for sure he was right."

"Let's get her into the clinic and we'll see what is going on," I suggested.

When Old Nell finally reached the clinic floor it dawned on me that I was going to have trouble making an examination. Her hind quarters were so high that I couldn't see over them. She must have weighed close to a ton if she weighed a pound. I knew my arm could not be extended sufficiently while I was standing on the clinic floor to examine the contents of the uterus. While she seemed quiet and gentle, as do most working breeds of horses, under stressful conditions one couldn't know her response.

"Well, she's too tall for me to examine without getting up on something like a ladder," I explained. "Do you suppose she'll stand for that?"

Ed looked at me for a moment pondering whether or not I was "funning" with him, but when he saw I was serious he said, "I think she'll stand for that all right. She's put up with lots of crazy things from kids over the years. She'll probably just think you're one of them." He guffawed at what he considered a good joke. "Anyways," he added chuckling, "if she does kick, you'll be up high enough not to get hit. The ladder would get it first." Then he burst forth in a hearty laugh which lasted for several minutes.

With Ed's reassurances I decided to chance an examination of the mare. The only other alternative was to give her an anesthetic and lay her down. I didn't want to do that on the off chance the foal was still alive. The anesthesia would pass to the foal, also, and I didn't want that.

Once my decision was made, I went to the house and picked up the stepladder. As I was leaving with it tucked under my arm, Harriet looked up from her book work and asked me what I was doing. When I told her briefly my intentions she laughed and said, "You've got to be kidding! What happens if she kicks the ladder out from underneath you?"

"She won't do that," I assured her. "Ed told me she was 'plumb gentle'." I paused, then said, "I guess if she does, I'll just have to pick myself up, won't I?"

The response I got from that remark was "Ha! Ha! Ha! Don't get the ladder dirty!"

When I returned to the clinic, Ed was still patiently holding the mare by the lead rope and when I placed the ladder behind her she wasn't even mildly curious.

"Tie her to the chute gate, Ed," I ordered, "and come around here and hold onto this ladder. When I have to push to get inside of her, I don't want it to fall over and scare her."

Ed responded quickly and as soon as I had carefully washed and prepped the mare and my hand and arm, I carefully entered her birth canal to make the examination. Other than an initial slight movement sideways, Old Nell stood perfectly still. The examination revealed my worst fear. The foal was presenting backward with both hind legs forward. I pulled its little tail through the vulvar opening to show Ed.

"What are you going to do now?" Ed asked with a worried look on his face.

"There's only one thing to do," I answered, stepping down off the ladder. "The only way I can work on her is to take her out back in the corral and lay her down. It's likely to be a rough job, as large as that foal felt upon examination."

Two bottles of anesthesia were required to make Old Nell groggy enough to lie down, and after nearly an hour and a half of very physical effort, the foal was removed without injury to the mare.

It was a great feeling after the task was completed and the mare was on her feet, even though the foal was dead. Ed appeared happy to have a live mare.

"There's always another year," he said philosophically. "As long as she's all right, that's the main thing." Then, almost as an after thought, he smiled and said, "Keep that stepladder handy, Doc. I got another mare out there about to foal, and she's a mate to Old Nell here, and just as big!"

THE BOLD INCISION
(or do-it-yourself veterinary surgery)

During my surgery rotation in veterinary school, I was taught that the best procedure was a bold incision, and rapid entry and exit to and from the surgical site. This practice, I'm sure, was based on the fact that traditionally there were few effective anesthetics and few good anti-infective agents. The idea was to "get in and get out" as rapidly as possible, thereby diminishing the pain and chances of infection. In human medicine this attitude persisted for a long period of time, though less so than in veterinary medicine. More effective drugs, along with improved procedures and facilities were available for physicians' use much sooner than for veterinarians.

One of my most vivid memories of small animal surgery in college was watching the professor spay a dog or cat from the initial incision to closure in three minutes. That the animal was under general anesthesia and the procedure conducted under the most sterile of conditions seemed of little importance; only the speed of execution, the bold incision philosophy, was paramount.

Veterinary practitioners when attending veterinary meetings often boasted of spaying animals in five or less minutes, or performing castration on a horse in five minutes or less. What began as a perceived or perhaps a real necessity became a fetish. Yet, I'm still victim to the "bold incision, get in and get out" philosophy, and I have a tendency to want to yell and scream or jump up and down when I witness a simple surgical procedure that takes half or three-quarters of an hour to perform.

Keep in mind this bit of background information as I tell you about the son of a client of mine. His name was Richard and I'd known him since he was a child. His dad had a cattle and sheep ranch about ten miles east of town. Richard was always active in 4-H, FFA, and other endeavors befitting a bright youngster bent on becoming a good rancher. I hadn't seen Richard around for a spell, but thought nothing of it until Nance, Richard's father, called me one day.

"I need to have you come out and see about some cows, if you've got the time." Typical of Nance, he didn't add more to his request.

"My schedule is pretty full," I said as I glanced at my schedule book. "I can make it out first thing in the morning, though, about seven o'clock. What seems to be the problem?"

"Danged if I know, Doc. Had a couple of cows slink their calves. They're not due to calve for another month or two yet. Can't think it could be Bang's 'cause we've been vaccinating for it going on three years now."

"How old are the cows that aborted the calves?" I was trying to get as much information as I could before going to the ranch.

"They were part of the older bunch. I bought them a year ago."

"Had they ever been vaccinated against Bang's, do you know?"

"Can't say for sure. I got them over at the sale at St. Onze, South Dakota. They had to be tested to come into the state and I got the papers here somewhere that says they're clean."

"See if you can find them. I'll want to look at them. By the way, have those cows been in the pasture where there are pine trees growing?" I asked as an afterthought when I suddenly remembered that one area on the ranch not far from the sheds was heavily populated with Ponderosa pines. Cattle seem to migrate, as if pulled by a magnet, to the needles from these trees, especially during this time of year. Cattle often abort their calves after feasting on pine needles.

"Haven't noticed them being in the trees, but I'll ride through them this afternoon and see if there's any sign of 'em being in there. They just might work them at night when I can't see 'em. I'll tell you in the morning what I find."

"Okay, I'll see you in the morning then."

When I arrived at the ranch the next morning, Nance was just coming out of the house with son Richard trailing behind. Richard, I noticed, had his left arm in a sling.

Nance hurried ahead to the corral in order to open the gate so that I could pull my pickup in close to the squeeze chute. We needed this equipment to catch the cattle and hold them during examination.

Richard came over to the pickup and climbed into the front seat with me. He wasn't looking too perky, so I supposed he chose to ride to the corral.

As he got in I said to him, "Haven't seen you around for a spell. What happened to your arm?"

"I've been up to Sheridan working with the vets up there," he said. "I'd heard they needed a hand to work around their clinic cleaning out stalls and the like and I figured it would be good experience to learn a little about vet work, as long as I'm going to be a rancher."

By the time he finished this part of his explanation we had reached the chute and the conversation was interrupted when we got out of the pickup and moved over to the side of the corral where Nance was already waiting.

"Well, Doc," Nance announced, "I rode through those pine trees yesterday after talking to you. There was no sign of cattle being in there at all. The snow hadn't been disturbed by cattle, that's for sure. No droppings or footprints around anywhere, 'cept maybe for a rabbit."

"All right, then. Let's get those cows that lost their calves. I'll want to examine them and take some blood samples." I turned back to the pickup to get the necessary equipment and the blood vials.

Richard followed me and while I was readying the equipment I started the conversation again. "So you've been working with Pete and John. (Both were the vets at Sheridan who had a clinic.) How are they getting along?" I asked. We veterinarians saw one another only a couple of times a year at vet meetings and any first-hand information about a fellow practitioner was always of interest.

"Oh, they're fine," Richard replied. "I'm the one not doing so hot," he added with a little chuckle.

"Yah, I can see that," I said, taking a good look at the arm in the sling and noticing that it was encased in a plaster cast.

Nance had gotten one of the cows in the chute and was waiting for me to get on with the work, but Richard was still talking. He asked, "You remember here a couple of weeks ago I asked you to order me a real sharp knife, like you vets use to castrate calves and the like?"

I remembered it and recalled that he had picked the knife up just a few days earlier. What, I wondered, had that to do with the story he was telling me?

"Well," Richard continued, "I wanted to use it to open up an abscess on the shoulder of one of our horses. That horse standing over there in the round corral, in fact." He pointed to a sorrel gelding standing with its head over the corral fence. Probably looking for something to eat.

"Why don't you fellows talk later!" Nance hollered. "I've got extra work to do now that Richard is 'stove up', I can't stand around here all day."

We stopped our conversation and hurried over to the chute, where I drew a blood sample from the cow's jugular vein and recorded in my notebook the number I found on her ear tag. Then I took her temperature and did a rectal examination and determined that whatever had caused her to abort was not bothering her at this time. We released her from the chute, loaded in another of the afflicted cows, and repeated the procedure. Nothing of an obvious nature was present in any of the several we examined.

From the chute I walked to the middle of the corral to take a good look at the remainder of the herd. Nance and Richard followed. The cattle started to move around the perimeter of the corral, almost in single file, and because they were "half-way gentle" and calm, I was able to get a very good look at each individual. What I was looking for in particular was any evidence of vaginal discharge or swelling of the vulva—a sign of a recent or pending abortion, and a symptom more typical of pine needle abortion than that of Bang's disease. Again, there was an absence of any kind of clue to the problem. Looking at Nance I said, "Well, there's nothing different to see among this bunch, but keep them handy for a few days until I get the results from the blood tests. Then we can decide what to do."

"They'll be right here where we can get at 'em," Nance responded. "Sure hope it's nothing serious." He walked toward the corral gate to let the herd out onto the feed ground.

Richard and I walked over to look at the horse he had "operated on," and as we approached I could see the wound from the "surgery." The wound wasn't on the shoulder, as Richard had described, but was on top of the shoulder in the area called the withers—the withers being the name used by stockmen to locate the area. The minute I saw the position of that wound I suspected the cause of the problem with the cows. It would, I thought, be a waste of time to send the blood samples to the laboratory, but I would do it anyway as it would confirm my suspicion.

"I want you to look at him and see if that abscess needs to be opened some more," Richard said as we neared the sorrel. "I'm not sure I got a good enough job done. You see, Dad was holding him by the halter, just like I used to hold the horses for the vets at Sheridan when they had this sort of quick surgery to do. I guess I didn't learn enough about opening abscesses up there, because I had no sooner stuck the knife in and the fluid began to fly when that sucker whirled on me and Dad so quick we both ended up in a heap. Before we did, though, he caught me with one of his heels. That's when I got this broken arm." He was acting sort of chagrined at the whole affair.

It's the same old story, I thought to myself. In the hands of professionals, most things look easy. No comment seemed required so I didn't say anything for a minute; rather, I peered over the fence at the horse. The condition he had was not a simple abscess but rather a malady known in veterinary medicine as fistulas withers: an inflammation of the bursae (little sacs) that hold ligaments off of the shoulder blades. The inflammation is thought to be infectious in origin because the fluid contained in the swelling often proves to be brucella abortus organisms—those same bacteria that cause Bang's disease in cattle and undulant fever or brucellosis in man. That's why I said to myself it would probably be a waste of time to send to the laboratory the blood samples just taken from the cows. I was almost certain the cows were suffering from Bang's disease.

The operation to correct fistula of the withers is very extensive and not really suitable to a ranch environment, though I'm sure it's been performed many times in barnyards, spreading the disease germs at random. Remedial surgery was even more extensive and extremely difficult since many of the anatomical landmarks were obliterated by scar tissue and exudate.

In response to Richard's idea that I might open the abscess further, I decided it was time to teach the young man some facts concerning the abscess in relation to the cattle. Nance was able to hear my educational reply as he had come back to the corral after releasing the cattle. When I finished the lesson I told them I could operate on the horse but it would have to be done at the clinic where I could treat the animal intravenously for several days following surgery. In order to confirm the relationship of the horse's fistula to the problem with the cows, I drew a blood sample from the horse, and with that, I left them and asked that they wait to make the decision about the horse's surgery until we received the results of the blood tests.

The blood samples for both the cattle and horse showed high titers for Bang's disease. As a result, it became necessary for me in my role as a regulatory veterinarian to return to the ranch to brand the infected cows and to take blood samples from the rest of the herd. Two more cows showed up with the condition and they, too, had to be branded.

The horse? Well, I never did learn what happened to the horse. I saw it on the second trip out to the ranch but never thereafter. Neither Nance nor Richard ever offered an explanation, and they were not the kind of folks you would ask for an explanation.

Richard's arm healed without complication and, as far as I know, I assumed the role of "chief of surgery" for their ranch as long as I remained there in practice. There was no more of that "quick" surgery for Richard.

ADVERSE REACTIONS

Unwanted and unanticipated reactions to drugs are a constant yoke around a practitioner's neck. By yoke, I mean it is a constant emotional burden. Some drugs are much worse than others—for example, anesthetics and tranquilizers, products that affect the nervous system. Vaccines and serums also have a fair incidence of unwanted effects. Most of the information about these reactions is taught in school as well as appearing on the labeling accompanying a product.

Nevertheless, when untoward reactions occur, one's knowledge doesn't relieve the anxiety of the moment; sometimes, it hardly makes it bearable. When totally unexpected and unreported reactions occur, it is doubly agonizing for both owner and veterinarian. Sometimes as a result of such reactions, lawsuits are brought against drug manufacturers and/or veterinarians.

One afternoon about two o'clock, I was at the railroad yard checking over a group of lambs on their way to feedlots in Illinois and awaiting the arrival of three trailer loads of yearling cattle needing shipping inspection. These were routine inspections for interstate shipment.

Of particular interest to me were the yearling cattle. They belonged to Sid Parker, a rancher who lived thirty miles south of town. He had called me that morning and said they planned to be in with the cattle about three o'clock and wanted me to examine them and issue the necessary permits for entrance into the State of Iowa, their destination. I was particularly interested in the shipment because Sid had stopped at the clinic several weeks earlier and asked me to order a special tranquilizer that the buyer had requested be given the cattle prior to shipment.

"Doc, do you know anything about using these new drugs called tranquilizers for shipping cattle?" Sid had inquired, as his way of introducing the subject when he came into the clinic that fall afternoon. "The fella in Iowa who's been buyin' my cattle these past four years wants me to give them some of that stuff before we load. He says the cattle he's bought with it in 'em have done a lot better for him after arrival, better than those that don't. He figured that with cattle traveling so far it might be even better."

I had been reading a little about the use of tranquilizers for such use, but I hadn't seen any studies reported in our scientific journals. Most of the material was in stockmen's publications and written by someone in the manufacturing firm who was touting their particular product. My response to Sid's question concerning its use was, "I haven't used any of those drugs in that manner, just on individual animals to calm them down a little when they're excited. I have seen some reference to its use for that purpose, but no controlled studies have been reported in the scientific literature."

"Well, can you get me some? The fella said it was only available through vets. He's going to pay for it, so just go ahead and order some of it. I think he said Tranvet was the best kind."

"I know the product. How many yearlings do you have and about what will they weigh? The dose is calculated on a weight basis."

"There'll be 150 head going," Sid replied, adding, "They'll weigh a good 650 pounds. Leastwise, that's what I'm figurin' on for pay weight."

"When are you planning on loading them to bring them to the yards? It will make a difference on when you give the drug as to how soon it takes effect. It usually takes about an hour for full effect, then four to five hours to wear off … or, at least, for the animal to get so it doesn't stagger around."

"Well, Doc, I got the trucks called for two o'clock. It shouldn't take them longer than an hour to get to the shipping yards. The train doesn't leave until five-thirty. That gives you and the brand inspector plenty of time to look at them and make out your papers. Course, I have to weigh them off the truck. That'll take a little time."

"In that case, you'll want to give them their shots about ten-thirty or eleven o'clock. Then they should have plenty of time to get used to it before they're loaded," I advised. "I'll get the medicine ordered and call you when it comes in."

With that, Sid departed and I calculated the amount of drug that would be needed and called in the order. When it arrived, I called Sid. His wife picked up the order the same day. I had written the directions on a piece of paper and placed it in the bag. I wanted to make sure Sid would give the drug in the muscle over the hip as close as he could to two hours before the trucks arrived. Mrs. Parker acknowledged the presence of the instructions before she left and I heard nothing from the Parkers thereafter until the day I was walking among the lambs making my inspection.

Suddenly I heard the blaring of air horns and the roar of diesel engines. I looked up to see three tractors and their trailers running at high speed across the railroad tracks and toward the shipping yards. They were fair-flying and so was the dust as they moved toward the unloading chutes.

Directly behind the semis, Sid followed in his pickup. He, too, was laying on his horn.

Everyone in the yard started to migrate toward the cattle chutes. Not a one present had ever seen trucks with full loads on them handled in such a manner. All the spectators were dumbfounded.

Sid was the first to pull over to the corrals. Skidding to a stop, he jumped out of the pickup and started shouting at the driver of a truck that blocked access to the unloading chute, a truck that had unloaded sheep but hadn't pulled away as yet.

"Get that truck out of the way!" Sid hollered at the top of his lungs. "We've got a bunch of cattle down in those trucks and they have to be unloaded before they all smother!"

All hands present in the yard ran toward the unloading chutes to help in any way they could. The sheep truck was hurriedly removed and two of the semis quickly backed up to the gates for unloading. I was standing on the chute ramp when the first truck stopped. Sid was there also and grabbed the rope to lift the overhead door at the rear end of the trailer. The door was only halfway opened when in horror I saw the yearlings laying all over each other as if they were indeed dead. Not a critter was standing, not one! All were down.

"G—, Doc," Sid moaned, "I think they are all going to die!" Quickly he pulled out his pocket knife and opened it in one swift jerk, then reached down, grabbed the closest animal by its nose, twisted its head around and cut its throat! Blood came pumping out of both jugular arteries as Sid dropped the head and reached for another.

"Wait a minute, Sid!" I shouted among the now rising crescendo of voices and noise of the diesels. "Wait a minute! Let me look at them. You can't cut all their throats."

I pushed Sid aside and stepped in front of him in order to look over the mass of dormant animals. As I looked more closely I could see first one and then another take a deep breath and lie still for awhile. The movement was repeated again in a few minutes.

"Quick!" I shouted over my shoulder. "Everybody grab a hold of their ears and tail and drag them out. They're still alive! We've just got to get them more room or those on top will smother those underneath!"

Fortunately there were some eight or ten husky hands present and they didn't wait for a memo to commence action; they jumped right in and did as I instructed. It wasn't long before half the calves on each trailer were lying in the corral; the rest were asleep in the trucks. Prodding and cajoling the sleepers in the truck for an hour resulted in all of them finally staggering off. Once on their feet and no longer staggering, they appeared as if nothing had happened. Sid remarked that the calves didn't look any "worse for the wear." It was just he and the help that looked beat up.

During the lull that followed, and after we had deposited the dead yearling in the meat processing plant, I said to Sid, "What happened out there on the ranch? How much tranquilizer did you give?"

He looked at me with consternation and said, "I did just like you instructed. About ten o'clock we started running them through the chute to give them their shots. We used the dose you told us. They worked real fine and we finished with them about eleven-thirty. Then we went to the house and had a bite to eat and the trucks were right on time ... two o'clock. They loaded good, too. Only a few staggered a little, that I noticed. It wasn't until we were close to halfway in when the lead driver stopped to check his load that we saw we were in trouble. I'd say close to a quarter of them were down by then and even though we poked through the slats on the side of the trailer with hot shots trying to make them get up, they just laid there like zombies. Well, sir, we stopped a couple of more times and each time it was worse. Finally we just made a run for it."

One of the drivers listening to Sid spoke up and stated, "It's just as he said, Doc, only worse. When we were coming up the Four J Road we almost run over Jim Houseman in his damned old pickup. Probably couldn't hear the horns, as deaf as he is. I've been hauling cattle for nigh onto ten years and this is the worst mess I've ever been in. I don't think the insurance we carry covers anything like this, either. From now on, believe me, before I load one more critter I'm going to ask the rancher if they have given them any of that dope like Sid gave his cattle and if they have I'm leavin'—I'm not haulin' anything like that again!! No, Siree!!"

By the time the cattle were ready to load on the train they were walking about as if nothing had happened. They loaded without a stagger.

Sid later reported that the calves had arrived at their destination in good shape and that the buyer was well pleased with them.

Some time later in that season, a colleague practicing in the western part of the state had a similar experience, with an entirely different outcome, however. Those cattle weighed some 1,000 to 1,200 pounds—fat cattle—and when they went down, those beneath the pile smothered. There was no adequate equipment or space for unloading them and they were all too heavy to move by hand. In spite of radioing ahead to have empty trucks on hand for transferring those alive that were on top of the pile and could stagger out of the pileup, the loss was terrific: forty or fifty, as I recall, half of them or better.

The owner of the cattle brought suit against the drug company for the damages the drug had inflicted, but I'm ignorant as to the outcome of that suit.

Unlike now, drugs in those days used either in human or animals were not tested for efficacy. Safety data and a little utility information was all that was required for FDA drug approval. In regard to the drug I've just cited, I learned that information on only five calves had been submitted for the utility portion of the drug approval and it was carried out essentially under laboratory conditions; no field trials were conducted. Once a drug gained approval, however, that drug could and would be used in thousands of head of cattle under many different conditions. Under the conditions for FDA drug approval that existed at that time, is it any wonder that back then many professionals, in both human and veterinary medicine, waited to use newly marketed drugs until they could learn more about the product from reputable sources or from data presented in professional journals and at scientific meetings?

"Wrecks" still occur from time to time, even today with all the additional requirements for FDA drug approval. Usually, however, there is an immediate response by both government and the drug firm to remove the product from the marketplace or to quickly propagate information on the safe use of it. Nevertheless, adverse reactions still occur often enough to be a shadow in the mind of the practitioner. Maybe not a yoke as in bygone days, but a shadow nonetheless.

ABOUT THE AUTHOR

Robert A. Baldwin was born in Fitchburg, Massachusetts in 1923 and raised in Lunenburg and Fitchburg. He left to enter the U.S. Army in 1943, after attending the Stockbridge School of Agriculture for one semester.

Upon returning from the Asiatic-Pacific theatre of World War II in 1946, he entered Massachusetts State College for a brief period before transferring to the Veterinary College at Michigan State College (Now Michigan State University) in East Lansing, where he earned a Doctor of Veterinary Medicine degree in 1951.

Doctor Baldwin and his wife Harriet returned to her home state, Wyoming, to spend the next 15 years: he in private veterinary practice; she as a wife, mother and storekeeper. They lived first in Sundance and then in Gillette, leaving there in 1964 for Bob to enter a Master of Science program at Colorado State University in Fort Collins.

In 1966, after obtaining a master's degree, Bob moved back East to take a position with the U.S. Food & Drug Administration in Arlington, Virginia, then Rockville, Maryland. He remained with that agency until 1984, rising to the position of Associate Director for the Center for Veterinary Medicine.

Currently, he operates a 155-acre farm in the beautiful Shenendoah Valley of southwest Virginia. Between chores, he writes stories of his experiences as a private veterinary practitioner.

978-0-595-47637-
0-595-47637-6